Novell® Linux Desktop 9 Administrator's Handbook

EMMETT DULANEY

N

Novell
PRESS™

Novell®

Published by Pearson Education, Inc.
800 East 96th Street, Indianapolis, Indiana 46240 USA

Novell® Linux Desktop 9 Administrator's Handbook

Copyright © 2006 by Novell, Inc.

International Standard Book Number: 0-672-32790-2

Library of Congress Catalog Card Number: 2004195535

Printed in the United States of America

First Printing: July 2005

08 07 06 05   4 3 2 1

Trademarks

All terms mentioned in this book that are known to be trademarks or service marks have been appropriately capitalized. Que Publishing cannot attest to the accuracy of this information. Use of a term in this book should not be regarded as affecting the validity of any trademark or service mark.

Novell, NetWare, GroupWise, ManageWise, Novell Directory Services, ZENworks and NDPS are registered trademarks; Novell PRess, the Novell Press logo, NDS, Novell BorderManager, and Novell Distributed Print Services are trademarks; CNE is a registered service mark; and CNI and CNA are service marks of Novell, Inc. in the United States and other countries. All brand names and product names used in this book are trade names, service marks, trademarks, or registered trademarks of their respective owners.

Warning and Disclaimer

Every effort has been made to make this book as complete and as accurate as possible, but no warranty or fitness is implied. The information provided is on an "as is" basis. The author and the publisher shall have neither liability nor responsibility to any person or entity with respect to any loss or damages arising from the information contained in this book.

Bulk Sales

Que Publishing offers excellent discounts on this book when ordered in quantity for bulk purchases or special sales. For more information, please contact

> U.S. Corporate and Government Sales
> 1-800-382-3419
> corpsales@pearsontechgroup.com

For sales outside of the U.S., please contact

> International Sales
> international@pearsoned.com

Acquisitions Editor
Jenny Watson

Development Editor
Scott Meyers

Managing Editor
Charlotte Clapp

Project Editor
Seth Kerney

Copy Editor
Rhonda Tinch-Mize

Indexer
Erika Millen

Proofreader
Heather Arle

Publishing Coordinator
Vanessa Evans

Designer
Gary Adair

Page Layout
Brad Chinn

Contents at a Glance

Table of Contents

Preface

When Novell began purchasing leaders in the open source world, they committed to creating and releasing the best software offerings on the market. To this end, they refined the SUSE server, released Open Enterprise Server, and—best of all—brought an open source–friendly solution to the desktop with Novell Linux Desktop 9.

This powerful operating system incorporates the best of the SUSE desktop with features of Ximian and the engineers at Novell. To say that it will meet your needs is an understatement akin to saying that a luxury car will take you to the grocery store—it will do all that and so much more.

This book is an administrators' handbook, designed to be your reference to the operating system. It takes the stance that you are and/or have been a Novell administrator, and are probably new to Linux and open source. With that in mind, it walks through the elements of the operating system that you need to know in order to effectively manage it.

This book contains overviews, installation procedures, configuration options, and reference materials—all that you should need in order to successfully incorporate Novell Linux Desktop into your environment and administer it. After you read this book, keep it on a shelf nearby and use it when you need to find reference information to make your job easier.

About the Author

Emmett Dulaney is the author of the *Novell Certified Linux Professional (CLP) Study Guide*, also from Novell Press, and a number of other Linux and Unix titles. A columnist and reviewer for UnixReview and CertCities, he holds several vendor certifications and is working on a doctorate. He can be reached at edulaney@iquest.net.

Dedication

This book is dedicated to my family. Were it not for their patience, contributions, and understanding, I would not be able to accomplish a fraction of the little I do.

Acknowledgments

A great deal of thanks is owed to Jenny Watson for giving me the opportunity to write this book. I appreciate her confidence and encouragement to step out from the DE role once in a while. Thanks are also due to Scott Meyers, the development editor. His comments, insight, and help proved invaluable time and time again, and I cannot thank him enough.

We Want to Hear from You!

As the reader of this book, *you* are our most important critic and commentator. We value your opinion and want to know what we're doing right, what we could do better, what areas you'd like to see us publish in, and any other words of wisdom you're willing to pass our way.

You can email or write me directly to let me know what you did or didn't like about this book—as well as what we can do to make our books better.

Please note that I cannot help you with technical problems related to the topic of this book. We do have a User Services group, however, where I will forward specific technical questions related to the book.

When you write, please be sure to include this book's title and author as well as your name, email address, and phone number. I will carefully review your comments and share them with the author and editors who worked on the book.

Email: feedback@novellpress.com

Mail: Mark Taber
            Associate Publisher
            Novell Press/Pearson Education
            800 East 96th Street
            Indianapolis, IN 46240 USA

For more information about this book or another Novell Press or Que Publishing title, visit our website at www.quepublishing.com. Type the ISBN (excluding hyphens) or the title of a book in the Search field to find the page you're looking for.

Introduction

What Is Covered in this Book

This book is divided into 13 chapters. Each chapter builds on the ones that have come before it.

Chapter 1 explores just what the Novell Linux Desktop is and why you should consider it.

Chapter 2 explains how to install Novell Linux Desktop. It also looks at ways to update it with service packs and keep it current.

Chapter 3 explains the graphical interfaces. Two graphical desktop environments, GNOME and KDE, are included with NLD, and you can choose either or both with which to interact.

Chapter 4 introduces the command line—a source of great power in Linux—and introduces you to the most popular utilities that can be run from it.

Chapter 5 introduces Yet Another Setup Tool (YaST). This interface simplifies configuration settings and provides a unified interface for many administrative tasks.

Chapter 6 looks at hardware devices, such as printers, and how NLD interacts with them.

Chapter 7 explains how NLD works with filesystems.

Chapter 8 explains the files that exist in NLD and how to create and work with them.

Chapter 9 discusses Boot, Initialization, Shutdown, and Runlevels.

Chapter 10 focuses on Linux administration and the tasks you will likely face on a regular basis.

Chapter 11 looks at networking and how NLD interacts with other operating systems.

Chapter 12 introduces security.

Chapter 13 discusses how NLD interacts with other environments and how to use it in the real world.

What this Book Is Not

This book is not designed to be a programmer's guide or focus on such topics as kernel tweaking. Those are not part of the normal administrators role and thus not included in an *Administrator's Handbook*. This is not a reference work for network theory, protocols, or architectures.

This book focuses on the implementation of Novell Linux Desktop and the administration of it after that implementation.

## CHAPTER 1

What Is the Novell Linux Desktop?

The book you hold in your hands is about Novell Linux Desktop—
a desktop computing environment powered by the SUSE Linux
operating system. This book describes how to use NLD, as well as
how to administer it. Before you can truly be good at either of
those, however, you need to understand what it is and the legacy
that it comes from.

This chapter offers a brief look at the history of Linux, and the
product that you have chosen to adopt for your desktop.

Ancient History

Long before there was Linux, there was Unix. The Unix operating
system came to life more or less by accident. In the late 1960s, an
operating system called MULTICS was designed by the
Massachusetts Institute of Technology to run on GE mainframe
computers. Built on banks of processors, MULTICS enabled infor-
mation-sharing among users, although it required huge amounts of
memory and ran slowly.

Ken Thompson, working for Bell Labs, wrote a crude computer
game to run on the mainframe. He did not like the performance
the mainframe gave or the cost of running it. With the help of
Dennis Ritchie, he rewrote the game to run on a DEC computer
and, in the process, wrote an entire operating system as well.
Several hundred variations have circulated about how the system
came to be named what it is, but the most common is that it is a
mnemonic derivative of MULTICS (Multiplexed Information and
Computing Service).

In 1970, Thompson and Ritchie's operating system came to be
called Unix, and Bell Laboratories kicked in financial support to
refine the product in return for Thompson and Ritchie adding text-
processing capabilities. A side benefit of this arrangement was that
it enabled Thompson and Ritchie to find a faster DEC machine on
which to run their new system.

By 1972, 10 computers were running Unix, and in 1973, Thompson and Ritchie rewrote the kernel from assembly language to C language—the brainchild of Ritchie. Since then, Unix and C have been intertwined, and Unix's growth is partially because of the ease of transporting the C language to other platforms. Although C is not as quick an assembly language, it is much more flexible and portable from one system to another.

AT&T, the parent company of Bell, was not in the computer business (partially because it was a utility monopoly at the time and under scrutiny from the government), so it could not actively attempt to market the product. Instead, AT&T offered Unix in source-code form to government institutions and universities for a fraction of its worth. This practice led to Unix eventually working its way into more than 80 percent of the universities that had computer departments. In 1979, it was ported to the popular VAX minicomputers from Digital, further cementing its way into universities.

The subsequent breakup of the AT&T monopoly in 1984 enabled the former giant to begin selling Unix openly. Although AT&T continued to work on the product and update it by adding refinements, those unaffiliated individuals who received early copies of the operating system—and could interpret the source code—took it upon themselves to make their own enhancements.

Much of this independent crafting took place at the University of California, Berkeley. In 1975, Ken Thompson took a leave from Bell Labs and went to practice at Berkeley in the Department of Computer Science. It was there that he ran into, and recruited, a graduate student named Bill Joy to help enhance the system. In 1977, Joy mailed out several free copies of his system modifications.

While Unix was in-house at Bell, enhancements to it were noted as version numbers—Versions 1 through 6. When AT&T began releasing it as a commercial product, system numbers were used instead (System III, System V, and so on). The refinements done at the university were released as Berkeley Software Distribution, or BSD (2BSD, 3BSD, and so on). Some of the more significant enhancements to come from Berkeley include the vi editor and the C shell. Others include increased filename lengths; AT&T accepted 14 characters for filenames, and Berkeley expanded the limit to 25.

Toward the end of the 1970s, an important moment occurred when the Department of Defense announced that its Advanced Research Projects Agency would use Unix and would base its version on the Berkeley software. This achievement gave Unix a national name and put a feather in the cap of the Berkeley version. One of the demands on the operating system placed by the DOD was for networking, and Unix thus moved farther along the line of technological advancements.

Bill Joy, in the meantime, left the campus setting and became one of the founding members of Sun Microsystems. The Sun workstations used a derivative of BSD known as the Sun Operating System, or SunOS.

In 1988, Sun Microsystems and AT&T rewrote Unix into System V, release 4.0. Other companies, including IBM and Digital Equipment, fearful of losing their positions in the Unix marketplace, countered by forming a standards group to come up with a guideline for Unix. Both groups incorporated BSD in their guidelines but still managed to come up with different versions of System V.

In April 1991, AT&T created a spin-off company called *Unix System Laboratories (USL)* to market and continue development of Unix. Immediately, Novell bought into the company. Later that year, a joint product, UnixWare, was announced that would combine Unix with some of the features of NetWare's connectivity. It finally came to market in November 1992, and in December of that same year, Novell purchased all of USL from AT&T.

In the early 1990s, Berkeley announced that it was in the business of providing education and was not a commercial software house—no more editions of BSD would be forthcoming. Sun Microsystems, one of the largest providers of Unix in the world, quickly moved to the System V standards that had grown from enhancements to the original AT&T Unix. Sun's commitment to System V was the birth of Solaris and the beginning of the end for SunOS, which still stumbled on for a while.

The History of Linux

At the heart of any operating system is the kernel. The kernel is responsible for all low-level tasks and handles all system requests. You must have a kernel in order to have an operating system.

In 1991, Linus Torvalds, a computer science student at the University of Helsinki, made freely available a kernel that he had written. The kernel he wrote mirrored many of the features of Unix and Minix—a version of Unix that was in used in many university learning environments.

Developers and programmers around the world took to the concept of an open-source operating system and quickly began writing and adding features. The kernel version numbers quickly incremented from the 0.1.1 that was first made available to the 2.6.x versions available today. To this day, Linus Torvalds continues to oversee the refinement of the kernel.

The GNU General Public License (GPL) that governs Linux continues to keep it open source and free to this day. To summarize the license, it states that everyone is given the same set of rights and anyone may make modifications as long as they make those modifications available to all.

Ray Noorda, one of the first CEOs of Novell, saw the value of the Linux operating system early on and formed another company—Caldera—to pursue opportunities there. This company eventually grew to purchase the SCO Group, and change its name to SCO.

In 2003, Novell purchased Ximian, a cutting edge Linux company formed by Miguel de Icaza and Nat Friedman—two visionaries in the Mono movement for an open-source platform. In 2004, Novell purchased SUSE—the biggest vendor of Linux in Europe.

The Novell Linux Desktop

The Novell Linux Desktop (NLD) came into being by Novell combining the best features of the incredibly stable SUSE Linux with elements from Ximian and other Novell products. Not only is it one of the very best operating systems on the market today, but also one of its unique attributes is its inclusion of office productivity software in the core product. The Open Office software from OpenOffice.org is included along with support for the standard Microsoft Office file formats.

In addition to the items already mentioned, the Novell website lists the following features/selling points to consider during migration contemplation:

- AutoYast automated installation tool
- Familiar look and feel
- Typical installation in under one hour

Factor in that NLD also includes the following, and you can see the elasticity of the operating system to fit almost any need:

- Mozilla Firefox browser
- Novell iFolder for file sharing and mobility
- 2.6 Linux kernel
- Acrobat Reader, Macromedia Flash Player, RealPlayer 10, and so much more

This book looks at NLD and walks you through the use and administration of it. Whether you are new to Linux, or just new to NLD, one thing is for certain: You'll be delighted with your choice of a desktop operating system and astounded by all that it can do.

Understanding What the Linux Kernel Is

The following information is intended to provide a little more depth on what the Linux Kernel actually is. If you are experienced with other versions of Linux, but not NLD, you can skip this section and move on to Chapter 2, "Installing Novell Linux Desktop 9."

On the other hand, if you are new to Linux, you should read this section for there will be times when you need to have an understanding of how the operating system is working. This will allow you to tweak existing module parameters for performance or functionality. Often this is necessary when you add proprietary modules provided for specific devices (typically video and Ethernet cards), build your own kernels, and so on.

NOTE

In some instances, you must build your own kernel in order to get proprietary modules working. Before doing so, however, you should check to verify that this will not void Novell's support commitment. It is possible that they will adhere to only supporting their own kernels as shipped.

In order to understand how the Linux operating system works, it is helpful to understand the heart of it. The kernel is a software component of the operating system that acts as the system supervisor. The kernel provides all system services to the applications and commands users execute. This includes allocation of CPU time, memory management, disk access, and hardware interfaces. Users are not typically aware of the kernel functions as they are hidden from their view by the applications, such as the shell, that the user interacts with. The system administrator becomes familiar with the kernel as he or she perform the jobs.

When a system administrator executes a command such as **ps**, the kernel accesses the system table to provide information regarding the currently running processes. More commonly however, system administrators interact with the kernel to handle the installation of new hardware.

Unlike other Unix implementations, the Linux kernel makes use of loadable modules to add new features or support for specific hardware. This provides the administrators with the flexibility to reconfigure their systems as required. Typical Unix implementations require the administrator to build a new kernel whenever a change is required to the kernel. Although some changes do require building a new kernel, most do not.

Loadable modules are kernel components that are not directly linked or included in the kernel. The module developer compiles them separately and the administrator can insert or remove them into the running kernel. The scope of actual modules available has grown considerably and now includes filesystems, Ethernet card drivers, tape drivers, PCMCIA, parallel port IDE, and many printer drivers. Using loadable modules is done using the commands listed in Table 1.1.

TABLE 1.1
Loadable Module Commands

COMMAND	DESCRIPTION
lsmod	List the loaded modules
insmod	Install a module
rmmod	Remove a module
modinfo	Print information about a module
modprobe	Probe and install a module and its dependents
depmod	Determine module dependencies

The commands affect the modules in the currently running kernel and will also review information available in the /proc filesystem. lsmod is used to list the currently loaded modules.

The output of lsmod includes some header text identifying the different columns of data. Column one specifies the module that has been loaded, column two is the size of the module in bytes, column three indicates the number of references to the module, and column four specifies the modules that call this module.

Removing a module with rmmod requires that you specify the module to be removed. The modinfo command is used to query information from the module file and report to the user. modinfo can be used to report

- The module author
- The module description
- The typed parameters the module accepts

Bear in mind that many modules do not report any information at all. If the module author does not provide the information when the module is developed, there is nothing for `modinfo` to report. You can use the `-a` option to get as much information as possible, but some modules will still report `<none>`.

The `depmod` and `modprobe` commands can also be used to load modules. Although the method previously reviewed can be tedious and frustrating, it is worthwhile to understand the relationships between the modules. `depmod` is used to determine the dependencies between modules.

The `/etc/modprobe.conf` file is a text-based file that can be used to store information that affects the operation of `depmod` and `modprobe`. When modifying or reading this file, remember:

- All empty lines and all text on a line after a # are ignored.
- Lines can be continued by ending the line with a backslash (\).
- The lines specifying the module information must fall into one of the following formats:

```
keep
parameter=value
options module symbol=value ...
alias module real_name
pre-install module command ...
install module command ...
post-install module command ...
pre-remove module command ...
remove module command ...
post-remove module command ...
```

In the preceding list, all values in the "parameter" lines will be processed by a shell, which means that "shell tricks," like wildcards and commands enclosed in back quotes, can be used during module processing. For example,

```
path[misc]=/lib/modules/1.1.5?
path[net]=/lib/modules/`uname -r`
```

These have the effect of values to the path to look for the system modules. Table 1.2 lists the legal/allowed parameters.

TABLE 1.2
Allowed Configuration Parameters

PARAMETER	DESCRIPTION
keep	If this word is found before any lines containing a path description, the default set of paths will be saved, and thus added to. Otherwise the normal behavior is to replace the default set of paths with those defined on the configuration file.
depfile=DEPFILE_PATH	This is the path to the dependency file created by depmod and used by modprobe.
path=SOME_PATH	The path parameter specifies a directory to search for the modules.
path[tag]=SOME_PATH	The path parameter can carry an optional tag. This tells us a little more about the purpose of the modules in this directory and allows some automated operations by modprobe. The tag is appended to the path keyword enclosed in square brackets. If the tag is missing, the tag misc is assumed. One very useful tag is boot, which can be used to mark all modules that should be loaded at boot time.
Options	Define options required for specific modules.
Alias	Provides an alternate name for a module.
pre-install module command ...	Execute a command prior to loading the module.
install module command ...	Install the following module.
post-install module command ...	Execute a command after the module is loaded.
pre-remove module command ...	Execute a command prior to removing the module.
remove module command ...	Remove the named module.
post-remove module command ...	Execute a command after the module has been removed.

If the configuration file is missing, or if any parameter is not overridden, the defaults are assumed.

SUSE-based systems always look in /lib/modules/kernel-version-default, then in /lib/modules/kernel-version-override, and then any other directories that you've specified using path commands in modprobe.conf.

Summary

This chapter looked at the basics of Linux and Novell Linux Desktop. The next chapter walks through the steps involved in a standard installation.

## CHAPTER 2

Installing Novell Linux Desktop 9

It should come as little surprise that installing the Novell Linux Desktop (NLD) product is as straightforward and easy as using it. In this chapter, we'll examine the system requirements for the operating system and walk through its installation.

Minimum System Requirements

You can choose to install NLD in a number of different environments. For a standard installation, the requirements are

- Pentium II+ 266MHz or any AMD64 or Intel EM64T processor
- 128MB RAM
- 800MB free hard drive space
- 800×600 or higher resolution

Though the preceding numbers are the minimum, the following requirements are more realistic for an environment you can be comfortable working within:

- Pentium 3 1GHz processor
- 512MB RAM
- 20GB free hard drive space
- 1024×768 or higher resolution
- 100Mb/sec Ethernet card

Installing the Operating System

Novell Linux Desktop is presently available in both the DVD and CD formats. With the exception of not needing to switch media with DVD (everything fits on a single disk)—and needing to do so with CDs (there are currently three disks)—the installation routine is the exact same regardless of which media you use. For the purpose of this discussion, the CD media is used.

To begin the installation, insert the first CD into the drive and boot the workstation. A Welcome screen will quickly appear, as shown in Figure 2.1, followed by a screen offering a boot options menu, as shown in Figure 2.2.

FIGURE 2.1
The splash screen quickly appears when booting.

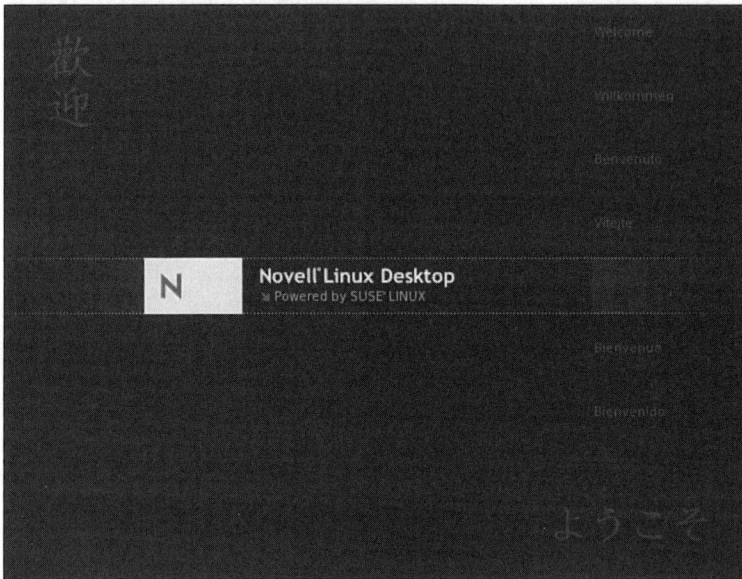

By looking at the Welcome screen, you'll notice that Novell Linux Desktop is built on SUSE LINUX and available for a number of languages.

The welcome menu offers the following choices:

NOTE

The workstation BIOS must be configured to boot from the media in order to begin this installation. If the boot options menu does not appear, reconfigure the BIOS on the workstation to make the drive bootable.

FIGURE 2.2
Upon first booting, there are a number of choices to choose from.

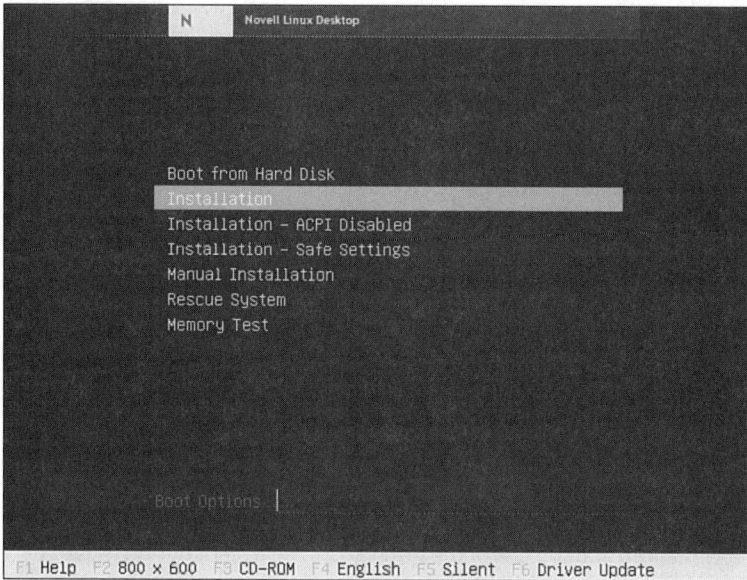

- **Boot from Hard disk**—This choice is the default, and the one to use if you accidentally arrive at this menu and truly do not want to make any changes.

- **Installation**—The choice to use to begin the installation routine.

- **Installation - ACPI Disabled**—This option sets `acpi=off` and is used only if you are having trouble with power savings interfering with the installation routine.

- **Installation - Safe Settings**—Among other things, this sets `acm=off`, `acpi=off`, and `barrier=off` and is used when you are having a great deal of trouble getting an installation to take. These settings disable certain advanced features such as power management and advanced hard drive settings during the installation process. Use this choice as a last ditch effort for a successful installation, and use it only after you have exhausted the previous two options.

- **Manual Installation**—This lets you walk through only the aspects of the installation you want to tweak.

- `Rescue System`—This recovers a system with corrupted boot files.

- `Memory Test`—This does not do any installation, but simply checks the memory.

To begin a standard install, choose Installation. If your system cannot be recognized as meeting the minimal requirements, a text-based installation will begin (skip to the "Text-based Installs" section later in this chapter and continue from there).

The License Agreement appears next. Scroll through the choices, and you can click either on the command button labeled I Agree or the command button labeled I Do Not Agree. If you choose the latter, the installation will not continue.

Note

In addition to the two command buttons directly linked to the License Agreement, two others also appear on this screen—Abort (which immediately stops the installation altogether, and Accept. These two command buttons remain present throughout all the remaining screens (though on some, Accept is labeled as Cancel) and the rest of the installation. The Accept button is used to proceed to the next dialog screen, but nothing is really accepted until you confirm all your choices and settings on the last installation screen.

After agreeing to the License Agreement, YaST2 identifies itself as "The Installation and System Administration Program," and you must select your language. Your hardware is then analyzed, and you are given radio buttons allowing you to choose either GNOME or KDE for the default desktop. Neither is preselected, and you cannot choose to install both at this time, though you can always go back and do so at a later time.

Tip

KDE is the traditional desktop used on SUSE systems, whereas GNOME is now preferred by much of Novell for internal use. If you are not familiar with either, and have no valid reason to select one or the other (such as being a site-wide desktop standard), GNOME is probably the "right" choice, and the one this book will mostly focus on.

A summary of the installation settings you have chosen appears next. This lists information about

- The system itself (processor, memory)
- Mode (new installation)
- Keyboard layout
- Mouse
- Partitioning
- Software to install (including default desktop)
- Booting (GRUB is the default boot loader)
- Time zone
- Language
- Default runlevel (5 is the default; graphical multiuser with network and the X Window system)

You can alter any of the configurable settings by clicking the Change button, or agree to them as they are by clicking Accept. As soon as you click Accept, a warning appears telling you that YaST2 has all the information needed and can now start the installation. You can click Yes, Install to commit to the installation and the choices you made up to now, or click No to go back to the previous dialog and make any changes that you want to.

Once you click to start the actual installation, the hard disk starts being prepared. Following that, you can watch the status of the installation for each of the CDs through progress bars. At the end of this phase, basic installation finishes with the following automatic steps:

1. Update configuration
2. Copy files to installed system
3. Install boot manager
4. Prepare system for initial boot

The system reboots and continues on with the installation (often asking that you install the next install CD at this point). Packages are now installed including RealPlayer, Acrobat Reader, Red Carpet, and OpenOffice.org, among others.

You are prompted to enter, and verify, a password for the root user. Because this is the account that has the most power on the system, and the one that most people intent on inflicting harm to the system will attempt to access, it is imperative that good password rules, such as mixing case and including non-alpha characters, be applied to this password. In addition to letters, digits, and blanks, the password can include the following characters: #*,.;:- _+!$%&/|?(){[]}=. A command button entitled Expert Options also appears on this screen and if you click it, you can choose between three encryption types:

- DES (Linux default)—Restricted to eight characters; technically, you can type in as long a string as you want, but only the first eight characters are used in the hash.

- MD5

- Blowfish

Note

These are three very different encryption-hashing functions. MD5 and Blowfish differ algorithmically, and both are harder to crack than DES because they use longer passwords. DES is the default because it offers the ability to interact with legacy systems such as those that use NIS.

After the root password is configured, the system next turns to network configuration. A scan is done for network interfaces, DSL connections, ISDN adapters, Modems, Proxy, and VNC Remote administration. You can accept the results (values) that are found and given on the summary screen, or make any changes to them that you want before accepting. Upon clicking Next, the network configuration is written and you are offered the opportunity to test the Internet connection. This is useful if you want to download the latest release notes and updates, but you can also choose to skip this test.

Note

The default network configuration model is automatic IP address configuration with DHCP.

Three choices are offered for an authentication mode:

- NIS—Network Information System—Select this option if you are using an NIS server to store information about your users.

- LDAP—Lightweight Directory Access Protocol—Select this option if you are using an LDAP server to store information about your users.

- Local (/etc/passwd)—Select this option if you want the passwords stored in the /etc/passwd and /etc/shadow files.

After clicking Next, you can add a new user account. While it is possible to add all of your users at this point, that is not truly the best use of this screen. At this point, you should add at least one account that can be used in place of root, complete the installation, and then add your other users later.

To add this user, you are prompted for the following:

- Full User Name—This is free text in which you can add any value, but it is usually the first and last name of a user.

- User Login—If you have no idea what you want to use, a Suggestion command box will return a possibility based on the value entered in the Full User Name field.

- Password—All the characters that can be used for the root user can be used for this and all other users.

You must give the password again to verify that you entered it correctly, and you can check a box if this user is to receive system mail. The first user you add will have a User ID (uid) of 1000, and all others will increment by 1 from there (1001, 1002, and so on).

SuSEconfig now starts and writes the system configuration files as they stand at this point; after which Release Notes are displayed. You can scroll through and read the Notes if you prefer, or access them at any later point in time at /usr/share/docs/release-notes/RELEASE-NOTES.en.rtf.

Hardware configuration occurs next, as such items as graphic cards, printers, and sound cards are searched for and identified. Once again, you can make any changes on the summary screen that you want to or accept what is there and click Next. At this point, the installation is complete and all that is left to do is click Finish. Once you do so, the system reboots and comes to the Novell Linux Desktop login screen prompting you for a username and password that you must now supply (see Figure 2.3). After you do so, the desktop (GNOME or KDE) is loaded, and you are in business.

FIGURE 2.3
After a successful installation, you can login and begin using the desktop.

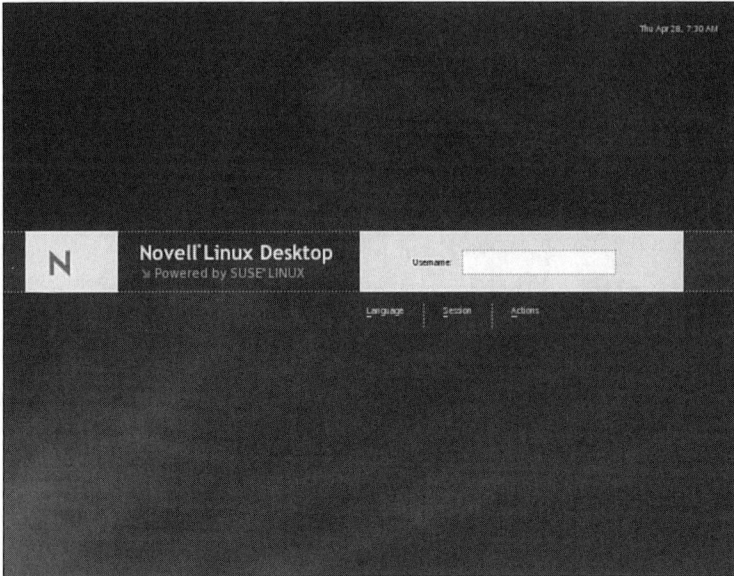

Tip

At the login prompt, you can choose the Language and Actions to take when you login, as well as choose a desktop other than your default, if it is available.

For information on working with the graphical interfaces and customizing the desktop, see Chapter 3, "Working with the Desktop Environments."

Text-based Installs

A text-based installation is necessary when the minimal system requirements are not met. After choosing Installation from the boot menu choices, you will see an error screen similar to that shown in Figure 2.4.

Choose OK, and the License Agreement appears next. You can choose I Agree or I Do Not Agree. You must choose the former to continue the installation. The next step is to choose the language to use, as shown in Figure 2.5.

FIGURE 2.4
The text-based version of YaST must be used for the installation.

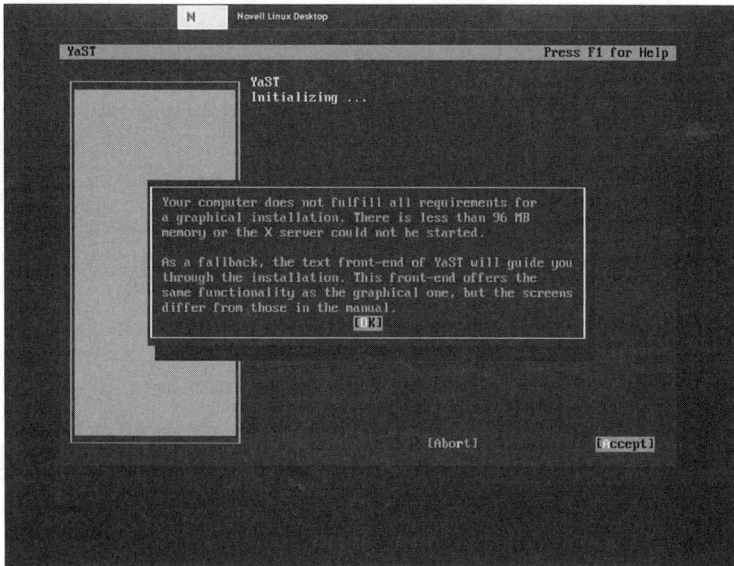

FIGURE 2.5
Choose the language during installation.

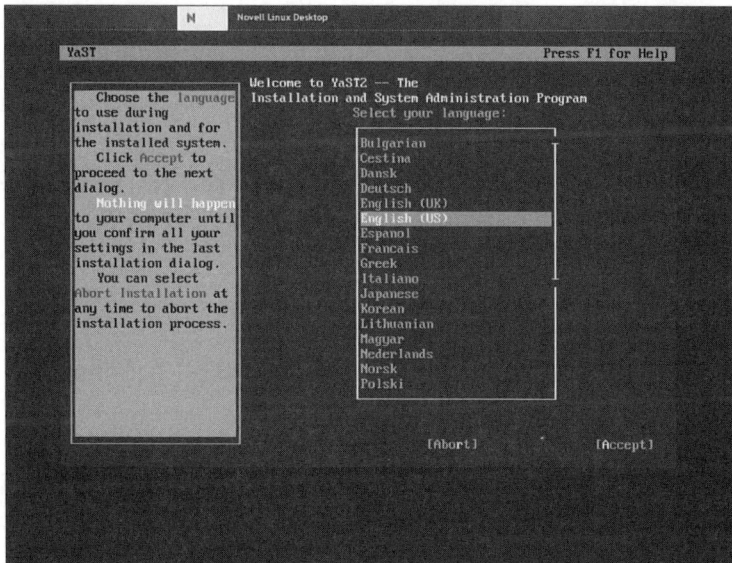

Hardware is analyzed next, and then you must choose your default desktop, as shown in Figure 2.6.

FIGURE 2.6
Choose GNOME or KDE for your default desktop.

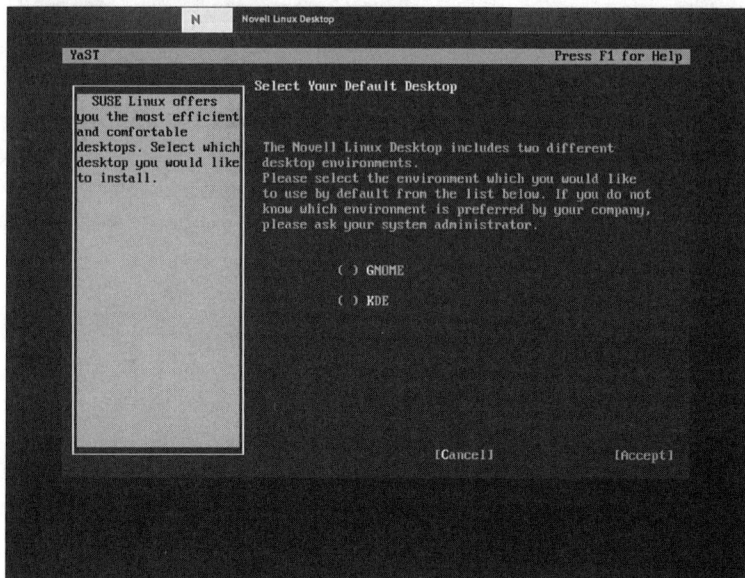

Choose Accept after selecting the default desktop of your choice (remember that Novell prefers GNOME, but KDE is also a valid choice), and the installation settings are summarized for you. Choose Accept and a warning appears (as shown in Figure 2.7) indicating that the settings you have selected will now be carried out.

Installation is now done as you play disc jockey and swap the CDs into the machine, as shown in Figure 2.8.

When the swapping is complete, you must enter a root user password (as shown in Figure 2.9). If you choose the Expert Options, you can choose between DES (the default), MD5, or Blowfish password encryption methods.

The system is analyzed. Network cards, if present, are detected: DSL connections, modems, and so on are searched for—with the end result being the summary configuration information presented to you, as shown in Figure 2.10.

FIGURE 2.7
You must accept the installation settings before they are applied.

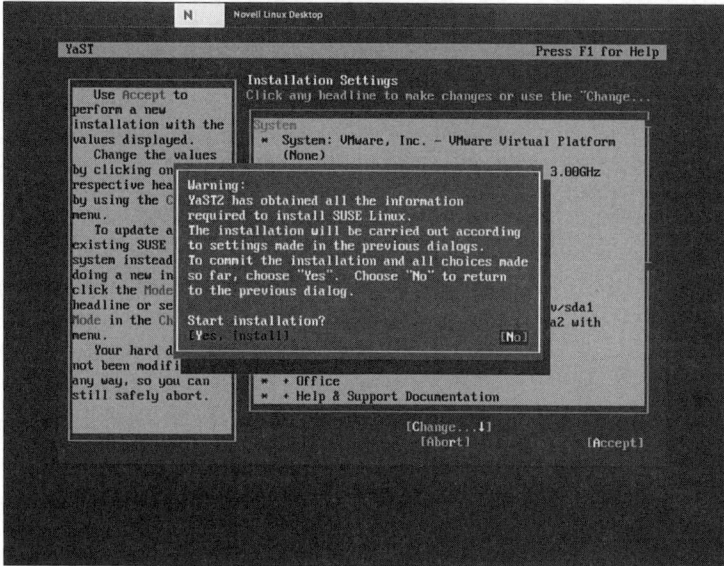

FIGURE 2.8
You are prompted to swap the set of CDs to complete the installation.

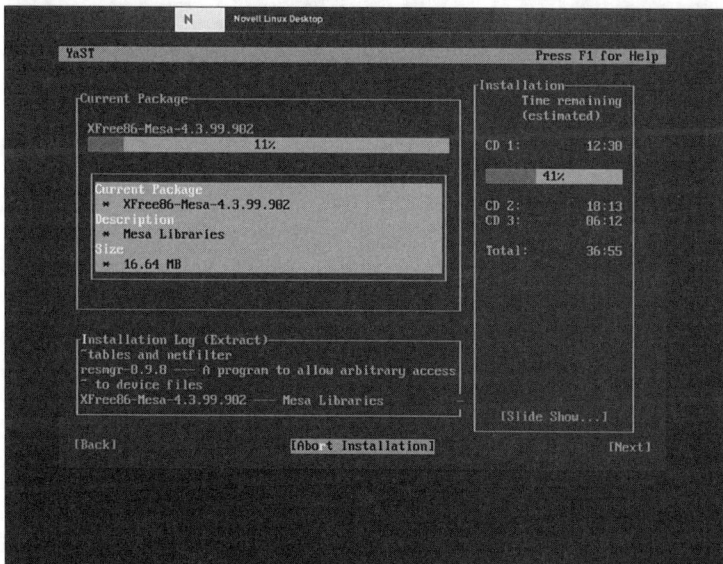

FIGURE 2.9
Configure the root user account.

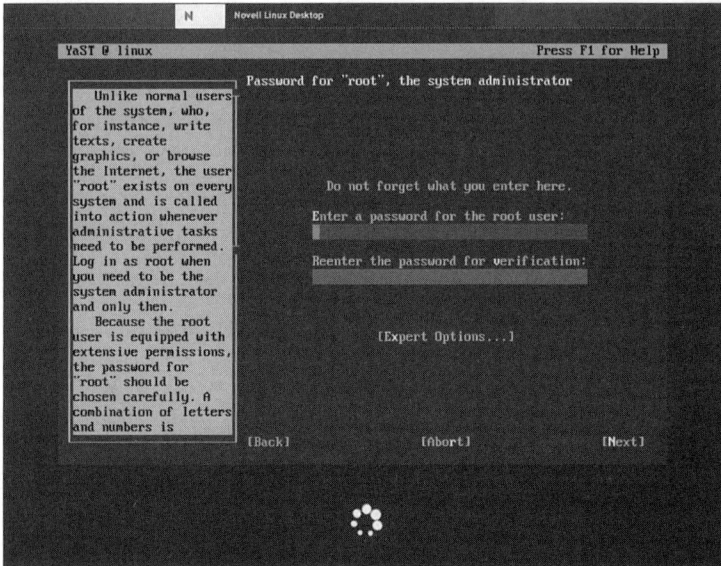

FIGURE 2.10
Network devices are typically automatically detected.

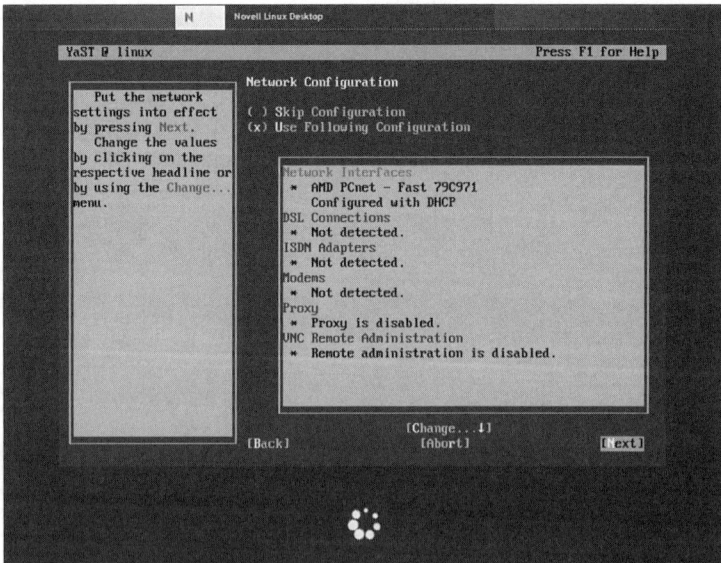

After the network configuration is written, you are given the chance to validate your Internet access and choose your authentication method. Three choices are offered:

- NIS—Network Information System—Select this option if you are using an NIS server to store information about your users.

- LDAP—Lightweight Directory Access Protocol—Select this option if you are using an LDAP server to store information about your users.

- Local (/etc/passwd)—Select this option if you want the passwords stored in the /etc/passwd and /etc/shadow files.

You are given the choice to enter another system user (besides root), and system configuration is then written out. Release notes are displayed, and hardware configuration begins. A summary screen shows the graphics cards, printers, and sound cards found (any of which can be changed).

Installation is now complete. Upon clicking Finish, the system reboots and comes to the Novell Linux Desktop login screen, prompting you for a user-name and password. After you do so, the desktop (GNOME or KDE) is loaded and you are in business.

Customizing the Installation

As an administrator, there are times when deploying preconfigured system images, rather than running each installation independently, makes more sense. For those time, it is possible to work with the Firstboot utility and configure certain elements of the installation to fit your needs.

If you want to change the settings that appear during the installation on the Welcome screen, License Agreement, and Finish dialog, you can create a custom script file to show different values. The ability to do this is not enabled by default, and you must first install the Firstboot utility by installing the yast2-firstboot package on a master machine, as shown in Figure 2.11.

Check the box and click Accept. If it is not already in the drive, you will be prompted to install CD 1. Once it has copied over, you must perform the following steps:

1. Touch the `/etc/reconfig_system` file and turn firstboot on. Both of these steps are shown in Figure 2.12.

FIGURE 2.11
Install the Firstboot package.

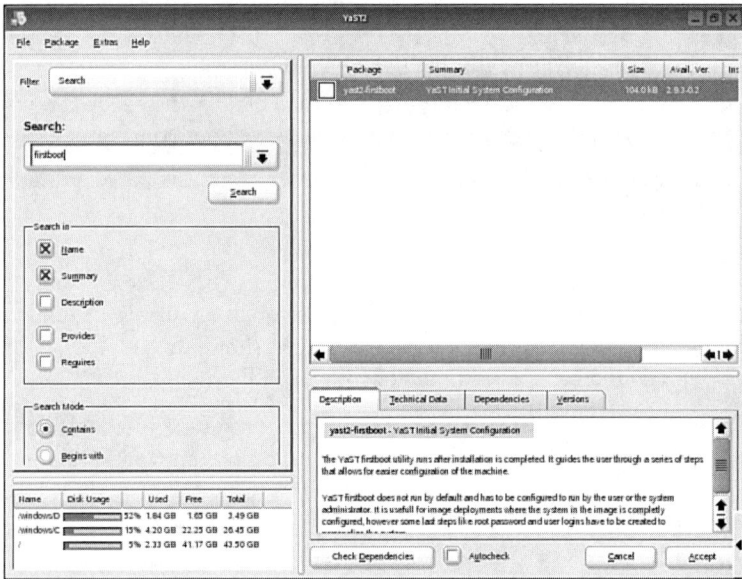

FIGURE 2.12
Touch the configuration file and turn firstboot on.

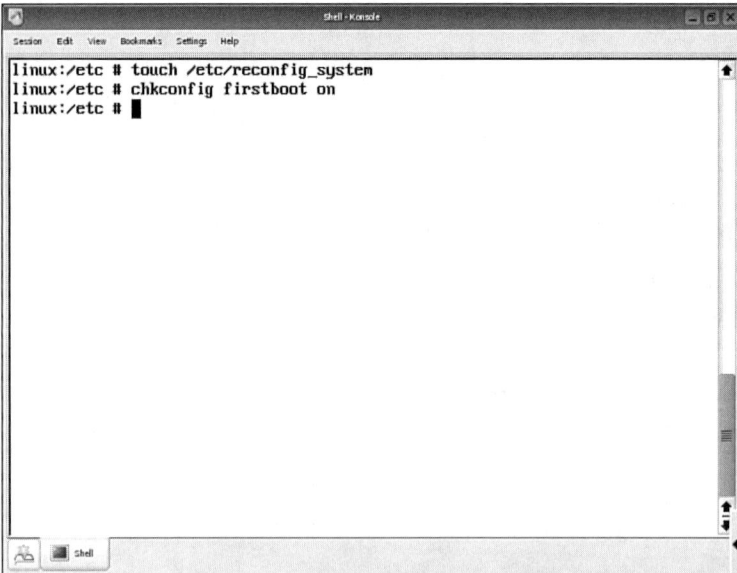

2. You can now edit the `/etc/sysconfig/firstboot` file, shown in Figure 2.13, and set the options that you want.

FIGURE 2.13
Modify the configuration file to have the settings you want.

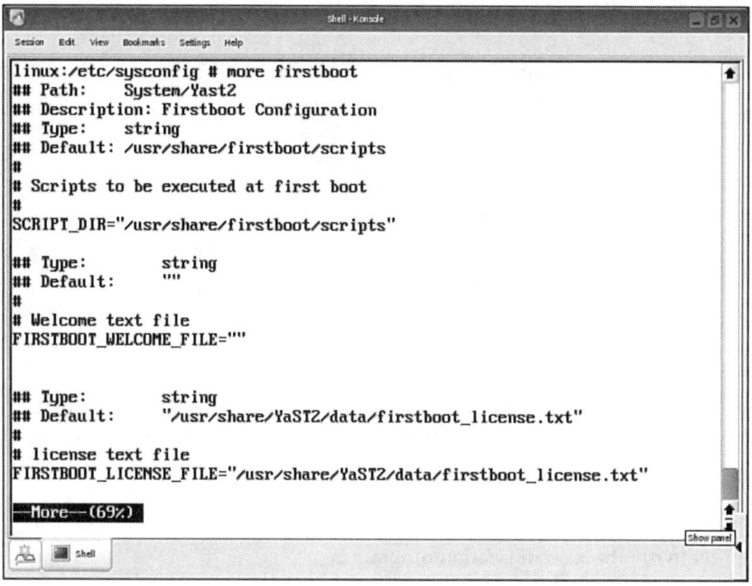

```
linux:/etc/sysconfig # more firstboot
## Path:        System/Yast2
## Description: Firstboot Configuration
## Type:        string
## Default: /usr/share/firstboot/scripts
#
# Scripts to be executed at first boot
#
SCRIPT_DIR="/usr/share/firstboot/scripts"

## Type:          string
## Default:       ""
#
# Welcome text file
FIRSTBOOT_WELCOME_FILE=""


## Type:          string
## Default:       "/usr/share/YaST2/data/firstboot_license.txt"
#
# license text file
FIRSTBOOT_LICENSE_FILE="/usr/share/YaST2/data/firstboot_license.txt"

--More--(69%)
```

This configuration file can now be used in place of the standard file for installations at your site. For more information on the Firstboot utility, see the Novell Linux Desktop online documentation.

Troubleshooting Installation Problems

Most installations are completed without any problems at all. When there are problems, usually they are related to legacy hardware or a failure to meet minimum requirements. This section looks at two somewhat related problems: an inability to start the X server, and a monitor that does not work well with the operating system.

X Server Problems

If there is a problem with the X server, it will usually rear its head when you first reboot the system after completing the installation. An error message similar to that shown in Figure 2.14 will appear.

FIGURE 2.14
An error indicates that X server cannot be started.

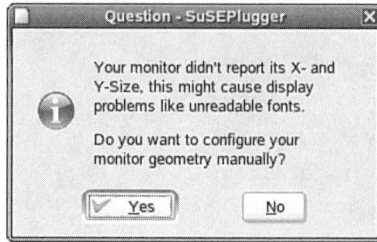

The first dialog box asks if you want to view the log files, which might or might not be of any use given that the operating system has just completed the installation. Following this, you are given the option of running the X configuration program (see Figure 2.15), to which you want to answer Yes.

FIGURE 2.15
The option to run the X configuration program is given.

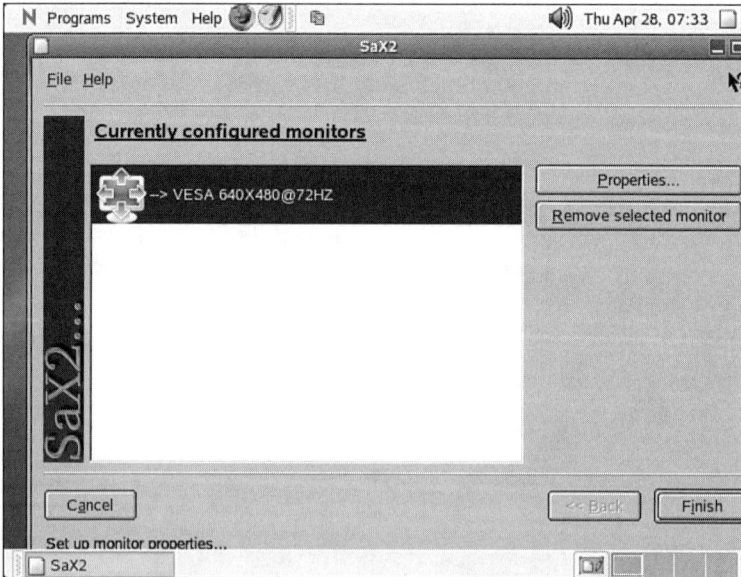

After choosing Yes, you must give the root user password before you can go any further. Following this, an attempt will be made (often more than once) to restart the X server again. If the attempts are successful, the X server will start. If the attempts are unsuccessful, a dialog box will inform you that the X server is now disabled and encourage you to try configuration again.

Monitor Problems

If there is a problem with the monitor, it will usually show up the first time you login, as illustrated by the dialog box in Figure 2.16.

FIGURE 2.16
An error indicates that the monitor is not properly configured.

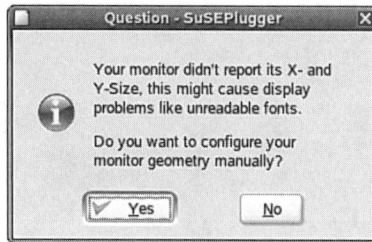

When you choose Yes, the SaX2 utility is started, as shown in Figure 2.17. There are several things to note in this figure—the first is that not all of the dialog box is present because of the inability to properly configure it for the monitor. Clicking the resize button does make it possible to work within the confines of the space available.

The second thing to notice in the figure is that the monitor is identified as VESA. Monitors that cannot be recognized typically default to VESA.

You can change the properties of the monitor to your actual monitor—make, model, resolution, and so on—then choose to accept that. You will be given the opportunity to test the configuration you have selected (see Figure 2.18), and then save it.

You should never save a configuration without first testing it. After you have done these steps, the new configuration will be active the next time the X server is restarted.

FIGURE 2.17
The SaX2 utility is used to configure the monitor.

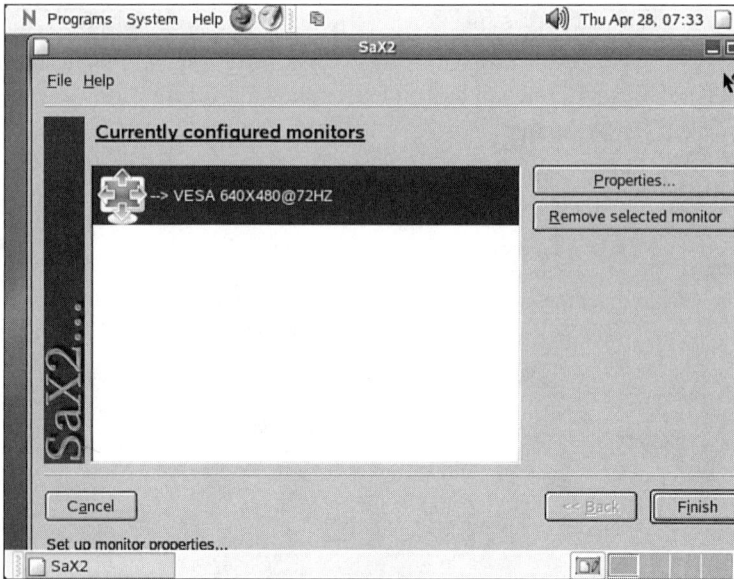

FIGURE 2.18
The SaX2 final steps.

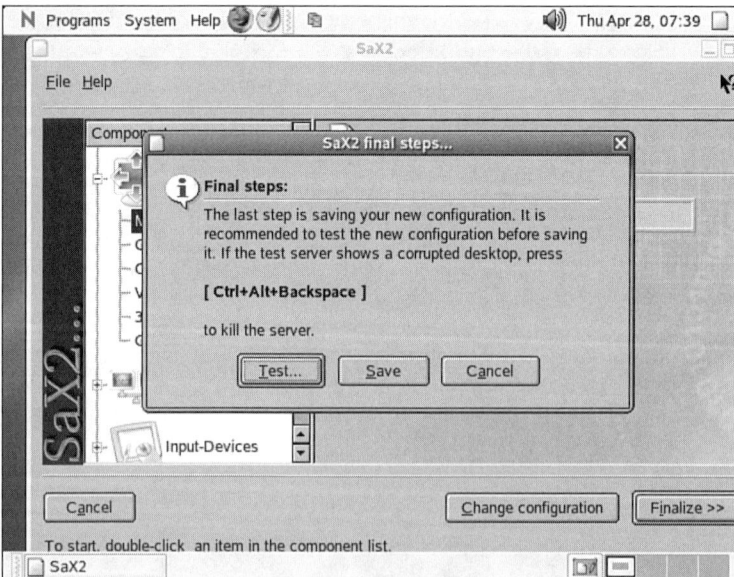

Upgrading During Installation

One of the benefits of choosing to test Internet connectivity during the installation—whether performing a graphical or text-based installation—is that a check is performed to see if updates are available for the system. If such updates are available, you will be notified, as shown if Figure 2.19.

FIGURE 2.19
You can choose to update the system during the installation.

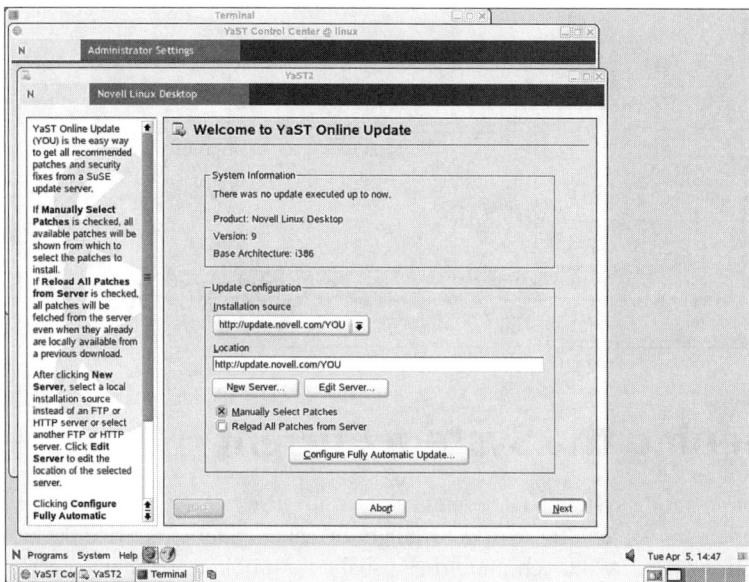

Note

The text-based updates are shown in this section because they are the most difficult to work though. The graphical updates follow the same steps and simply involve clicking **Next** or **OK**.

Choosing to continue, by default, downloads the updates from http://update.novell.com/YOU and notifies you when the system is current, as shown in Figure 2.20.

FIGURE 2.20
After the updates are download/applied, the system is current.

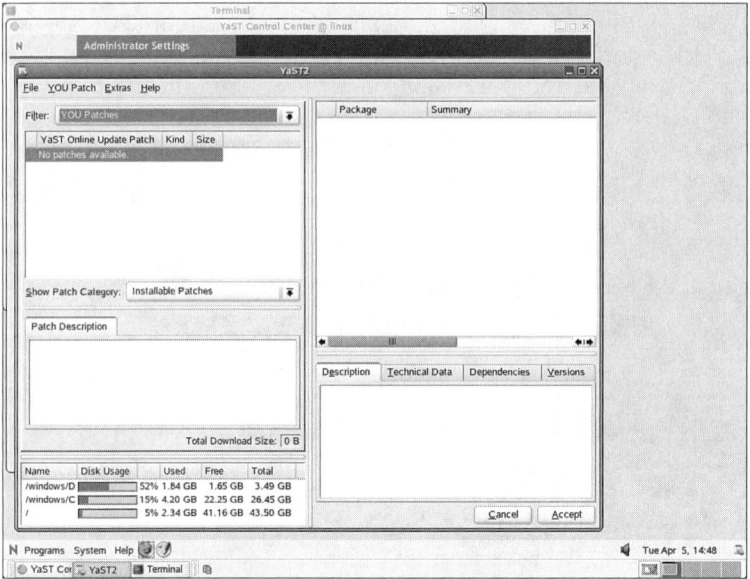

Keeping the System Current

Every operating system has updates released for it occasionally. Depending on the operating system, these updates might be called patches, service packs, or something entirely different, and they usually fix problems that have been found and/or add additional functionality to the operating system.

In Novell Linux Desktop, you can keep the system up-to-date through two methods. Each of these methods is discussed in the sections that follow.

Using Online Update

You can check for updates and keep the system current using the YaST2 (Yet Another Setup Tool) interface. From the System menu, choose Administrator Settings. When the Control Center opens, choose Software (if it is not already selected), followed by Online Update. This brings up the dialog box shown in Figure 2.21.

FIGURE 2.21
The Online Update options.

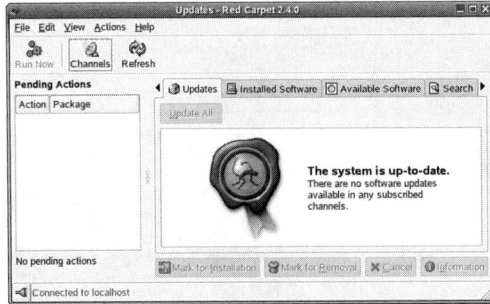

You can choose to manually select the patches to be applied (the default) or reload all patches from the server. If any patches are available, they are presented for you to select: Otherwise, you are notified that the system is currently up-to-date, as shown in Figure 2.22.

FIGURE 2.22
The system is current, and there are no patches to apply.

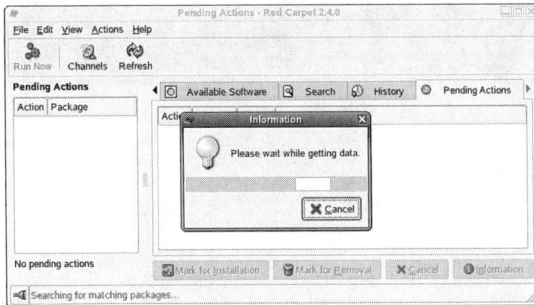

Using Red Carpet

Novell Linux Desktop also includes the Red Carpet utility to allow you to check for updates and keep the system current. To start this utility, from the System menu, choose Software Update.

A check will be done of the system, as shown in Figure 2.23, and you will be notified if there are any patches to download. If there are no new patches, you will be notified that the system is up-to-date, as shown in Figure 2.24.

FIGURE 2.23
A quick scan is performed.

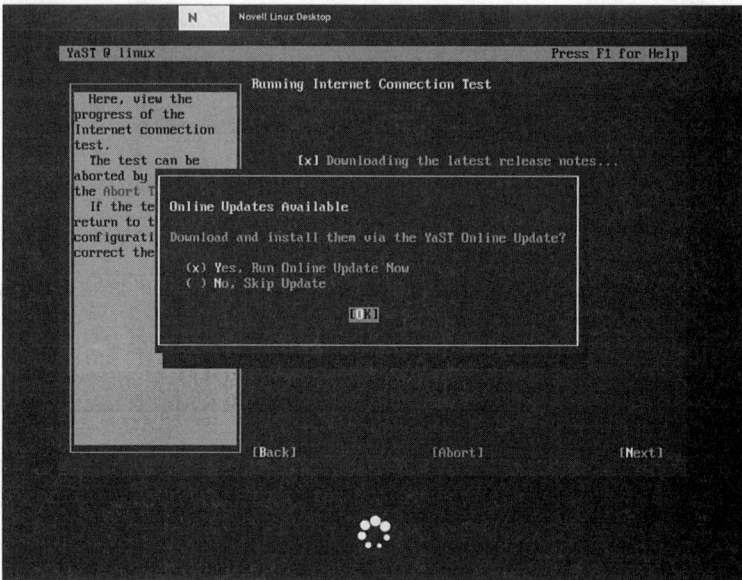

Using an Update CD

Novell Linux Desktop can be updated manually with a patch CD. Normally, when you install the CD into the caddy, NLD will recognize that the patch CD is present and ask if you want to run it (see Figure 2.25). If the CD is not recognized, you can still start the installation manually. To do this, from the System menu, choose YaST, and then Software, and Patch CD Update.

Once YaST begins, the installation source defaults to the CD, and you need only choose Next to begin the installation. Information about new updates is retrieved from the CD and you can select which patches/packages to install. Click Accept and the progress log will show the actions taking place. If there is more than one CD, you will be prompted to swap them as necessary.

FIGURE 2.24
There are no patches to install.

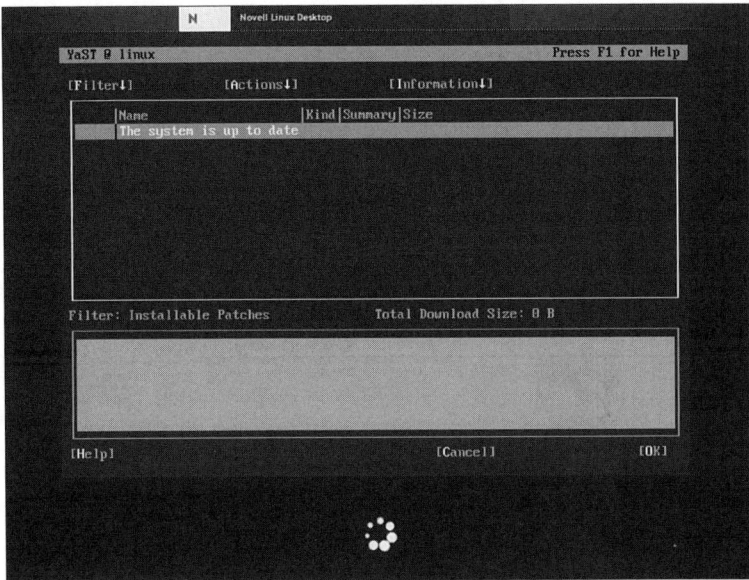

FIGURE 2.25
An Update CD can be used to patch the system.

Tip

Occasionally, an error will occur that a particular patch cannot be installed. When this happens, choose to skip it. After the processes complete, you can run update again and it will only list the patches that were not installed—thus giving you another chance to install them. The vast majority of the time, they will install on a subsequent try without error.

When the updates are finished installing, and SuSEconfig has run, you will often need to reboot. Following that, the system will be running with the latest patches in place.

Note

You should check http://www.novell.com/linux/ for information related to new patches or releases.

Summary

This chapter looked at the requirements for installing the Novell Linux Desktop and walked through the steps in a standard installation. The next chapter focuses on the graphical side of NLD and examines how KDE and GNOME are used.

## CHAPTER 3

Working with the Desktop Environments

Although many administrators are perfectly content to work at the command line, Linux does offer a number of excellent graphical interfaces to choose from based on the X Windows System. Novell Desktop Linux includes two of these: KDE and GNOME. During installation, you can choose which of the two you want to install, and you can always add the other at any point after the installation (see Chapter 5, "Working with YaST"), if you choose to do so.

Each desktop has its own set of equivalent applications, and you can even run applications for one desktop under the other if the right libraries are present. As mentioned in Chapter 2, "Installing Novell Linux Desktop 9," KDE is the desktop environment that is most widely used with SUSE Linux, but Novell is leaning more toward GNOME on Novell Linux Desktop, and most new tools are written for it.

In this chapter, we'll first look at the GNOME interface and the elements of it. Following that, we'll look at the KDE interface.

An Overview of GNOME

During installation, you can choose either KDE or GNOME as the default desktop environment for your system. GNOME is chock-full of features, and Figure 3.1 shows the opening screen, whereas Figure 3.2 shows the Nautilus browser graphically depicting the computer.

NOTE

If both KDE and GNOME are installed, you can click on Session on the Novell Linux Desktop login screen and choose between GNOME Desktop or KDE Desktop. A third choice, Failsafe, also appears and is used for troubleshooting.

FIGURE 3.1
The default GNOME desktop environment.

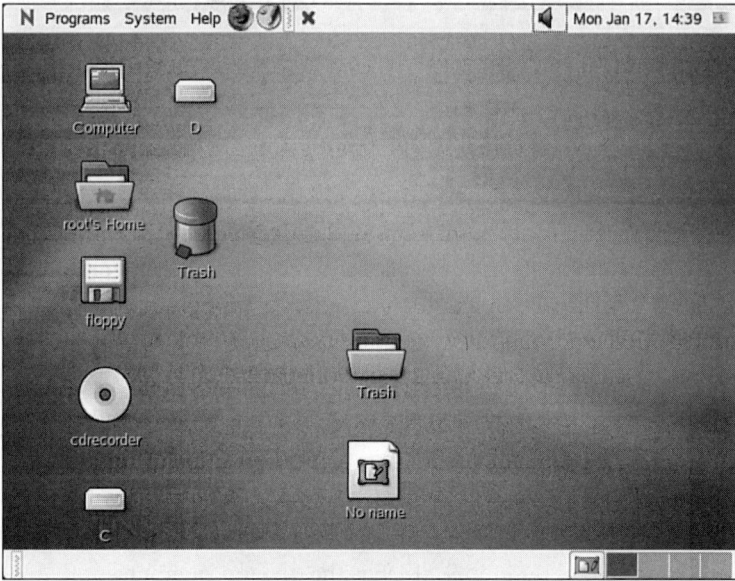

FIGURE 3.2
You can access the drives through the browser.

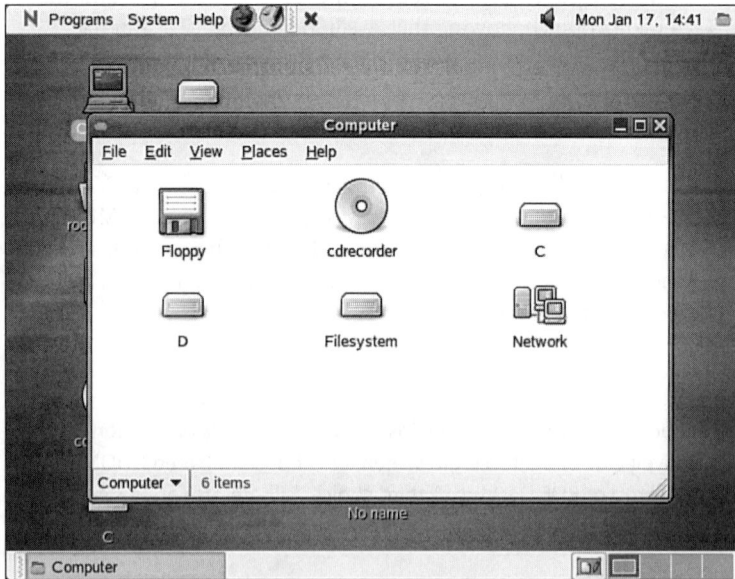

With GNOME, the clock appears in the upper right corner on what is known as the *panel*, and the menu options and hot buttons are along the top left of the screen by default. This is the normal location for the panel, but it can be easily changed by dragging it to the bottom or either side of the screen or changing the properties.

By right-clicking on the panel, you can choose to add or remove items from it. Figure 3.3 shows the pop-up menu of items that can be added to the panel, whereas Figure 3.4 shows the properties that can be configured for the panel.

FIGURE 3.3
You can add additional items to the panel.

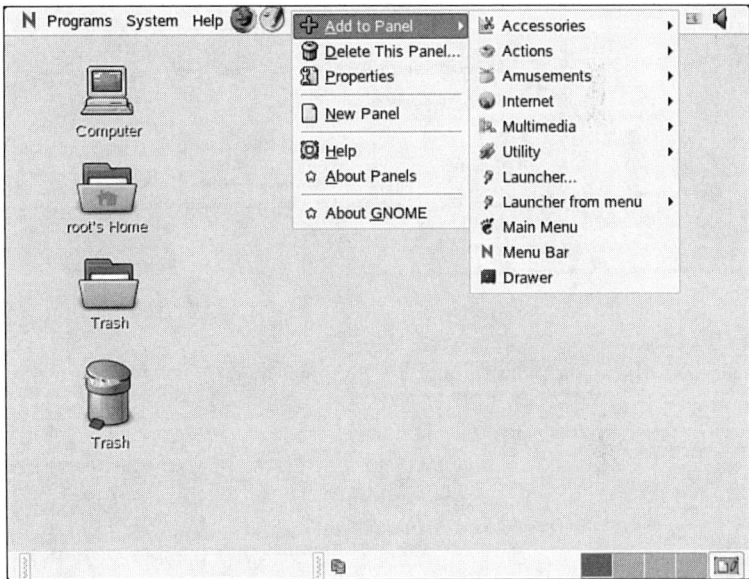

The bottom panel, by default, shows the running applications and offers you the ability to choose between them. In the rightmost corner is an icon of a desktop that you can click to hide all windows and show the desktop.

The Programs menu, shown in Figure 3.5, holds the known applications.

Of key importance on the System menu is the Administrator Settings choice. This opens the YaST (Yet Another Setup Tool) interface, as shown in Figure 3.6. This tool is thoroughly discussed in Chapter 5, "Working with YaST."

FIGURE 3.4
You can configure items for the panel.

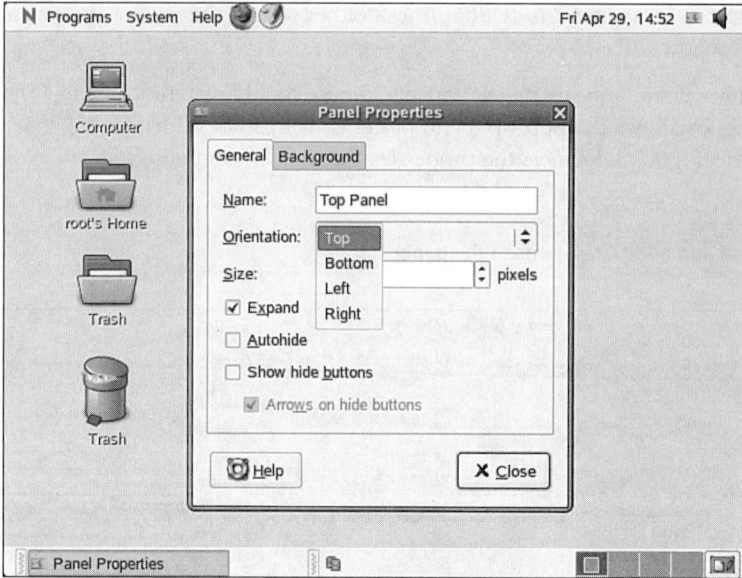

FIGURE 3.5
You can access the applications through the Programs menu.

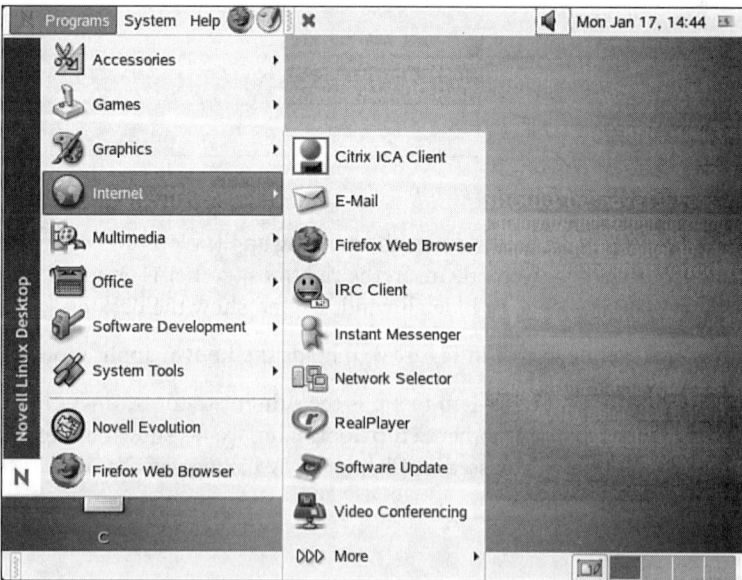

FIGURE 3.6
Administrator Settings offers an easy way to access YaST.

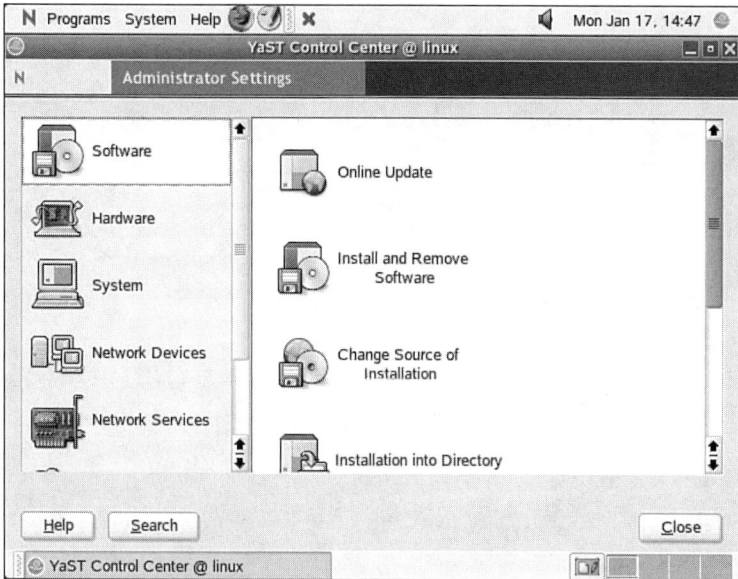

If a user attempts to access this utility, he must provide the root password, and is prompted to do so, as shown in Figure 3.7.

Other choices on the System menu are

- Personal Settings—Allows the user to configure such things as the screen resolution, sounds, shortcuts, and so on.

- Search for Files—Find files, folders, and documents on the computer.

- Recent Files—See, and access, the most recently viewed files.

- Software Update—As discussed in Chapter 2, this is used to install patches and updates.

- Run Program—Runs a program by filename without going through the menu choices.

- Log Out—Exits this user and brings up the login screen for another user to log in.

FIGURE 3.7
You must have root access to run Administrator Settings.

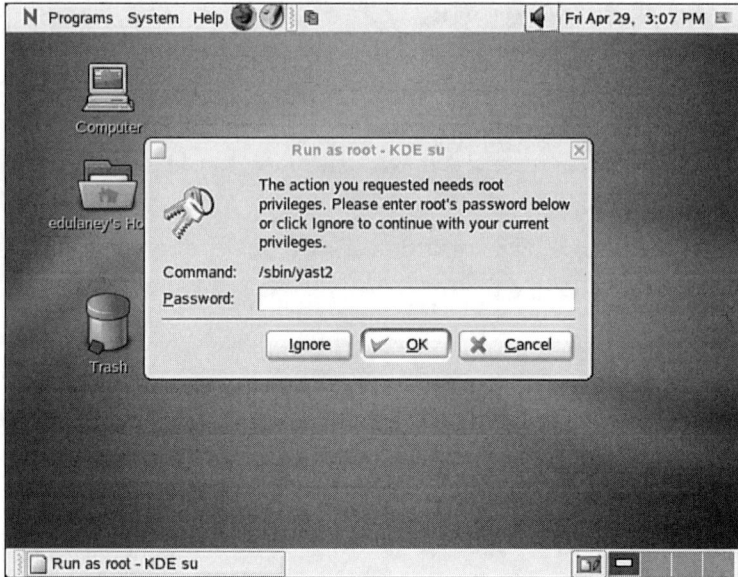

NOTE

If a user other than root is logged in, a choice of Lock Screen also appears. When this is chosen, the password associated with the user account must be given in order to unlock the screen.

The Help menu choice opens the User Manual, whereas the icon of the world starts the Firefox web browser. The icon of a circle with a pencil starts the OpenOffice word processor.

Administering the GNOME Desktop

Under normal circumstances, you typically allow users to work with the desktop and make any changes to it they want that can make them more productive. Under certain circumstances, however, you not want them to have the ability to make changes to certain elements.

Most users can access the Personal Settings option on the System menu and be able to change their desktop background, fonts, screensaver, and such, as shown in Figure 3.8. The same configuration for Desktop Background can also be accessed by right-clicking on the desktop and choosing Change Desktop Background from the popup menu.

FIGURE 3.8
Users can change their display settings.

The Config Editor can be used with GNOME to change configuration values if you want to apply a more uniform appearance; this tool is discussed further in the KDE section that follows. Additionally, you can use the `gconftool-2` command-line utility to configure a plethora of options, as shown in Figure 3.9.

`gconftool` is extremely complex, and it is not suggested that mere mortals even attempt to use this tool. Read the man page carefully for this utility to find the option to use to set a particular option.

FIGURE 3.9
You can change most GNOME settings with gconftool-2.

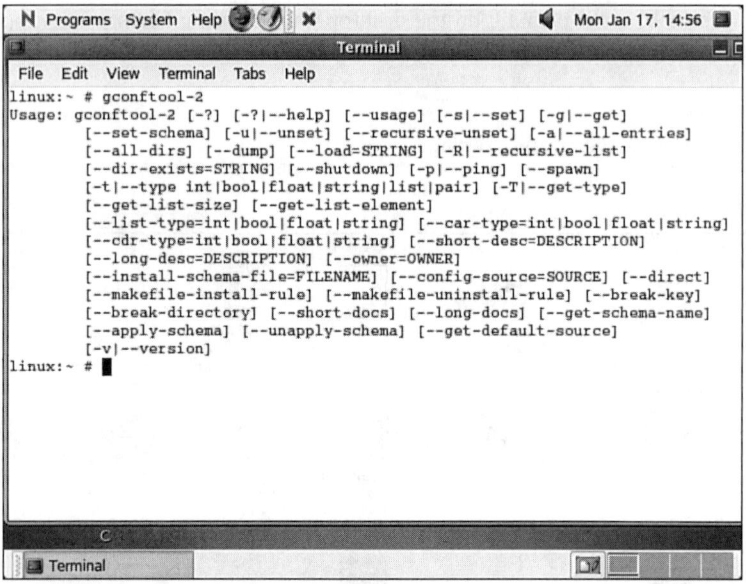

```
N  Programs  System  Help  🌀 🕐 ✕                    🔊  Mon Jan 17, 14:56  ▣

▣                                    Terminal                                ▬▢
 File  Edit  View  Terminal  Tabs  Help
linux:~ # gconftool-2
Usage: gconftool-2 [-?] [-?|--help] [--usage] [-s|--set] [-g|--get]
        [--set-schema] [-u|--unset] [--recursive-unset] [-a|--all-entries]
        [--all-dirs] [--dump] [--load=STRING] [-R|--recursive-list]
        [--dir-exists=STRING] [--shutdown] [-p|--ping] [--spawn]
        [-t|--type int|bool|float|string|list|pair] [-T|--get-type]
        [--get-list-size] [--get-list-element]
        [--list-type=int|bool|float|string] [--car-type=int|bool|float|string]
        [--cdr-type=int|bool|float|string] [--short-desc=DESCRIPTION]
        [--long-desc=DESCRIPTION] [--owner=OWNER]
        [--install-schema-file=FILENAME] [--config-source=SOURCE] [--direct]
        [--makefile-install-rule] [--makefile-uninstall-rule] [--break-key]
        [--break-directory] [--short-docs] [--long-docs] [--get-schema-name]
        [--apply-schema] [--unapply-schema] [--get-default-source]
        [-v|--version]
linux:~ # █

                  C
 ▣ Terminal                                              ▢▢ ▭▭ ▯ ▮
```

An Overview of KDE

If you've never worked with Linux before, but have experience working with the Windows environment, you'll find that you are quickly able to understand the KDE desktop and work effectively within it. Figure 3.10 shows the basic desktop.

Notice that icons appear on the desktop for entities that can be accessed. The two appearing in Figure 3.10 are the Trash (where deleted files are temporarily stored), and the CDWRITER. A green arrow at the bottom right of the CDWRITER icon indicates that it is mounted (available), and the lack of such an arrow beneath the icon would mean that it is not yet mounted.

Right-clicking on the icon for the device will bring up a context-sensitive menu, which will include such choices as Mount and Unmount. You can add icons for the Floppy or other devices as they are needed.

In Figure 3.10, you will see a number of icons in a frame along the bottom of the screen—this area is historically known as the *kicker*, but commonly called the *panel*. The button that is a Red N brings up a menu of all configured programs and functions and is known as the KDE menu. The blue house is a hardwired shortcut to bring up the home directory in Konqueror (the KDE file manager). The monitor with the shell in front of it is used to open a terminal session (an interactive shell). The life preserver icon starts the KDE HelpCenter. The globe with gear teeth starts the Konqueror web browser. The icon of an envelope and a calendar page brings up the Kontact personal information manager.

FIGURE 3.10
The basic KDE desktop.

To the right of these icons are two boxes—white and gray. They represent the virtual desktops; views that you can switch between. To the right of that is an area known as the taskbar, where active tasks are listed. To the right of that is the System Tray, where items such as the clock, loudspeaker, and so on can appear. The three arrows to the far right are used to scroll left, scroll right, and hide the panel (the entire lower area starting with the kicker).

KDE Menu

The KDE menu, shown in Figure 3.11, is divided into three sections. The first section lists the most frequently used applications, and the second section offers access to all applications. The third section provides shortcuts to some commonly performed tasks.

FIGURE 3.11
The KDE menu.

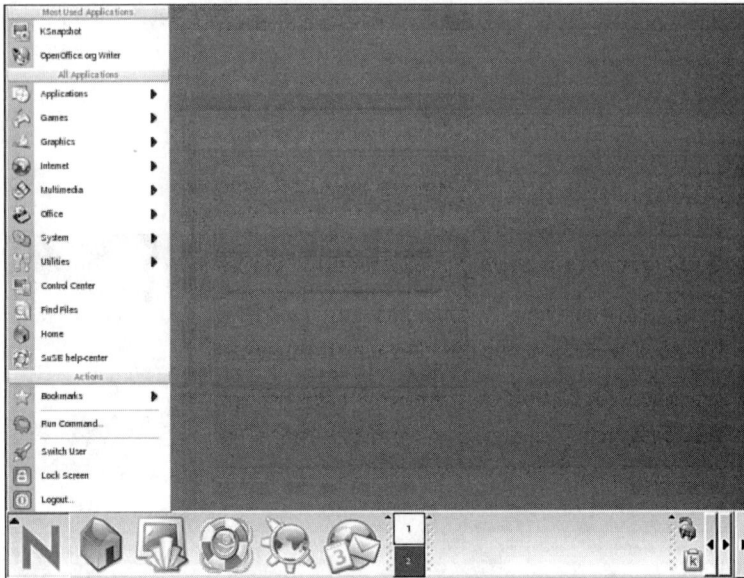

Konqueror

The Konqueror file manager, shown in Figure 3.12, is an object browser of sorts that allows you graphical access to all entities (file objects, http objects, network objects, network protocol objects, and so on). It automatically takes you to your own home directory when it is accessed through the Home short-cut. In the upper-right corner, there are four button choices. The question mark is used to access help. The underline is used to minimize the window. The square is used to restore the window to its regular size. The X button is used to close the window.

A number of icons appear below the menu bar. Starting from the left, the up arrow is used to take you to the next higher level; for example to /etc from /etc/cups. The left arrow moves you back to where you were previously. The right arrow moves you forward (after you've gone back). The house icon takes you to your home directory. The circle icon reloads, or refreshes the display. The X icon stops loading the current page. To the right of this are icons for cutting, copying, pasting, printing, and changing icon sizes and views.

A number of icons appear along the left frame. Starting from the top, the wrench icon allows you to configure the navigation area. The star shows your bookmarks. The cubes show your devices. The clock shows history. The house shows the home directory. The connected globe shows the network, including access available Windows networks if SMB has been configured. The folders icon shows the root directory, and the flags show special KDE services.

FIGURE 3.12
The Konqueror file manager.

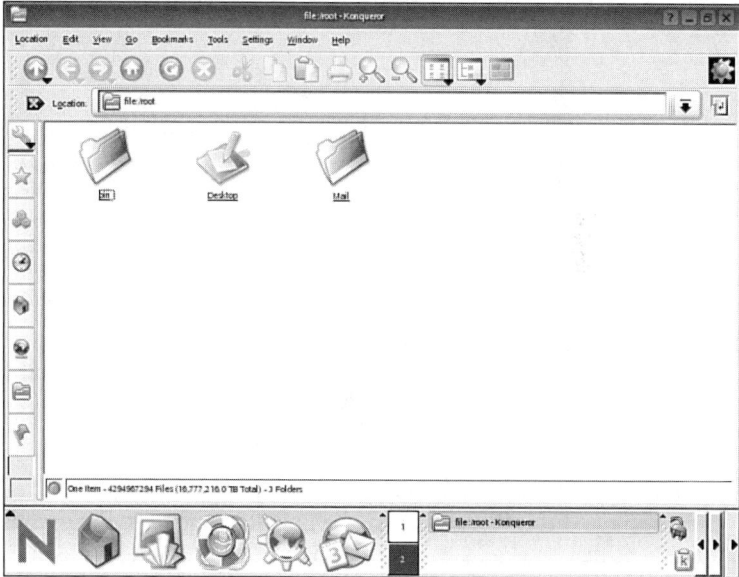

Right-clicking on any item in the display area brings up a context-sensitive menu from which you can make choices such as copy, paste, and so on. Just clicking on the item will open it, or double-clicking on a folder will open it and show the entries beneath it.

Shell

Choosing to open a shell, by clicking on the third icon in the kicker/panel, brings up an interactive shell, as shown in Figure 3.13. The shell can be thought of as a command-line interface.

The menu options along the top are: Session (open a new shell, new Linux console, print the screen, and so on), Edit (copy, paste, history, and so on), View (monitor for activity), Bookmark (add, edit), Settings (keyboard, fonts, size, and so on), and Help.

FIGURE 3.13
You can interact with the command line by opening a shell.

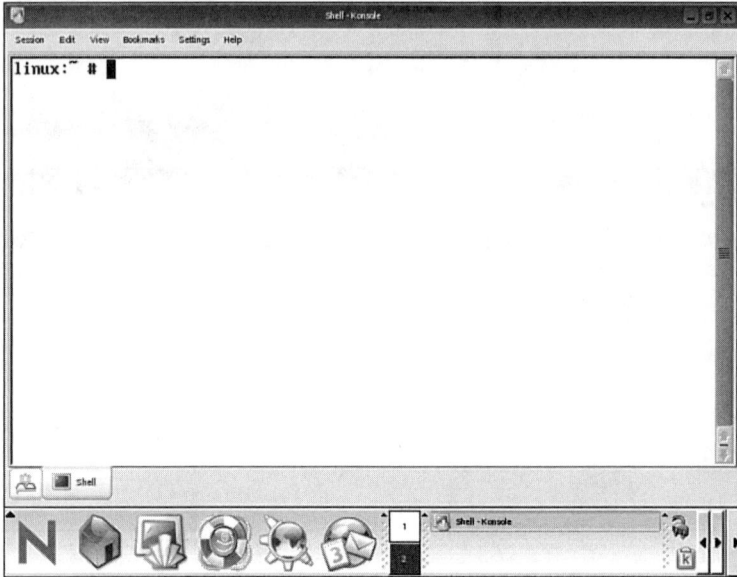

You can open as many shell sessions as you want, and the icon, just above the kicker, will automatically start a new shell session. Shell sessions are just individual shells that you can switch between by selecting the appropriate tab.

KDE HelpCenter

The KDE HelpCenter, shown in Figure 3.14, is the quickest way to access the Admin Guide, as well as application manuals, documentation for developers, and online resources.

In the left frame, there are tabs allowing you access to the TOC, Glossary, and a Search widget where you can search for particular entities.

Web Browser

The Konqueror web browser, shown in Figure 3.15, resembles the file manager and offers the same icons and menu items for a good reason. It is exactly the same application, just used to look at a different type of object (http versus file).

FIGURE 3.14
The KDE HelpCenter.

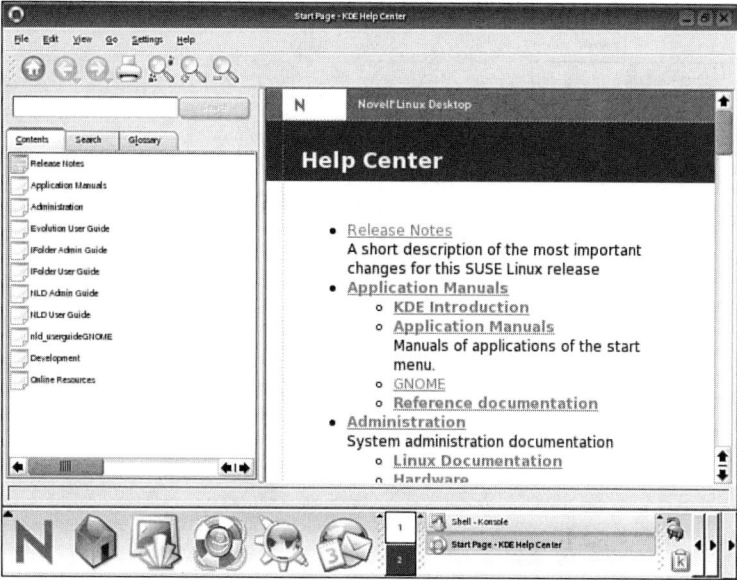

FIGURE 3.15
The Konqueror web browser.

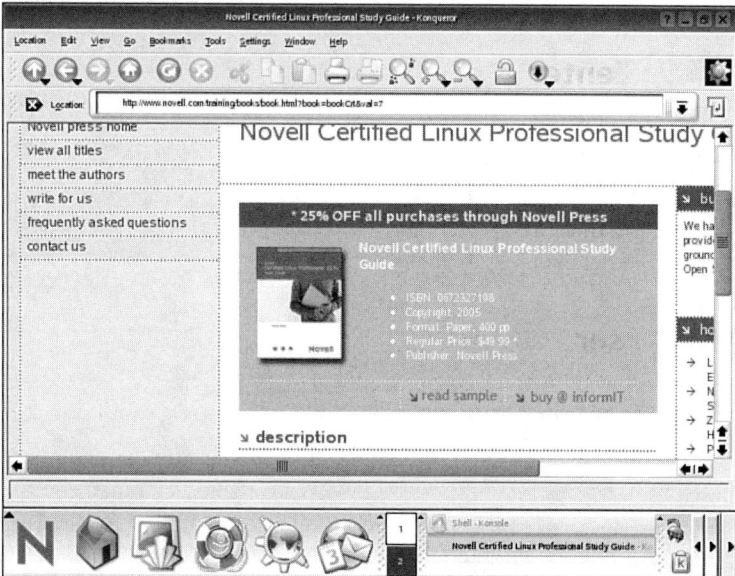

Figure 3.15 shows a sample web page. By default, this icon isn't associated with a specific web page.

(E)KONTACT

The Kontact utility, shown in Figure 3.16, offers a simple-to-use personal information manager (PIM). Among the application choices are

- Mail
- Contacts
- Todo List
- Calendar
- Notes

FIGURE 3.16
The Kontact utility.

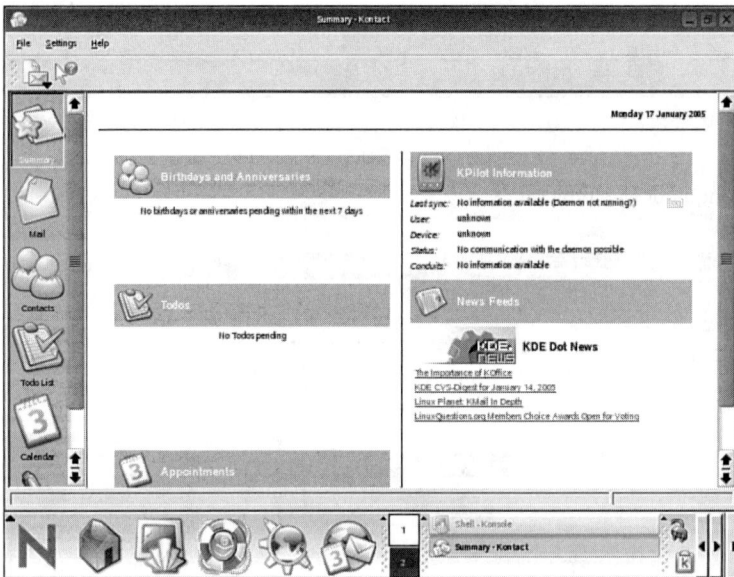

Configuring the Desktop

You can access the configuration options for the KDE desktop in a number of different ways. The simplest of these methods is to right-click on an empty spot on the desktop and choose Configure Desktop from the pop-up menu. This brings up the configuration interface shown in Figure 3.17.

FIGURE 3.17
You can configure the desktop to your liking.

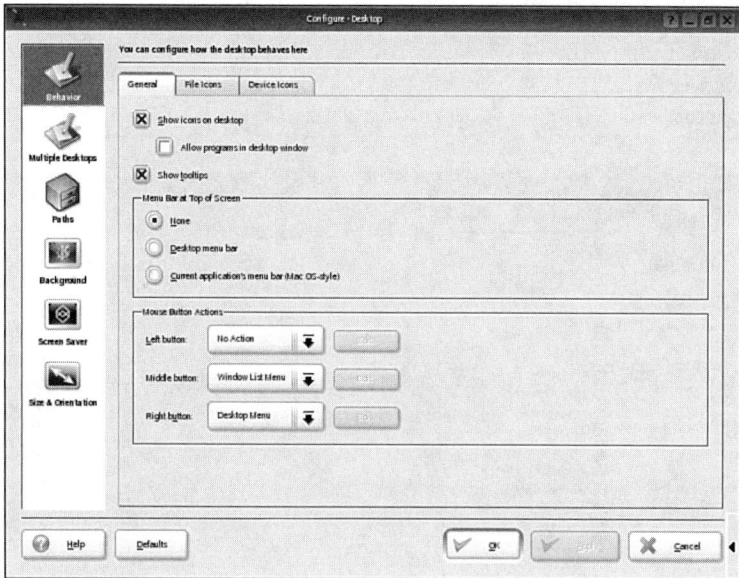

The configuration choices are divided into the following categories:

- Behavior—Icon settings and mouse actions.
- Multiple Desktops—Configure how many virtual desktops there are.
- Paths—Set the path for the desktop, trash, autostart, and documents.
- Background—Choose from a number of different pictures or select your own.
- Screen Saver—Configure and test screen saver settings.
- Size & Orientation—Set the screen size, refresh rate, and related variables.

To add icons to the desktop for other devices installed, you have two choices—manual and automatic. The easiest method is to go the automatic route. To do this, click on the Device Icons tab, shown in Figure 3.17, and click the Show Device Icons check box, as shown in Figure 3.18.

NOTE

This only works when the Behavior configuration choice is selected, as it is by default when you first start the Configure Desktop item.

FIGURE 3.18
You can easily add additional devices to your desktop.

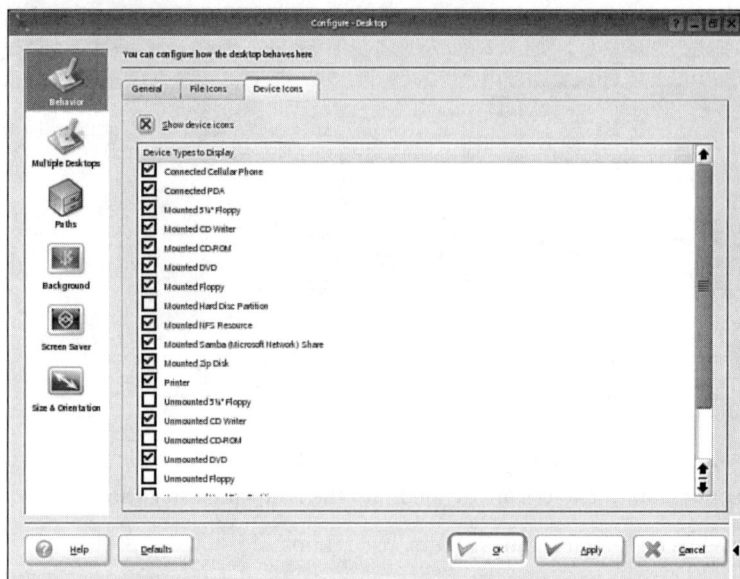

This automatically highlights all devices for which icons are available on your system, and when you click Apply, you will see additional devices on your desktop, as shown if Figure 3.19 (contrast with Figure 3.10).

You can add them manually by right-clicking on the desktop and choosing Create New, Device, and then the type of device, as shown in Figure 3.20. You will need to add any necessary parameters based on the type of device added.

TIP

You will only want, or need, to add them manually if you have not enabled Show Device Icons or have added new hardware to your system that is in a category which was not previously highlighted when you enabled Show Device Icons.

FIGURE 3.19
The new devices appear on the desktop.

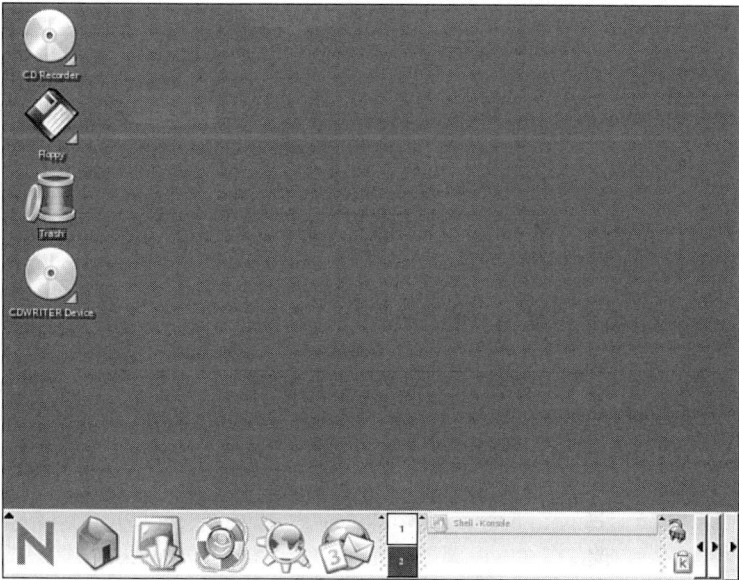

FIGURE 3.20
You can manually add a device to the desktop.

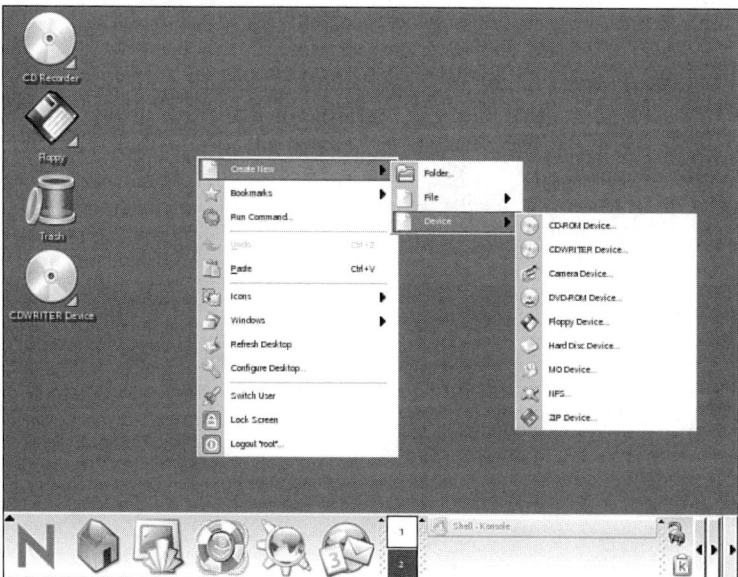

Administering the KDE Desktop

Under normal circumstances, you typically allow users to work with the desktop and make any changes to it they want that can make them more productive. The KDE Control Center is the most common way for users to configure their desktop environment. It provides access to the Configure Desktop items discussed in the previous section, as well as to the Appearance & Themes items, and many other more granular configurable items.

Under certain circumstances, however, you don't want them to have the ability to make changes to certain elements. KDE uses a number of text files to configure its environment, and it is possible to painstakingly edit those for changes you want to make. A far better option, however, is to use two utilities designed for such a purpose:

- The Kiosk Admin Tool
- The Config Editor

Both of these are fairly obscure configuration tools, and the purpose of the following section is only to introduce you to their existence and what can be done with them. The level of complexity of each requires a depth of knowledge beyond the scope of this book.

The Kiosk Admin Tool

Although very rare, it is possible to use KDE in Kiosk mode in the most restrictive environments. This is typically only used by system administrators who want a number of systems deployed to be similarly locked down, and can clone one configuration to a number of machines since manually configuring kiosks is a very time-consuming undertaking.

The KDE Kiosk Admin Tool can be started on the command line with the command `kiosktool`, and opens to the first screen shown in Figure 3.21.

Figure 3.21 shows the default profiles, and more can be easily added by using the Add New Profile button on the right. This brings up the dialog box shown in Figure 3.22.

The power of the tool lays in the Configure button, which allows you to store profiles under a different directory and choose whether or not profiles are uploaded to a remote server upon exit. Figure 3.23 shows the `kiosktool` configuration. Once you create a profile, many aspects of it can be configured. You get to this panel by double-clicking on a profile.

FIGURE 3.21
You can lock down the desktop with the Kiosk Admin Tool.

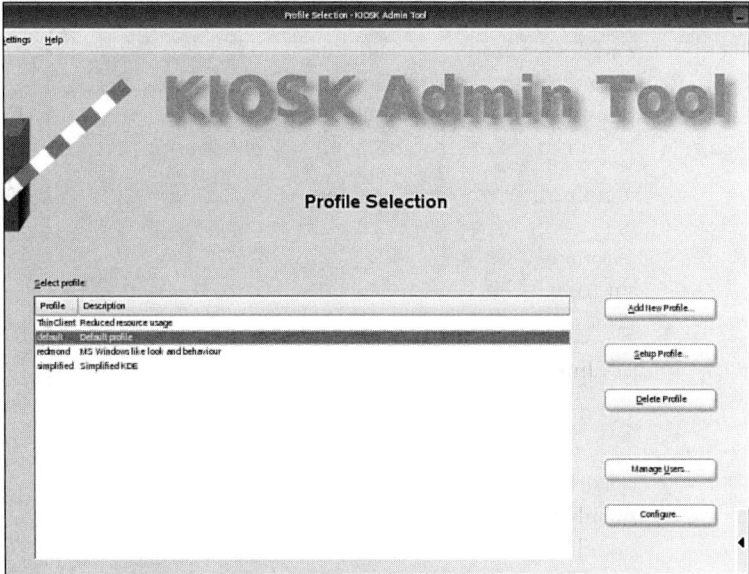

FIGURE 3.22
Adding a new profile requires filling in only a few fields.

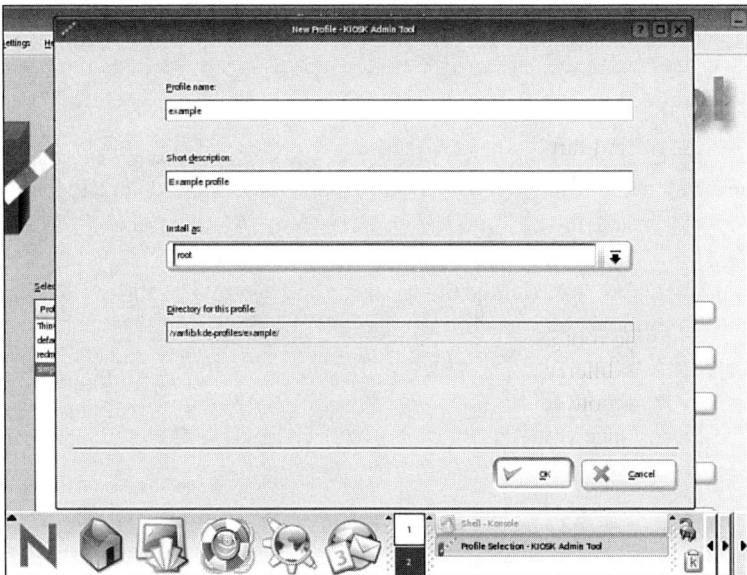

FIGURE 3.23
A number of configuration options are available.

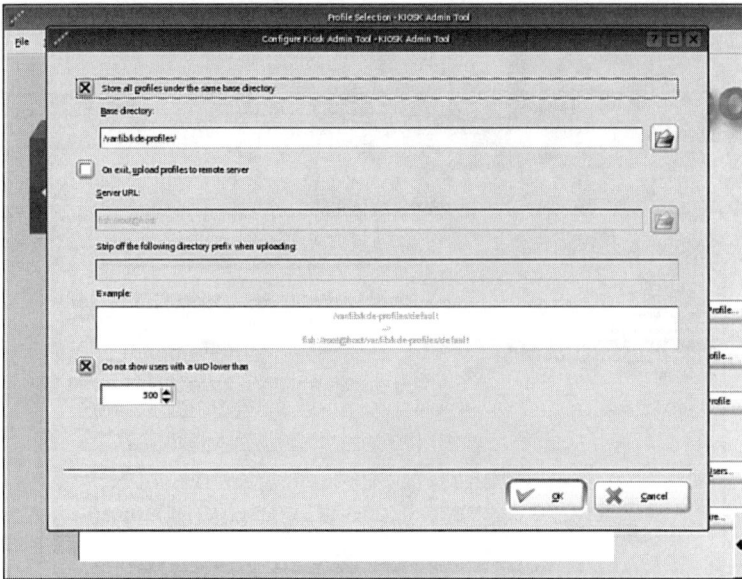

The Config Editor

The KDE Config Editor is rarely used by anyone except experts, as it is the KDE equivalent of Windows' regedit. It can be started on the command line with the command kconfigeditor, and opens to the first screen shown in Figure 3.24.

NOTE

It cannot be stressed enough that this is an experts-only tool, and not a tool for normal users.

Using this tool, you can change the value for any key in a configuration file. There are hundreds of keys with very specific meanings, and it would take an entire book to document them; the purpose here is to merely make you aware of the existence of such a tool.

FIGURE 3.24
You can change values with the Config Editor.

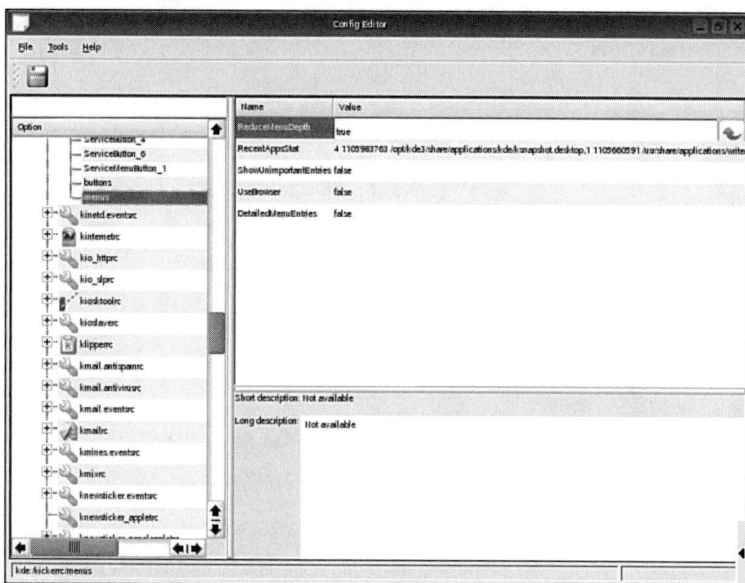

NOTE

As mentioned at the beginning of this chapter, the Config Tool also works with GNOME settings and can be used to make configuration changes for that desktop as well.

Summary

This chapter focused on the graphical side of the Novell Linux Desktop and examined how KDE and GNOME are used. Both desktops are included with NLD, and you can choose which one you are most comfortable with. The next chapter looks at the command line and the most used utilities you will need to know to effectively administer the system.

## CHAPTER 4

Working on the Command Line

The lowest common denominator across all versions and implementations of Linux is the command line. This chapter provides you with the core set of skills that you must know in order to be able to work effectively with any Linux implementation.

Basics of the Command Line

To understand the command line and work there effectively, you must understand the processes that are taking place. Within Linux, the shell is the command interpreter. It takes commands that a user gives, processes them (or sends them to the appropriate utility/interacts with the kernel), and formats the finished results for the user. Thus, the shell is the mediator between the operating system and the user. Not only can it interpret commands, but it can also handle redirection (input and output), filename generation, some programming, variable substitution, piping, and a host of other services.

A number of different shells (interpreters) are available, and different distributions include different combinations of choices with their operating systems. The simplest of all is the Bourne shell (sh), which is one of the earliest ones created for the Unix platform and it offers the smallest number of features. The Korn shell (ksh) was one of the first to expand on, and deviate from, sh, and it includes a larger number of options. The Bourne Again shell (bash) took many of the features from Korn, and some new ones, and combined them with sh, while trying to reduce deviations. The Z shell (zsh) is the largest shell of all and added a whole new set of features to the Korn shell.

Not to be overlooked are shells created to make the environment more friendly to those familiar with the C programming language. The first of these was the C shell (csh), which added C-like features to the interpreter and deviated greatly from the Bourne shell. It has been expanded on by Tom's C shell (tcsh).

As a generalization, every distribution includes more than one shell for the user to choose from, but rarely do they include all the available shells. In many versions, there are three prevalent shells:

- bash
- tcsh
- zsh

Note

All shells reside in the /bin directory, and the default can be specified for the user in the user's /etc/passwd file entry. The /etc/shells file lists the shells that each user can have as valid login shell entries in /etc/passwd.

There are slight deviations in the way each shell carries out its tasks, but all perform a core set of functions. Throughout this section, we will look at the core functions for all shells and discuss any relevant differences, as they apply.

Command-Line Interaction

When a command is entered, the shell must determine if the command is for it (built-in, or internal) or not (external). If the command is an internal one, it does the processing and sends the output back without further interaction being needed. If the command cannot be found within the shell itself, it is assumed to be an external utility (such as ls, cat, cal, and so on). The command syntax for external commands is always assumed to be

```
{program name} {option(s)} {argument(s)}
```

Although it is not always the case, usually there are three components that can be given to a command. The simplest command to give is simply the name of the utility, for example:

```
ls
```

This will return an output list of files and directories similar to

```
Desktop     sample     snapshot01.gif     snapshot02.gif
```

In this case, only the program name was given, and no options. This results in a listing of all files within the present directory being shown in the default format. An option can be specified to change the display to include/exclude information and/or change the format of the display. An example would be

```
ls -l
```

This changes the output to

```
total 34
drwx---    5   root    root    1024    Jul 19 16:34 Desktop
-rw-r-r-   1   root    root    155     Jul 19 16:48 sample
-rw-r-r-   1   root    root    12497   Jul 19 16:39 snapshot01.gif
-rw-r-r-   1   root    root    17257   Jul 19 16:50 snapshot02.gif
```

Here, the program name has been specified (ls), as well as an option to use with it (-l) to change the listing to the "long" format.

Note

It is important to understand that whitespace must always be used to separate the parameters from one another. Whitespace can be either one or more space characters or tab characters.

If the command were given as ls-l, an error message would be generated because there is no utility by the name of ls-l, and the interpreter would not be capable of distinguishing the program name from the option.

Note

The man and info commands can be used to find information (manual pages) on most commands. For example, to see information on the use of the ls command: man ls

The options, as well as the arguments, are optional and never required. To complete the example, an argument can also be used with the command:

```
ls -l *.gif
```

This will result in the following display:

```
-rw-r-r-   1   root    root    12497   Jul 19 16:39 snapshot01.gif
-rw-r-r-   1   root    root    17257   Jul 19 16:50 snapshot02.gif
```

Note

Alternatively, the argument can be used without the options, like this:

```
ls *.gif
```

The number of arguments that can be given is not limited to one. Although there may be limitations on the number of parameters an individual utility will accept, typically you can string multiple requests together. For example, instead of specifying

```
ls -l sa*
```

as one command and then following it with

```
ls -l *.gif
```

you can accomplish the same operation with

```
ls -l sa* *.gif
```

The result of the operation becomes

```
-rw-r-r-   1   root   root    155    Jul 19 16:48 sample
-rw-r-r-   1   root   root   12497   Jul 19 16:39 snapshot01.gif
-rw-r-r-   1   root   root   17257   Jul 19 16:50 snapshot02.gif
```

If the number of arguments you are giving becomes too long to be easily readable on the command line, or if you simply want to break up the entry a bit, you can use the backslash character to signify that you are continuing from one line to the next. For example,

```
ls -l sa* \
*.gif
```

Tip

The backslash actually just prevents the newline from being interpreted by the shell, which is usually expressed as "escaping the newline." The backslash must be the last character on the line before the newline in order to work this way.

If you were giving hundreds of such arguments, you would use the backslash following each entry to separate each. This would make entry easier to view and the command would not execute until the Enter key is pressed without being preceded by a backslash. For example,

```
ls -l sa* \
*.gif \
*.ead \
*.txt \
*.doc
```

Connecting Commands

In all the examples thus far, the Enter key is used to inform the shell that you have given a command that needs to be processed. You are not, however, limited to giving the shell only one command at a time.

Multiple commands, not connected to one another in any way, can be given on the same line as long as the semicolon (;) is used as a command separator. For example, it is possible to see all the files in the current directory and the current date by giving the following two commands in succession:

```
ls
date
```

These are unrelated commands in that the output of the second has absolutely nothing to do with the output of the first. You can combine them on a single command line with a semicolon between the two and get the same result:

```
ls ; date
```

The semicolon is a special character signaling that multiple commands are on the same line. This character allows you to break the whitespace rule on both sides of it (`ls;date`) while giving you the same result.

If the commands *do* have something in common—the output of one is to become the input of the next—they are connected using a pipe (|). For example, if a list of files within a directory is too long to fit on one screen, you can view a screen at a time by using this command:

```
ls -l | more
```

Here the output of the `ls -l` command becomes the input of the `more` command. If the first part of the entire command line fails, the second part cannot possibly be executed successfully.

Note

The second part of a failed pipe will always attempt to execute and fail, usually complaining that it has "no input."

Wildcards

Wildcards are characters used to signify other characters that the shell fills in. The two most common wildcard characters are the asterisk (*) and question mark (?). Although they are often confused, their meanings are different and can lead to completely different results.

The asterisk is used to signify any and all; anything and nothing; alpha and omega. For example,

```
ls s*
```

will find all entries (files and directories) within the current directory starting with the letter "s" and having any number of alphanumeric characters following—including none. Possible results it could generate in the display include

```
s    sa    sam    samp    sampl    sample    samples    samples.gif
```

Note that it finds "s" alone, and "s" with any number of entries following it. In contrast, the question mark is a placeholder for one character, and only one character. Using the same file possibilities, the following command

```
ls s?
```

will only find entries (files and directories) in the current directory starting with the letter "s" and having only one character following. The resulting display generated is

```
sa
```

If you want to find only five-letter entries beginning with "s," the command to use would be

```
ls s????
```

To recap, the asterisk means all or none, and the question mark always means one. These two wildcards are not mutually exclusive, and can be used in combination with one another as the need arises. For example, to find only files with three-letter extensions, regardless of the filename, the command would be

```
ls *.???
```

To muddy the waters a bit, you can also use brackets ([]) to specify possible values. All the possible values must reside within the brackets and are used individually. For example,

```
ls [de]*
```

will find all entries that start with either "d" or "e" and have an unlimited number of characters following. To find only three-character entries that start with "d" or "e," the command would become

```
ls [de]??
```

The number of characters within the brackets can be virtually unlimited. Therefore, if you wanted to find all entries that start with a lowercase

letter instead of a number (or other character), you could use
"[abcdefghijklmnopqrstuvwxyz]." However, because this is a range,
a much simpler way to signify it would be "[a-z]":

```
ls [a-z]*
```

The ranges need not be a complete set (though complete sets are easier to specify), and can jump around if needed. For example, if you only want to look for
entries that fall within the range from "d" to "t," you could use either
"[defghijklmnopqrst]" or "[d-t]." If the entry could be between the two
values upper- and lowercase, you can either use
"[DEFGHIJKLMNOPQRSTdefghijklmnopqrst]" or "[D-Td-t]."

Some more examples follow:

- All letters (upper- and lowercase): [A-z]

Note

"[A-z]" is the same as saying "[A-Z]" and "[a-z]."

- All numbers [0-9]
- All letters and numbers [A-z0-9]
- Not a number [!0-9]
- Not a letter [!A-z]

The Path Statement and Other Variables

When you enter a command at the command prompt and the shell cannot find
it internally, it must look for a utility by that name externally. It does this by
searching directories specified in the PATH variable, in the order they are listed,
until it finds the first match. If no match is found after all listed directories
have been searched, the result is an error message ("command not found").

Note

All Unix/Linux shells support internal variables that are typically known as environment variables. The most common of these is PATH, which is a colon-separat-
ed list of directories that the shell should search for commands.

The way in which environment variables are set is shell-specific—bash, ksh,
sh, and ash share one convention whereas csh and tcsh share another. This
chapter—and this book—focuses on bash.

There are several important things to know about the path:

1. You can view your path by using the **echo** command:

   echo $PATH

2. The path does not, by default, include the present directory. Thus, you can create an executable file in your home directory, see it right before you (with **ls**), and when you type its name, you will be told that the command cannot be found. To circumvent this, you can give the full path to the file, add your home directory to your **PATH** variable, move the file to a directory in the path statement, or add the present directory variable (.) to the **PATH** variable.

3. Entries within the path are separated by colons (:).

4. The order of the **PATH** search should always include the most common directories where executables can be found first (the **bin** directories) and the user-specific directories (if any) at the end.

To add another directory to your path, you can redefine the entire statement, or simply append the new directory with the command

PATH=$PATH:{new directory}

Thus to add the directory **/home/edulaney** to the path, the command would be

PATH=$PATH:/home/edulaney

Or you can add a variable that signifies you always want the directory you are currently working in to be searched for the utility:

PATH=$PATH:.

Note

For security reasons, it is always recommended that you not include the current directory in your path. If you must do so, however, it should be at the end of the PATH statement—as shown in the preceding example—and not at the beginning.

For example, if your current PATH is equal to /sbin:/usr/sbin:/usr/local/sbin:/root/bin:/usr/local/bin:/usr/bin, you want the new PATH to look like /sbin:/usr/sbin:/usr/local/sbin:/root/bin:/usr/local/bin:/usr/bin:./ and not

./:/sbin:/usr/sbin:/usr/local/sbin:/root/bin:/usr/local/bin:/usr
/bin because the directories are always searched in the order they appear in
PATH.

Common Variables

Any variable that exists can display its values using the following syntax:

echo ${variable name}

Thus the command

echo $MAIL

will show the mail directory, $HOME the home directory, and so on. To see a
complete list of the environmental variables that are defined, you can use two
commands—env and set. Although the displays can differ slightly (environmental variables only versus local variables), for the most part the output of
env is a subset of the output of set. Some of the variables that can display
include the following:

- HOME—The directory you begin in, and where you end up when typing
  cd without any other parameters
- LINES—Number of lines within the display before pausing (more)
- LOGNAME—The username under which the current user is logged in
- PWD—The present working directory, or where you are now
- SHELL—Which interpreter you are using
- TERM—The type of terminal, or emulation, in use
- USER—Which rarely differs from LOGNAME but can if you the user are
  using a command such as su, which enables you to temporarily execute
  commands as another user

Note

As a general rule, predefined system variables are always in uppercase.

You can change the value of variables as needed or add your own to be referenced in programs or at the command prompt. For example, to create a new
variable called TODAY, use the following syntax:

TODAY=Wednesday

You can now see the value of the variable by using the command

```
echo $TODAY
```

the result will be **Wednesday**. If you now use the command

```
set
```

the variable will appear there. However, if you use the following command, it will not:

```
env
```

The variable has been created locally, and can be referenced locally. In order for it to be accessible in subroutines and child processes, you must move it from local status into the environment, and this is accomplished via the **export** command:

```
export TODAY
```

This moves the variable to where it can be found in the environment, as well as locally, and accessed by subroutines and child processes. The variable, and its value, will be available for the duration of the session, and lost when you log out. To make the value permanent, you must add the entry to a profile.

To change the value of the variable, simply define its new value:

```
TODAY=Monday
```

Because it has already been exported, this need not be done again, and the new value will apply locally as well as in the environment. Should it be necessary to remove a variable, you can use the **unset** command.

Among those variables present and definable are those that present the prompt. The prompt is the visual message from the shell that tells you it is ready for input. The default prompts include

- **$** as the last character for Bourne, BASH, and Korn shells
- **%** as the last character for C shell and Z shell
- **>** as the last character for **tcsh**

The primary prompt is either the variable **PS1** or **prompt**, based on which shell you are using. In **bash**, a typical value for **PS1** is

```
[\u@\h \W]\$
```

Note

PS1 is also usually followed by a space, to separate it from what the user types. You can see this if you type **echo \"$PS1\"**.

Dissected into its components, **PS1** is equal to the following:

- The left bracket ([)
- The name of the current user
- The at symbol (@)
- The name of the current host
- A space
- The present working directory
- The right bracket (])
- The dollar sign ($)

An example of this prompt would be

```
[edulaney@server7 home]$
```

The backslash (\) character is used to signify that a special value should be used. Different values that can be used for the prompt include those shown in Table 4.1.

TABLE 4.1
Variables to Define the Prompt

VALUE	RESULT
\d	Current date
\h	Name of host to first period
\n	New line
\s	Shell
\t	Time
\u	Username
\W	Current directory
\!	History number
\#	Command number
\$	Default prompt—$ for standard users, and # for root
\\	An actual backstroke (literal)
ABC	ABC (the value of that text, or any text given)

Looking at the variables on the system, you will find that more than **PS1** exists. For example, earlier in this chapter, we discussed ending a line with a backstroke to signify that you are not finished entering input yet. If we look at the sequence of events, and include prompts, it would look like this:

```
[edulaney@server7 home]$ ls -1 *.gif \
> *.fig \
> *.bmp
```

Note that the prompt changed from **PS1** to a greater-than sign (>). If it had stayed **PS1**, you would not know that it was still accepting input, so it changed from the primary prompt to a secondary prompt to signify the change in mode. The prompt represented (by default) by the greater-than sign is **PS2**. Its value can be changed from the default to any value you want, including all the special values given in the earlier table. Within most shells, there are three to four layers of prompts.

By now you've realized that the dollar sign ($) is used to signify a variable; when you have a variable named **EXAMPLE**, you view its contents by examining **$EXAMPLE**. Three other variables exist for a shell that can be useful in determining your environment.

- The first—**$$**—will show the process ID number of the shell now running:

  ```
  echo $$
  ```

- The second —**$?**—will show the results of the last command that you ran in terms of whether it was successful (0) or not (1). For example, the `ls` utility accepts an option of `-F` that will differentiate between directories and files by putting a slash behind the name of directories. The `ls` utility does not have a `-z` option. Given this knowledge, the following sequence shows how **$?** can be utilized and includes the prompts and output of each operation:

  ```
  [edulaney@server7 home]$ ls -F
  Desktop\    sample    snapshot01.gif    snapshot02.gif
  [edulaney@server7 home]$ echo $?
  0
  [edulaney@server7 home]$ ls -z
  ls: invalid option - z
  [edulaney@server7 home]$ echo $?
  1
  ```

- The third variable—**$!**—will show the process ID number of the last child process started in the background. If no child processes have been started in the background, the result will be empty. For this discussion, it is useful to know that placing an ampersand (&) at the end of the command will execute the command in the background. For example,

```
[edulaney@server7 home]$ echo $!

[edulaney@server7 home]$ ls -F &
[edulaney@server7 home]$ echo $!
19321
[edulaney@server7 home]$
```

In the first instance, no job had been sent to the background, so the returned value was empty. A job was then sent to the background, and its process ID number could be found by echoing $!.

Quoting

One of the most difficult components of the shell to understand is often the use of quotes. There are a few rules to remember to make understanding the concept easier:

1. There are three types of quotes—double quotes ("), single quotes ('), and back quotes (`). Each has a different and distinct meaning. Double quotes are used to disable all characters except ', \, and $. Single quotes disable all characters except the back quote. The back quote substitutes the value for a command.

Note

"Disabling" is used to mean overriding the expansion/interpretation of characters that otherwise have special meanings to the shell.

2. Quotes must always be used in even numbers. If you give an odd number, the shell believes that you have not finished with input yet and waits for more.
3. You can mix and match different types of quotes and embed them within one another.

Let's examine each rule in order. If you have a file named `sample of the worlds best cigars`, and you give this command,

```
cat sample of the worlds best cigars
```

The `cat` utility will first try to open a file named `sample`, and then one named `of`, followed by four other files: `the`, `worlds`, `best`, `cigars`. The whitespace between the words is interpreted as delimiters between different filenames. In order to be able to see the file, the command must be changed to

```
cat "sample of the worlds best cigars"
```

The double quotes cancel the default meaning of the whitespace and allow the value between them to be interpreted as a single entry. The double quotes cancel the meaning of most special characters, but not all. For example, suppose there is a variable named EXAMPLE that is equal to 25:

```
echo $EXAMPLE
```

This will return "25". Likewise, the following will also return "25":

```
echo "$EXAMPLE"
```

To prevent the interpretation of the '$' sign as a special character by the shell, you would use single quotes; so the following will return "$EXAMPLE":

```
echo '$EXAMPLE'
```

The single quotes go above and beyond the double quotes and also cancel out the meaning of the dollar sign.

Going in another direction:

```
echo 'date'
```

will return "date". Substituting the single quotes for back quotes will have a different result:

```
echo `date`
```

will return the results of the date command. An alternative to the backquotes in the newer shells is to place the command within parentheses and treat it as a variable. The parentheses actually execute the command in a subshell and display the result via the environment. Thus the date can be echoed as in the preceding example with the command:

```
echo $(date)
```

If you fail to use an even number of any quote set, PS1 is replaced by PS2, and continues to be so until the total number of quotes used (each set) is an even number. This can be useful when you have a lengthy entry you want to break into lines during entry. The following example includes the prompts and also shows the use of one set of quotes (back quotes) within another (double quotes):

```
[edulaney@server7 home]$ EXAMPLE="Hi, the date
> and time now
> are `date`."
[edulaney@server7 home]$ echo $EXAMPLE
Hi, the date and time now are Thu Aug 10 11:12:37 EDT 2000
[edulaney@server7 home]$
```

In many instances, the quotes need to be mixed and matched. One of the biggest problems you will encounter, however, is that special characters make it difficult to display them as output. For example, assume the end result of an echo operation to be

```
Evan says "Hi"
```

If you use the command

```
echo Evan says "Hi"
```

the result will be

```
Evan says Hi
```

The shell interprets the quotation marks as meaning that the text within them should be taken as a single entry. The shell performs the operation given it and loses the quotes in the process. To get around this, you must use the backslash (\) character to override the default meaning of the quotes:

```
echo Evan says \"Hi\"
```

Note that the backslash—literal—character must precede each incidence of the quotes, and is always only good for the character immediately following it.

Command History

The **bash** shell keeps a list of commands that you give it and allows you to reuse those commands from the list rather than needing to retype them each time. From the command line, you can use the up and down arrows to scroll through recent commands. You can also enter two bangs (!!) to rerun the very last command you gave.

Note

Many Unix/Linux geeks refer to the exclamation point as *bang*.

Typing **history** shows all the commands that are stored, with an incrementing number on the left. Typing a single bang and one of those command numbers will rerun that command, as in !205.

Note

Instead of seeing the entire history list, you can choose to see only the most recent entries by following the history command with the number of lines you want to see, like this:

```
history 5
history 10
```

Alternatively, you can type a bang followed by a set of characters, and the shell will rerun the most recent command starting with those characters. For example,

`!ls`

will rerun the most recent command that started with `ls`.

The shell saves its history in a file on the system, and important variables related to it are

- `HISTFILE`—Points to the file holding the history of commands. By default, it is `.bash_history` in each user's home directory
- `HISTSIZE`—The number of entries to keep each session.
- `HISTFILESIZE`—Identifies the number of commands history entries to be carried over from one session to another (letting you run commands in this session that you ran in the previous one).

Command Aliasing

Although a plethora of commands and utilities are available within the operating system and shell, you can create aliases that make more sense to you or that shorten the number of characters you have to type. For example, if you are familiar with working with the command line of Windows-based operating systems, you are accustomed to typing `dir` to see what files are there. A similar operation in Linux is possible with `ls -l`. It is possible to create an alias so that when you type `dir`, it is `ls -l` that runs using the following syntax:

`alias dir="ls -l"`

The syntax is always the alias followed by the actual command that will run when the alias is entered, separated by the equal sign (=). In rare instances, you can get away with not using the quotation marks around the aliased entry, but as a general rule, they should always be used.

Note

For aliases to survive a session, they should be added to the `.bashrc` file within a user's home directory. If you do not put them within a file that is executed upon login (thus re-creating them), the created aliases are lost when you log out.

Other Features and Notes

The Linux command line has a number of other features that should not be overlooked. Although they are not complicated enough to warrant a section of their own, it is useful to know of their existence:

- When typing a command, you can press the Tab key after entering a few characters, and the shell will attempt to complete the name of the command you were typing.

- The command-line history can be edited to alter commands before running them again. The default editor in **bash** is **emacs**, and in **zsh** it is **vi**. Editors are discussed later in this chapter.

- When you press the Enter key, the shell first scans the command line and determines what elements it has been given by looking for whitespace. It next replaces wildcards with any relevant filenames. Following that, it strips all quotes and substitutes variables. Last, it substitutes any embedded commands and then executes the entry.

- The **test** utility can be used in conjunction with **$?** to test almost anything and is often used within shell scripts. For example to see if a file exists and is readable, use this combination:

```
test -r snapshot01.gif
echo $?
```

  Complete syntax for all the **test** options can be found by typing **man test**.

- Two less-than signs (<<) are known simply as "here" and signify that processing is to wait until the string following them is given as a **PS2** prompt on a line by itself. For example,

```
cat << litter
```

  will accept input at a **PS2** prompt until the string "**litter**" is entered on a line by itself.

Processing Text

All the utilities that follow in this section are useful for common administrative tasks, such as viewing logs. They can be used independently of each other or in conjunction with one another.

The simplest text processing utility of all is **cat**, a derivative from the word
concatenate. By default, it will display the entire contents of a file on the screen
(standard output). However, a number of useful options can be used with it,
including the following:

- -b to number lines
- -E to show a dollar sign ($) at the end of each line (carriage return)
- -T to show all tabs as "^I"
- -v to show nonprinting characters except tabs and carriage returns
- -A to show the same as -v combined with -E and -T

To illustrate the uses of **cat**, assume that there is a four-line file named **example**
with the following contents:

```
How much wood
could a woodchuck chuck
if a woodchuck
could chuck wood?
```

To view the contents of the file on the screen, exactly as they appear in the
preceding example, the command is

```
cat example
```

To view the file with lines numbered, the command, and the output generated,
will be

```
cat -b example
     1    How much wood
     2    could a woodchuck chuck
     3    if a woodchuck
     4    could chuck wood?
```

Note the inclusion of the tab characters that were not there before, but were
added by the numbering process. They are not truly in the file, but only added
to the display, as can be witnessed with the following command:

```
cat -Ab example
     1    How much wood$
     2    could a woodchuck chuck$
     3    if a woodchuck$
     4    could chuck wood?$
```

The only nonprintable characters within the file are the carriage returns at the
end, which appear as dollar signs.

One of the most common uses of the cat utility is to quickly create a text file. From the command line, you can specify no file at all to display and redirect the output to a given filename. This then accepts keyboard input and places it in the new file until the end-of-file character is received (the key sequence is Ctrl+D, by default).

The following example includes a dollar sign ($) prompt to show this operation in process:

```
$ cat > example
Peter Piper picked a peck of pickled peppers
A peck of pickled peppers Peter Piper picked.
If Peter Piper picked a peck of pickled peppers,
Where's the peck of pickled peppers Peter Piper picked?
{press Ctrl+D}
$
```

The Ctrl+D sequence is pressed on a line by itself and signifies the end of the file. Viewing the contents of the directory (via the ls utility) will show that the file has now been created, and its contents can be viewed like this:

```
cat example
```

Note that the single redirection (>) creates a file named example if it did not exist before and overwrites it if it did. To add to an existing file, use the append characters (>>).

Note

The Ctrl+D keyboard sequence is the typical default for specifying an end-of-file operation. Like almost everything in Linux, this can be changed, customized, and so on. To see the settings for your session, use this command:

```
stty -a
```

and look for "eof = ".

head **and** tail

Two simple commands can be used to view all or parts of files: head and tail. The first, head as the name implies, is used to look at the top portion of a file. By default, the first 10 lines of the file are displayed. You can change the number of lines displayed by using a dash followed by the number of lines to display. The following examples assume that there is a text file named numbers with 200 lines in it counting from "one" to "two hundred":

```
$ head numbers
one
two
three
four
five
six
seven
eight
nine
ten
$
$ head -3 numbers
one
two
three
$
$ head -50 numbers
one
two
three
{skipping for space purposes}
forty-eight
forty-nine
fifty
$
```

Note

When printing multiple files, head places a header before each listing identifying what file it is displaying. The -q option suppresses the headers.

The `tail` command has several modes in which it can operate. By default, it is the opposite of **head** and shows the end of file rather than the beginning. Once again, it defaults to the number 10 to display, but that can be changed by specifying the number of lines that you want to see as an option":

```
$ tail numbers
one hundred ninety-one
one hundred ninety-two
one hundred ninety-three
one hundred ninety-four
one hundred ninety-five
```

```
one hundred ninety-six
one hundred ninety-seven
one hundred ninety-eight
one hundred ninety-nine
two hundred
$
$ tail -3 numbers
one hundred ninety-eight
one hundred ninety-nine
two hundred
$
$ tail -50 numbers
one hundred fifty-one
one hundred fifty-two
one hundred fifty-three
{skipping for space purposes}
one hundred ninety-eight
one hundred ninety-nine
two hundred
$
```

The `tail` utility goes beyond this functionality, however, by including a plus (+) option. This allows you to specify a starting point beyond which you will see the entire file. For example,

```
$ tail +50 numbers
```

will start with line 50 (skipping the first 49) and display the rest of the file—151 lines in this case. Another useful option is `-f`, which allows you to *follow* a file. The command

```
$ tail -f numbers
```

will display the last 10 lines of the file, but then stay open—following the file—and display any new lines that are appended to the file. To break out of the endless monitoring loop, you must press the *interrupt* key sequence, which is Ctrl+C by default on most systems.

Note

To find the interrupt key sequence for your session, use the command

```
stty -a
```

and look for "`intr = `".

Sort and Count

It is often necessary to not only display text, but also to manipulate and modify it a bit before the output is shown, or simply gather information on it. Two utilities are examined in this section: **sort**, and wc.

sort

The **sort** utility sorts the lines of a file in alphabetical order and displays the output. The importance of alphabetical order, versus any other, cannot be overstated. For example, assume that the **fileone** file contains the following lines:

```
Indianapolis Indiana
Columbus
Peoria
Livingston
Scottsdale
1
2
3
4
5
6
7
8
9
10
11
12
```

When a sort is done on the file, the result becomes

```
$ sort fileone
1
10
11
12
2
3
4
5
6
7
8
9
Columbus
```

```
Indianapolis Indiana
Livingston
Peoria
Scottsdale
$
```

The cities are "correctly" sorted in alphabetical order. The numbers, however, are also in alphabetical order, which puts every number starting with "1" before every number starting with "2," and then every number starting with "3," and so on.

Thankfully, the **sort** utility includes some options to add a great deal of flexibility to the output. Among those options are the following:

- -d to sort in phone directory order (the same as that shown in the preceding example)
- -f to sort lowercase letters the same as uppercase
- -i to ignore any characters outside the ASCII range
- -n to sort in numerical order versus alphabetical
- -r to reverse the order of the output

Thus by using the -n option, to do the numeric sorting correctly, the display can be changed to

```
$ sort -n fileone
Columbus
Indianapolis Indiana
Livingston
Peoria
Scottsdale
1
2
3
4
5
6
7
8
9
10
11
12
$
```

Note

The sort utility assumes all blank lines to be a part of the display and always places them at the beginning of the output. To suppress any effects of leading whitespace on sorting, use the -b option.

wc

The wc utility (named for "word count") displays information about the file in terms of three values: number of lines, words, and characters. The last entry in the output is the name of the file, thus the output would be

```
$ wc fileone
    17    18    86    fileone
$
```

You can choose to see only some of the output by using the following options:

- -c to show only the number of bytes/characters
- -l to see only the number of lines
- -w to see only the number of words

In all cases, the name of the file still appears; for example,

```
$ wc -l fileone
    17    fileone
$
```

The only way to override the name appearing is by using the standard input redirection:

```
$ wc -l < fileone
    17
$
```

Other Useful Utilities

A number of other useful text utilities are included with Linux. Some of these have limited usefulness and are intended only for a specific purpose, but are given because knowing of their existence and purpose can make your life with Linux considerably easier.

In alphabetical order, the additional utilities are as follows:

- file—This utility will look at an entry's signature and report what type of file it is—ASCII text, GIF image, and so on. The definitions it returns (and thus the files it can correctly identify) are defined in a file called `magic`. This file typically resides in **/usr/share/misc** or **/etc**.

- **more**—Used to display only one screen of output at a time.

- **pr**—Converts the file into a format suitable for printed pages—including a default header with date and time of last modification, filename, and page numbers. The default header can be overwritten with the **-h** option, and the **-l** option allows you to specify the number of lines to include on each page—the default is 66. Default page width is 72 characters, but a different value can be specified with the **-w** option. The **-d** option can be used to double-space the output, and **-m** can be used to print numerous files in column format.

- **uniq**—This utility will examine entries in a file, comparing the current line with the one directly preceding it, to find lines that are unique. Combining **sort** and **uniq** with a pipe is a powerful, and common, usage of this utility.

Basic File Management

In this section, you'll learn about a number of utilities used for managing files and directories. Some of these utilities—such as **cd** and **ls**—are of such importance that it was impossible to get this far in the book without using them in some of the examples. Here, we will expand on them and explore their functions and uses in greater detail.

Working with cd and pwd

The **cd** command is used to change the directory you are working in. If you enter the command with no parameters, it will move you to whatever directory is defined by the **HOME** variable. If you specify any parameter with it, it is seen as denoting the directory you want to change to.

Some characters that can be of great use with **cd** are the single period (**.**) and double period (**..**). The former represents whatever directory you are currently in, whereas the latter represents the parent directory of the current one.

The **pwd** utility shows the present working directory—the one you are currently in. The same value that it returns is contained in the environmental variable **PWD**.

The following are some examples of how these two utilities can be used:

```
$ pwd
/usr/bin
$ echo $HOME
/usr/home/edulaney
$ cd
$ pwd
/usr/home/edulaney
$
```

This sequence showed the present working directory to be **/usr/bin** and the HOME variable to be equal to **/usr/home/edulaney**. Entering **cd** without any parameters switched to that directory.

```
$ pwd
/usr/home/edulaney
$ cd /
$ pwd
/
$ cd /usr/home/edulaney
$ pwd
/usr/home/edulaney
$ cd ..
$ pwd
/usr/home
$
```

In this sequence, the first change is to the root directory (/), and then to /usr/home/edulaney. Using the shortcut for the parent of this directory, it was then possible to move back one directory.

Absolute and Relative Addressing

There are two methods of specifying paths to anything—files, directories, and so on: absolute and relative. When you give an absolute path, you take nothing into consideration, and you give a value that is always true. When you give a relative path, you take into account where you currently are, and you give a path relative to that.

To use an analogy, suppose that two people live in the same city and state: Muncie, Indiana. The first person lives at 1909 Rosewood, and the second lives at 4104 Peachtree. If the first person wants to find/visit the second person, he can find out where she is via an absolute path known as her mailing address:

4104 Peachtree Lane

Muncie, IN 47304

This address says to

1. Find Indiana.
2. Within Indiana, find Muncie.
3. Within Muncie, find the section of the city falling within the 47304 Zip Code.
4. Within all earlier confines, find Peachtree Lane.
5. On Peachtree Lane, go to house number 4104.

Note

Absolute addresses will never change and will point to the entity regardless of where you are coming from.

The absolute address is the same whether the person coming to visit lives in Muncie or in Alaska. Because the first person does live in Muncie as well, however, we can also tell him how to reach his destination using relative addressing:

1. Take Rosewood to Bethel and turn left.
2. Take Bethel to Jackson and turn right.
3. Take Jackson across the railroad tracks to the stop sign at Hawthorne.
4. Turn left on Hawthorne and go to the next stop, which is Peachtree.
5. Turn right on Peachtree Lane, and go to the first house on the right.

Note

Relative addresses will always change and are relative to where you are coming from.

Table 4.2 illustrates a few examples that can be used with the **cd** command.

TABLE 4.2
Examples of Using the cd Command

PRESENT WORKING DIRECTORY	NEW LOCATION	ABSOLUTE ADDRESS	RELATIVE ADDRESS
/usr/home/edulaney/ docs/proposals	/usr/home/ edulaney/docs	/usr/home/ edulaney/docs	..
/usr/home/edulaney/ docs/proposals	/usr/home/ edulaney	/usr/home/ edulaney	../..
/usr/home/edulaney/ docs/proposals	/usr/home/ edulaney/docs/ proposals/ law_order	/usr/home/ edulaney/docs/ proposals/ law_order	law_order
/usr/home/edulaney/docs/ proposals	/	/	../../ ../..

Working with ls

The ability to list files and directories is one of the most essential to any operating system, and the **ls** utility performs this function for Linux. When given by itself, it lists the names of files and directories beneath the current directory in a column-style format. Entries are always—by default—given in alphabetical order, and there is nothing to differentiate names of directories from names of files. An example would be

```
Desktop     emmett     filethree    junk2     questions
TestPro     errors     filetwo      mischief  sample
brio     example     Friday     myfile     sample of the world
dulaney     example2     garbage     numbers     simplesimon
eRRors     fileone     junk1     pull     snapshot01.gif
```

Note

The listings are always in alphabetical order by default, with all uppercase entries coming before lowercase entries.

A slew of options can be used with this command, and one of the most useful is -F, which will indicate what type of entry is being displayed:

```
Desktop/     emmett     filethree    junk2     questions
TestPro      errors     filetwo      mischief*  sample
```

```
brio     example    Friday    myfile    sample of the world*
dulaney   example2   garbage   numbers   simplesimon
eRRors    fileone    junk1     pull      snapshot01.gif
```

Entries without any trailing characters added are standard files. Entries with a / on the end—such as **Desktop**—are directories. Those entries with a trailing asterisk (*) are executable. Symbolic links are signified by an at (@) symbol.

Another useful option is -a, which will show all files. By default, hidden files are not displayed by ls. A hidden file is any file that has a period (.) as its first character:

```
.        Desktop    emmett    filethree    junk2     questions
..       TestPro    errors    filetwo      mischief  sample
.bash_history       brio      example      Friday    myfile     sample of the
world
.bash_logout        dulaney   example2     garbage   numbers    simplesi-
mon.fileone.swp     eRRors    fileone      junk1     pull       snapshot01.gif
```

Note

Periods can appear anywhere within a filename and appear as many times as you want. The only time they have any special significance is when they are the very first character of the name.

Filenames or directory names beginning with periods are typically used to hold configuration information for various programs.

If you use -A in place of -a, it will leave off the first two entries (". " and ".."). Undoubtedly, however, the most useful option of all is -l, which will display a long list of the files. Entries look like this:

```
drwx----   5   root   root   1024   Aug 30 11:12 Desktop
-rw-r--r--   1   root   root   548    Aug 23 22:01   TestPro
-rw-r--r--   1   root   root   28     Aug 22 10:26   brio
```

There are essentially seven columns here, and they can be broken out as follows:

1. The permissions on the entry. Permissions are more fully discussed throughout subsequent chapters, but for now it is important to realize that the first character identifies what type of entry it is. A "-" indicates a file, whereas a "d" is a directory. Other possibilities for the first character are "c" for a character special file (such as a terminal), "b" for a block special device (such as a tape drive), "l" for a symbolic link, or "p" for a named pipe.

2. The number of physical links to this file in the Linux filesystem.

3. The name of the owner who now owns the entity.

4. The name of the group owning the file.

5. The size of the file.

6. The date of creation, or of modification into the current format.

7. The name.

Table 4.3 offers some of the other options for ls and their purpose.

TABLE 4.3
Options for the ls Command

OPTION	PURPOSE
-c	Lists in order of time of last change/modification instead of alphabetical order.
-d	Lists directories.
-G	When used with -1, doesn't show the group.
-i	Shows the inode number (pointer) to each entry.
-n	Shows the owner and group by their numeric values instead of by name.
-o	Same as -1G.
-r	Reverses the order of the display.
-R	Recursively shows entries in subdirectories as well.
-S	Sorts.
-u	Sorts by last access time.
-w	Specifies screen width.
-x	Shows lines instead of columns.
-X	Alphabetizes by extension.

Standard Output and Input

Standard output is where displays usually go—to your screen. When you give the following command

```
ls -F
```

a listing of the subdirectories and files beneath the current directory is displayed on your screen. The default location for standard output, therefore, is to your screen. If you do not want the results displayed on your screen, however, you can redirect them to another location, such as a file. Redirection of standard output is possible through the use of the greater-than sign (>). For example, to send the results to a file, the command would be

```
ls -F > myfile
```

The first order of business the shell undertakes when given this command is that it creates a file named myfile with a size of zero. It then allows the ls utility to run and places the output within the newly created file rather than on your screen. It is important to note the order of operations. Suppose that you give a nonexistent command, such as this one:

```
ls -z > myfile
```

The file named myfile is still created with a size of zero that then stays at zero. The error appears on your screen, but this is after the file was created. This is also important because if you attempt to add more information to the file, the file will be overwritten first. To add more information, you must append to the file using two greater-than signs (>>):

```
ls -l >> myfile
```

This adds the new information to the end of the existing file and keeps the original contents intact. In some situations, you want a command to run but don't care at all about what the results are. For example, I might want a database to compile and need to run a utility for this to happen. I don't care about the messages generated—I just want the utility to run. When this is the case, you can send the results to nowhere by specifying /dev/null:

```
ls -F > /dev/null
```

The results are sent to this device, a special Unix/Linux device that discards all output sent to it.

Standard input is typically the keyboard, or interpreted to be among the arguments given on the command line. You can, however, specify redirection of standard input using the less-than sign (<). Rarely is there ever a need for this, but it is available. For example,

```
cat myfile
```

will give the same results as

```
cat < myfile
```

In the world of Linux, numerical values exist for these items as well. Standard input (abbreviated **stdin**) is 0, and standard output (abbreviated **stdout**) is 1. These numbers can be used with the redirection, but this is rarely done. An example would be

```
ls -F 1> myfile
```

Note

There can be *no space* between 1 and the > sign. If there is, the meaning is changed.

This example states that standard output is to be redirected to the file named myfile. The numbers are important for one reason only—because a third possibility exists as well. Standard error (abbreviated **stderr**) has a value of 2. For an example of standard error, think of the ls -z command you saw earlier. Even though the output was being sent to a file, the command was a nonexistent one and the error message appeared on the screen. The error could be sent to the file with the following command:

```
ls -z 2> myfile
```

The problem is that now the error will be sent there, but the output (in the absence of an error) will appear on the screen. To send both output and errors to the same file, the command becomes

```
ls -z > myfile 2>&1
```

This states that the output is to go to a file named myfile and further that standard error (2) is to go to the same location as standard output (1). Another alternative is to send errors to one location and output to another, like this:

```
ls -z > myfile 2>errors
```

Let's look at the order of operations here: The shell first creates two files (myfile and errors) with zero sizes (whether or not they existed before). If the command is successful, the output goes to myfile. If the command is unsuccessful, the errors go to errors. If these were truly log files, the only other modification might be to append rather than create each time the operation is run:

```
ls -z >> myfile 2>>errors
```

Working with Processes

In this section, you'll learn about utilities used to manage a process and see how processes are utilized for all transactions. In the previous sections, many utilities and commands were discussed—each time one of them is issued, a process is started to carry out the request, as you will see in greater detail.

What Is a Process

Crucial to understanding this section is knowing that a process is *any* instance, command, or utility in execution. When you issue the command `ls`, discussed earlier, a process is started to run the utility and return the results.

Even the shell with which you are interacting is running as a process. When you give a command to be carried out, the shell will look to see if it can do so without any outside help. (Assume that the command was really just an empty line: No other utilities are needed to return another prompt.) If your shell cannot perform the command, it will call another process to perform the action. The other process called is a child to your shell, which has become a parent to the new process.

When the child has completed performing its task, it returns its results to the parent, and then goes away. Because Linux is a multitasking operating system, there can be more than one child for any given parent. If the child cannot perform all the tasks on its own (think of compiling an annual report), the child might need to call one or more additional processes. When it does this, it becomes the parent to those child processes.

Note

Barring any restrictions coded into it, every process has the capability to be a parent or child, though many don't.

On a system, at any given time, there will be processes that you are running, there might be processes that others are running, and there will be processes that the system itself is running. The latter are often *daemons*—services that are running without interaction to provide functionality to the operating system. Examples of services daemons can perform include printing, running scheduled jobs, sending mail, monitoring run state, and so forth.

Working with ps

The **ps** command is the one key command for listing processes and process status. When run by itself (no options), **ps** will show the processes that you currently have running, with the last line always being itself. (It is a running process as well.) For example,

```
$ ps
PID     TTY     TIME      CMD
19605   pts/0   00:00:34  bash
30089   pts/0   00:00:00  vi
30425   pts/0   00:00:00  paste
32040   pts/0   00:00:00  cat
 1183   pts/0   00:00:00  awk
30679   pts/0   00:00:00  ps
$
```

The first column is the process ID number—this is a unique number assigned to every process that executes. Each process created on the system is assigned an incremental process ID by the system. This process ID is discarded when the process terminates. Process IDs are not reused until the system reaches the maximum process ID defined on the system; at which point, the system begins reallocating process IDs with the lowest process ID not currently associated with a running process.

The second column indicates the terminal with which the user responsible for the process is associated. This is because the default scope of **ps** is the current shell, not the current user. Users running multiple terminal sessions of xterms will only see the listing of processes spawned by the current shell, not all processes on the system associated with the current user.

The third column indicates the amount of processor time that the process is using. In most cases, processes can run quickly, sit idle, and so on, and use very little time. A very high time reading can indicate a process that is dragging down the performance of the system.

The fourth column is the name of the process (command) itself. In the first line, there is the user's shell—which must be there, or there would not be a user here at all: The user's shell is known as the session leader. The last line is the command that just executed. Those entries in between are other processes that the user is running.

The **ps** utility has a number of options to make it more flexible. The -a option removes obvious choices. For example, you know that you must have a shell running or you would not be interacting with the system, so it isn't really as important to see that as others. Using the -a option, the display changes just slightly:

```
$ ps -a
PID    TTY    TIME     CMD
30089  pts/0  00:00:00  vi
30425  pts/0  00:00:00  paste
32040  pts/0  00:00:00  cat
 1183  pts/0  00:00:00  awk
30685  pts/0  00:00:00  ps
$
```

Note

ps -a will show all processes associated with the current tty *except* the session leader. Also note that the PID associated with ps increments with every running, as each requires a new process. It does not increment by one, in this case, for several other processes ran (probably in the background) between the first and second running of ps.

Using either the -A or the -e option (all or everything), it is possible to see every process running and not just those linked to the current tty. There are several things to notice in the display that it produces. In no particular order, they are as follows:

- Processes started when the system came up have the lowest number PIDs (notice items 1 through 19). As a general rule, these are mission-critical processes, and if they were not there, some or all of the system would be unusable.

- Not all processes are tied to a terminal. If a question mark (?) is present, it indicates that the process is running on the system without terminal interaction and/or without a terminal being default standard output.

- For every terminal without a user, there is a getty, or mingetty, running. This process sits and waits for a user to attempt to log on. Even though no user is using tty1 through tty6, it is easy to see that six other terminals can be used. "getty" means "get tty"—wait to get login information from a tty/terminal. "mingetty" is "minimal getty." Most Linux systems use mingetty or agetty—getty.

Other options that can be used to determine what information to display are

- l to display a long listing (think of ls -l)
- u to show username and related stats
- f to show a full listing (add process, parent process, scheduling, and start time information)

The latter is often used, and favored by administrators, for the additional columns it adds to the display:

```
$ ps -f
UID      PID  PPID  C STIME TTY      TIME CMD
root    7054  7053  0 Oct12 pts/1   00:00:00 /bin/bash
root   13745  7054  0 09:45 pts/1   00:00:00 ps -f
$
```

There are four new columns that were not there before. The first column identifies the user ID associated with the process. The third column is the Parent Process ID—showing which process this one reports back to. The fourth column identifies whether scheduling is involved, and the fifth column is the time at which the process started.

Note

Notice that when using f, the CMD now lists the entire command and not just the first portion, as was done with the other displays.

These options can be combined with one another, and the most common combination is **ef**, which displays all processes in a full format.

Working with pstree **and** top

Two commands that are closely related to **ps** offer slightly different views of the processes. The first of these is **pstree**, which will graphically depict the relationship between the processes as shown in Figure 4.1.

This graphically depicts the children beneath the main processes and shows where each process fits in—the process hierarchy.

The second utility related to **ps** is **top**. Not only does it show the current processes, but it also stays active and continually updates the display. Additionally, the top of the screen depicts information about how many days the system has been up, the number of users, memory and swap statistics, and so on.

When **top** is running, you can press any of the following keys to interact with it:

- h—Help
- q—Quit
- s—Set the delay between updates (default is five seconds)
- spacebar—Update now rather than waiting for renewal interval
- u—Display a single user only

FIGURE 4.1
The pstree utility graphically shows the relationship between processes.

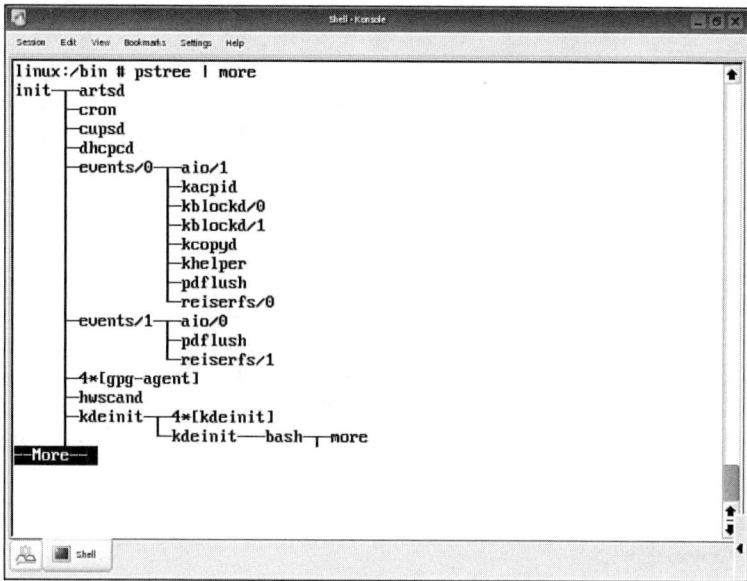

```
linux:/bin # pstree | more
init─┬─artsd
     ├─cron
     ├─cupsd
     ├─dhcpcd
     ├─events/0─┬─aio/1
     │          ├─kacpid
     │          ├─kblockd/0
     │          ├─kblockd/1
     │          ├─kcopyd
     │          ├─khelper
     │          ├─pdflush
     │          └─reiserfs/0
     ├─events/1─┬─aio/0
     │          ├─pdflush
     │          └─reiserfs/1
     ├─4*[gpg-agent]
     ├─hwscand
     ├─kdeinit─┬─4*[kdeinit]
     │         └─kdeinit──bash─┬─more
─More─
```

The columns show the standard PID information, as well as the amount of memory and the number of CPU processes being used.

Ending a Process

Processes are started in a plethora of ways. They are started automatically by the system as daemons, as well as started by the user in attempting to get a job done. Other processes start some processes, and the list goes on in ways that processes come to be.

Under normal circumstances, a child acts on behalf of, and reports to, a parent. When the child is no longer needed, it goes away on its own accord. There are situations, however, in which processes become runaways—they are no longer needed, yet they continue to run and consume processes.

A parent process cannot (or should not) cease as long as child processes are associated with it. Given that, a child process that fails to cease could keep a number of unneeded processes on a system. To illustrate, assume that a user's shell calls another process (A), which cannot do everything needed, and thus it calls another (B), and it in turn starts another (C).

Under normal conditions, when Process C finishes, it will report back to Process B and go away. Process B will massage the data, report back to Process A, and go away. Process A will do whatever it needs to with the data, and then return it to the user's shell and go away.

For a non-normal condition, assume that Process C has a glitch and does not end after reporting back to Process B. It continues to run: This prevents Process B from ending because it still has a child associated with it. We can assume that Process B returns its values to Process A, and it then returns its values to the user's shell. Process A, like Process B, cannot end because it still has a child associated with it. Because there is a glitch in Process C, three processes that are no longer needed continue to run.

Yet another possibility for the glitch (and it would depend on how applications are written) is that Process B could go ahead and end without Process C going away. Process A could do its task and go away as well. What happens in this instance is that only Process C remains a problem, but now it has nonexistent parents above it, and has no idea who it reports to—it becomes a true runaway.

To solve problems with erratic processes, there is the `kill` command. This utility works with the following syntax:

```
kill {option} PID
```

Thus to get rid of the `cat` process, the sequence would be

```
$ ps -f
UID          PID  PPID  C STIME TTY         TIME CMD
root       19605 19603  0 Aug10 pts/0    00:00:34 bash
root       30089 19605  0 Aug20 pts/0    00:00:00 vi fileone
root       30425 19605  0 Aug20 pts/0    00:00:00 paste -d fileone
filetwo?
root       32040 19605  0 Aug22 pts/0    00:00:00 cat
root        1183 19605  0 Aug23 pts/0    00:00:00 awk -F: questions
root       30900 19605  0 14:25 pts/0    00:00:00 ps -f
$
$ kill 32040
$
```

This "politely" asks the process to terminate. It is polite because there are 32 different ways to kill a process (*signals* to send), and this is the safest method of so doing. In a great many instances, the process will simply ignore the request and continue on. When that happens, you can use one of the other 32 ways by specifying the number to use. Among the possibilities are

- -1—On hangup/disconnect
- -2—Using an interrupt (Ctrl+C) sequence

- -3—Upon quit
- -9—Without regard—immediately
- -15—(the default)

Note

To see a list of signals on your system, use the command kill -l. The first 32 signals are standard, but many times a list of up to 64 is shown. Those signals between 33 and 64 are not standard and are intended for real-time application use.

To illustrate, assume that the cat process will not go away politely; the sequence of operations then becomes

```
$ ps -f
UID          PID  PPID  C STIME TTY           TIME CMD
root       19605 19603  0 Aug10 pts/0     00:00:34 bash
root       30089 19605  0 Aug20 pts/0     00:00:00 vi fileone
root       30425 19605  0 Aug20 pts/0     00:00:00 paste -d fileone
filetwo?
root       32040 19605  0 Aug22 pts/0     00:00:00 cat
root        1183 19605  0 Aug23 pts/0     00:00:00 awk -F: questions
root       30996 19605  0 14:25 pts/0     00:00:00 ps -f
$
$ kill 32040
$ ps -f
UID          PID  PPID  C STIME TTY           TIME CMD
root       19605 19603  0 Aug10 pts/0     00:00:34 bash
root       30089 19605  0 Aug20 pts/0     00:00:00 vi fileone
root       30425 19605  0 Aug20 pts/0     00:00:00 paste -d fileone
filetwo?
root       32040 19605  0 Aug22 pts/0     00:00:00 cat
root        1183 19605  0 Aug23 pts/0     00:00:00 awk -F: questions
root       30998 19605  0 14:25 pts/0     00:00:00 ps -f
$
$ kill -9 32040
[3]- Killed
$ ps -f
UID          PID  PPID  C STIME TTY           TIME CMD
root       19605 19603  0 Aug10 pts/0     00:00:34 bash
root       30089 19605  0 Aug20 pts/0     00:00:00 vi fileone
root       30425 19605  0 Aug20 pts/0     00:00:00 paste -d fileone
filetwo?
root        1183 19605  0 Aug23 pts/0     00:00:00 awk -F: questions
root       31000 19605  0 14:25 pts/0     00:00:00 ps -f
$
```

It is highly recommended that signal **15** (terminate) always be attempted before signal **9** (kill) is used. It is also highly recommended that you make certain there are no child processes beneath a process before killing it. If child processes exist, they should be removed first before proceeding further.

Just when you thought it couldn't get any more bloody, another command—killall—can be used to get rid of a process by name, versus PID. killall also has the capability (with the -w option) to wait for processes to die, and to require confirmation (with the -i option) before killing.

Background and Foreground

When a process is started, the default is for it to run in the foreground. In the foreground, it becomes the only job the user can work on and interaction is based on completion of the job. For example, when a user runs ls -l, the display appears on his terminal, and he is unable to issue another command until ls has finished.

To run a process in the background, simply add an ampersand (**&**) to the end—this allows you to run more than one command at the same time. For example, the sleep command simply enables the process to wait a given number of seconds before anything else happens, and it can be used by itself as a means of illustration:

```
$ sleep 90 &
[5] 31168
$
```

The number that appears in the brackets is equal to the number of jobs you currently have running in the background. The number following it (**31168** in this case) is the process ID number of this job.

Note

The PID of the last job placed in the background can also be referenced as $!. The scope of this is the current shell; this will be different in each shell.

Placing the job in the background allows the user to continue working and starting other processes. If you *must* wait for a process to finish before starting another, the **wait** command, used with the PID of the process, can cease processing until the specified process finishes. For example,

```
$ sleep 120 &
[5] 31175
$
$ wait 31175
```

The prompt does not return as long as **31175** remains a valid PID. The wait command is used often in shell scripts.

jobs

To see the jobs that you have running in the background, use the command jobs:

```
$ jobs
[1]   Stopped              vi fileone  (wd: ~)
[2]-  Stopped              paste -d' fileone filetwo ' (wd: ~)
[4]+  Stopped              awk -F: questions (wd: ~)
[5]   Done         sleep 120
$
```

Note

jobs is a shell built-in command, not an actual executable; therefore, it only applies to jobs started by or running in the current shell.

Jobs that were terminated (#3) do not appear, and jobs that have finished (#5) will only show up one time—the next time you press return in the shell after they have completed. (The next time **jobs** is run, #5 will not appear.) If the job is the most recent job that can run, or is running, a plus sign (+) will follow the job number brackets. The next most recent job is indicated by a minus sign (-). The **wd** information references the working directory.

The -1 option will add the PID numbers to the display, and the -p option can be used to show only the PID numbers of the processes. The -n option can be used to show only jobs that have been suspended.

fg

A job that is running in the background can be moved to the foreground through the use of the **fg** command. The syntax for **fg** allows reference to a job using a percent sign (%) and the job number. For example, the following sequence starts a two-minute sleep sequence in the background, and then moves it into the foreground:

```
$ sleep 120 &
[5] 31206
$
$ fg %5
sleep 120
```

Notice that the command being executed is echoed to the screen as it is brought to the foreground. Where **%5** was used, you can also reference the two most recent jobs by %+ and %-, respectively. If you don't know the job number (and can't remember to use the **jobs** command), you can refer to a job by a portion of its name when using it after the percent sign and question mark (%?). For example,

```
$ fg %?v
vi fileone
```

bg

The opposite of the foreground (**fg**) command is the background (**bg**) command. This allows you to take a job running in the foreground and move it to the background. Before you can do so, however, you must suspend the job (in order to get the prompt back).

Suspending a job is accomplished by pressing the keyboard sequence equal to the signal **sigsuspend**—Ctrl+Z, by default. When suspended, the job will stop and not start again until moved into the foreground or background. For example,

```
$ sleep 180
{Ctrl+Z pressed}
[5]+   Stopped        sleep 180
$
```

Issuing the **bg** command will now move the job into the background and change the status to Running.

Changing Priorities

When a process starts, it does so at a default priority of zero. This puts it on an even keel with all other processes competing for attention from the CPU and other resources. The priorities for the processes can be changed through the use of two utilities, **nice** and **renice**.

nice

Processes can be started at different priorities using the **nice** utility. There are forty different levels that **nice** can be used with (half negative and half positive), including

- 19 (lowest priority)
- 0 (default priority)
- -20 (highest priority)

A user can use only the negative numbers, meaning that the user can only lower a process and not raise it. You can also specify an increment (default is 10), with the -n option, that **nice** will use to change the priority over time. The root user (superuser) has the ability to give a negative increment, whereas users can only use the positive numbers to raise processes priority.

NOTE

Negative values are confined to use only by the superuser.

If only the **nice** command is given, it will show the scheduling priority used by default.

renice

The **nice** utility can only be used when starting a process and cannot be used with a process already running. That is where the **renice** utility comes into play. The utility uses the same priorities available to **nice** and is followed by one of three options:

- -p for PIDs
- -g for a process group
- -u for a group associated with a user

Working with grep

The utility with the funny name (something common in Linux) is really an acronym for the function that it performs: "Globally look for Regular Expressions and then Print the results." In layman's terms, it is one of the most advanced search utilities you can use. In order to be proficient with it, however, you must understand what a regular expression is and how to use it in searching for matches to a query.

There are a number of rules for regular expressions, and these eight constitute the most important:

1. Any non-special character will be equal to itself.
2. Any special character will be equal to itself if preceded by a backslash (\).
3. The beginning of the line can be signified by a caret (^), and the end of the line by a dollar sign ($).

4. A range can be expressed within brackets ([]).

5. A caret (^) as the first character of a bracket will find values not matching entries within the brackets.

6. A period (.) can signify any single character.

7. An asterisk (*) stands for anything and everything.

8. Quotation marks are not always needed around search strings, but can be needed, and should be used as a general rule. They are required around any search string containing a regular expression that the shell would otherwise expand.

Table 4.4 offers some examples and elaboration on each of the preceding rules.

TABLE 4.4
Using Regular Expressions

RULE	CHARACTERS	SEARCH RESULT
1	c (any character without a special purpose)	Matches "c" anywhere within the line.
1	apple	Matches "apple" anywhere within the line.
2	$	The end of the line (every line).
2	\$	Every line that contains a dollar sign.
3	^c	Every line that begins with the character "c."
3	c$	Every line that ends with the character "c."
4	[apple]	Every line that has an "a," "p," "l," or "e." (Because the brackets are interpreted as a range, the second occurrence of the "p" is completely ignored.)
4	[a-z]	Any lowercase letter.
4	[:lower:]	Any lowercase letter. Other special values that can be used include [:alnum;], [:alpha:], [:digit:], [:upper:].
5	[^a-z]	Everything but lowercase letters. Note that the caret inside a range negates it, whereas outside the range it is the beginning of line.

RULE	CHARACTERS	SEARCH RESULT
5	[^0-9]	Anything but digits.
6	c.	Two-letter words beginning with "c."
6	c..$	Three-letter words at the end of the line that begin with "c."
7	c*	Any word beginning with "c" (and including just "c")
8	"c*"	Any word beginning with "c" (and including just "c").
8	"c apple"	The letter "c" followed by a space and the word "apple."

To illustrate some of these operations using **grep**, assume that there is a small file named **garbage** with the following contents:

```
I heard about the cats last night
and particularly the one cat that
ran away with all the catnip
```

If you want to find all occurrences of the word cat, the syntax becomes

```
$ grep "cat" garbage
I heard about the cats last night
and particularly the one cat that
ran away with all the catnip
$
```

In this instance, the three-letter sequence "cat" appears in every line. Not only is there "cat" in the second line, but also "cats" in the first and "catnip" in the second—all matching the character sequence specified. If you are interested in "cat" but not "cats," the syntax becomes

```
$ grep "cat[^s]" garbage
and particularly the one cat that
ran away with all the catnip
$
```

This specifically removes a four-letter sequence of "cats" while finding all other three-letter sequences of "cat." If we truly were only interested in "cat" and no deviations thereof, there are a couple of other possibilities to explore. The first method would be to include a space at the end of the word and within the quotation mark:

```
$ grep "cat " garbage
and particularly the one cat that
$
```

This finds four-letter combinations equal to that given—meaning that nothing must follow. The only problem (and it is a big one) is that if the word given is the last entry in a line of a large file, it would not necessarily be followed by a space, and thus not be returned in the display. Another possibility is to eliminate "s" and "n" from the return display:

```
$ grep "cat[^sn]" garbage
and particularly the one cat that
$
```

This accomplishes the task, but would not catch other words in which the fourth character differed from an "s" or "n." To eliminate all fourth characters, it is better to use

```
$ grep "cat[^A-z]" garbage
I heard about the cats last night
and particularly the one cat that
ran away with all the catnip
$
```

This removes both the upper- and lowercase character sets.

Options for grep

The default action for **grep** is to find matches within lines to strings specified and print them. This can be useful for pulling out key data from a large display—for example, to find what port user **karen** is on:

Note

The who command, used in the following example, merely shows who is logged on to the system.

```
$ who | grep "karen"
karen     pts/2    Aug 21 13:42
$
```

From all the output of the **who** command, only those having the string "**karen**" are displayed. As useful as this is, there are times when the actual output is not as important as other items surrounding it. For example, if you don't care where **karen** is logged on, but want to know how many concurrent sessions she has, you can use the -c option:

```
$ who | grep -c "karen"
1
$
```

Note

You can also modify it to use a logical "or" (| |) to tell you if the user has not come in yet if the operation fails:

```
who | grep "karen" || echo "She has not come in yet"
```

The | | operator tests if the return code from the previous portion of the command was a "success" and does something else if not.

The -c option is used to *count* the number of lines that would be displayed, but the display itself is suppressed. The -c option is basically performing the same task as this:

```
$ who | grep "karen" | wc -1
1
$
```

But the –c option is much quicker and more efficient by shaving an additional operation from the process. Other options that can be used with **grep** are

- -f uses a file to find the strings to search for.
- -H includes in the display a default header of the filename from which the match is coming (if applicable) that appears at the beginning of each line, whereas -h prevents the header from appearing (the default).
- -i to ignore case. If this option did not exist, you would conceivably have to search a text file for **"karen"**, **"Karen"**, **"KAREN"**, and all variations thereof to find all matches.
- -L prints filenames that do not contain matches, whereas -1 prints filenames that do contain matches.
- -n to show line numbers in the display. This differs from numbering the lines (which **n1** can do) because the numbers that appear denote the numbering of the lines in the existing file, not the output.
- -q quiets all output and is usually just used for testing return conditions.
- -s prevents any errors that occur from displaying error messages. This is useful if you do not want errors stating that you have inadequate permissions to view something when scanning all directories for a match.
- -v serves as the "not" option. It produces the opposite display of what not using it would. For example, who | grep -v karen will show all users who are not **karen**.
- -w forces the found display to match the whole word. This provides the best solution to the earlier discussion of finding "cat" but no derivatives thereof.
- -x forces the found display to match the whole line.

The options can be mixed and matched, as desired, as long as one parameter does not cancel another. For example, it is possible to search for whole words and include header information by using either -wH or -Hw. You cannot, however, say that you want to see line numbers, and only see a final count (-nc), as the two options cancel each other out.

Some examples of how these options can be used follow. For the first, assume that we want to get a long list (ls -l) of the subdirectories beneath the current directory and have no interest in actual filenames. Within the output of ls -l, the first field shows the permissions of the entry. If the entry is a file, the first character is "-." and if it is a directory, it is "d." Thus, the command would be

```
ls -l | grep "^d"
```

If you want to know how many words are in the spelling dictionary, you can find out in a number of ways, including

```
wc -l /usr/share/dict/words
```

or

```
grep -c "." /usr/share/dict/words
```

Both of these generate a number based on the number of lines within the file. Suppose, however, that you want to find out only how many words there are that start with the letter "c" (upper- or lowercase):

```
grep -ic "^c" /usr/share/dict/words
```

Or you want to find words that are in the last half of the alphabet:

```
grep -ic "^[n-z]" /usr/share/dict/words
```

Note

The preceding example could also be expressed as

```
    grep -ci "^[^a-m]" /usr/share/dict/words
```

or

```
    grep -vci "^[a-m]" /usr/share/dict/words
```

Suppose that you have a number of different strings you want to find, not just one. You can search for them individually, requiring a number of operations, or you can place the search criteria in a text file and input it into **grep** using the -f option. The following example assumes that the file **wishlist** already exists:

```
$ cat wishlist
dog
cat
```

```
fish
$
$ grep -if wishlist /usr/share/dict/words
```

Approximately 450 lines are displayed as all matches of all combinations of the three words are displayed. You can also continue one line to another to input multiple search sequences by using an uneven number of quotation marks to put the shell into input mode (PS2 prompt):

```
$ grep -ic "dog
> cat
> fish" /usr/share/dict/words
457
$
```

fgrep

The first attempt to greatly enhance **grep** was **fgrep**—as in either "file grep" or "fast grep." This utility was created during the days of Unix and prior to Linux. It enhanced **grep** by adding the ability to search for more than one item at a time (something that **grep** has since gained with the -f option). The trade-off for gaining the ability to search for multiple items was an inability to use regular expressions—never mind what the acronym stood for.

Adding the additional functionality to **grep**, and facing the inability to use regular expressions here, **fgrep** still exists but is rarely used in place of **grep**. In fact, one of the options added to **grep** is -F, which forces it to interpret the string as a simple string and work the same way **fgrep** would. (The default action is -G for basic regular expressions.)

Note

For most practical purposes, grep -F is identical to fgrep.

egrep

The second attempt to enhance **grep** was **egrep**—as in "extended grep." This utility combined the features of **grep** with those of **fgrep**—keeping the use of regular expressions. You can specify multiple values that you want to look for within a file (-f), on separate lines (using uneven numbers of quotation marks), or by separating with the pipe symbol (|). For example,

```
$ cat names
Jan May
Bob Mays
```

```
Shannon Harris
Richard Harriss
William Harrisson
Jim Buck
$
$ egrep "Jim|Jan" names
Jan May
Jim Buck
$
```

It also added two new variables:

- ? to mean zero or one
- + to mean one or more

Assume that you can't recall how Jan spells her last name—is it May or Mays? Not knowing if there really is an "s" on the end, you can ask for zero or one occurrences of this character:

```
$ egrep "Mays?" names
Jan May
Bob Mays
$
```

Even though there was no "s," Jan's entry was found—as were those that contained the character in question. With the plus sign (+), you know that at least one iteration of the character exists, but are not certain if there are more. For example, does Shannon spell her last name with one "s" or two?

```
$ egrep "Harris+" names
Shannon Harris
Richard Harriss
William Harrisson
$
```

To look for values of greater length than one character, you can enclose text within parentheses "( )". For example, if you want to find Harriss and Harrisson (not Harris), the "on" becomes an entity with zero or more occurrences:

```
$ egrep "Harriss(on)?" names
Richard Harriss
William Harrisson
$
```

Since the creation of **egrep**—again, in the days of Unix—most of the features have been worked into the version of **grep** included with Linux. Using the -E option with **grep**, you can get most of the functionality of **egrep**.

Note

For most practical purposes, grep -E is identical to egrep.

Working with vi

When **vi** came into being, it was a revolutionary application. This was in the early days of Unix, and the editors that came with the operating system were incredibly crude and difficult to manage. Many times, you could not see the line you were working on (as with **ed**); instead, you would specify the line, specify the change, and then ask to see the line printed to tell if your change was correct.

The **vi** editor (pronounced "v—eye") was created by a graduate student named Bill Joy (later to become famous as one of the founders of Sun Microsystems). He created an editor that was *visual*—hence the "v"—and *interactive*—hence the "i." With this editor, you can see the lines in the file and see the changes being made *as you make them*.

Note

vi is a modal editor, and thus the same keys mean different things in different modes. For example, in command mode, i means "enter insert mode." In insert mode, it means the letter 'i.'

By today's standards, **vi** is now considered to be crude—who wants to work with such an application when such entities as WordPerfect and Microsoft Word exist? The answer is that you *must* know the basics of this editor because it is a powerful administrator's tool. The following points are among its benefits:

- Every version of Linux ships with this editor—you can be assured that it will reside on whatever machine you use.

- It has very low overhead. When a system is damaged and configuration files must be modified before it can be brought up, you are often pre-vented from starting large applications. This minimal overhead is possible because **vi** does not have the buttons and scrollbars common in GUI (graphical user interface) applications.

- Though considered a "screen" editor, **vi** also incorporates features from "line"-type and "command"-style editors.

The learning curve can be steep when first starting with **vi**. Lacking are the function keys and other niceties. In their place are mnemonics ("u," for example, stands for undo, and "o" for open a line, and so on.)

Note

The version of "vi" on Linux systems is actually a rewrite of "vi" called "vim" (vi improved). The "vi" command is usually a symlink to "vim."

There are many other Linux text editors besides vi—the most popular of which is emacs. emacs is not delivered by default as a part of NLD, but is available as a part of the freely downloadable NLD SDK (both terminal-oriented and X Window System versions).

Starting vi

You start **vi** by typing **vi** on the command line along with the name of a file to create (if it does not already exist) or edit (if it does already exist). If the file you want to work on is in a directory other than your present working directory, you can supply the full path to the file as well.

The following example starts **vi** in the current directory to create a file named first:

```
$ vi first
```

Because the file does not already exist, this brings up a blank screen with tildes (~) used to signify that you are working in the file that is currently empty. There is one tilde for each blank line on the screen. The information at the bottom of the screen (see Figure 4.2) gives the filename and the fact that it is a "New File."

If the file does exist, the lines of the file are shown (and any blanks within the screen are indicated by tildes), as shown in Figure 4.3. The bottom of the screen now reports the name of the file and the number of lines and characters.

Regardless of whether the file is new or existing, **vi** always starts automatically in command mode. This means that it is waiting for you to tell it to do something. You cannot just start typing away or begin making changes—you must first tell it what to do.

FIGURE 4.2
The vi utility can be used to create a new file.

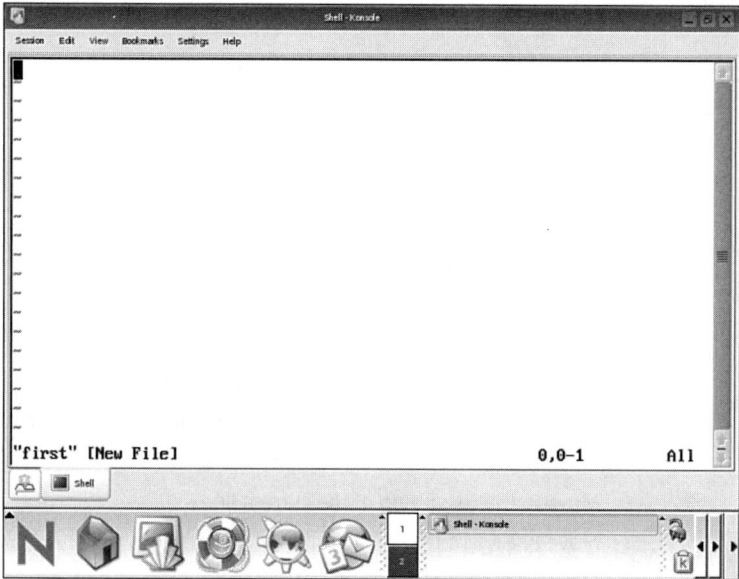

FIGURE 4.3
vi can be used to edit existing files.

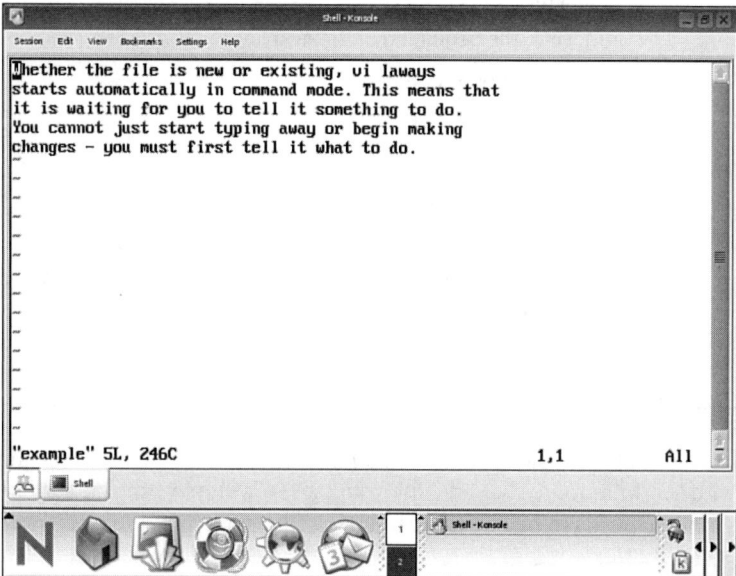

Navigation

The easiest commands involve navigation. Table 4.5 lists the navigation keys that can be used in vi.

TABLE 4.5
vi Navigation Keys

KEY	RESULT
-	Move to the first character of the previous line
$	Move to the last position of the current line
(	Move backward one sentence
)	Move forward one sentence
{	Move to the beginning of the previous paragraph
}	Move to the beginning of the next paragraph
^	Move to the first character of the current line (ignoring spaces)
+	Move to the first character of the next line
0	Move to the beginning of the current line
b	Move backward to the beginning of the previous word
B	Move backward to the beginning of the previous word, ignoring symbols and punctuation
e	Move to the end of the next word
E	Move to the end of the next word, ignoring symbols and punctuation
ENTER\RETURN	Move to the beginning of the next line
h	Move left one space
j	Move down one line
k	Move up one line
l	Move right one space
w	Move to the beginning of the next word
W	Move to the beginning of the next word, ignoring symbols and punctuation
G	Move to the last line of the file
xG	"Goto" line number x

The last entry of the table signifies that a line number can be used in conjunction with "G" to move to that line: for example, 5G will move the cursor from wherever it happens to be in the file to line 5. The ability to use numbers with commands is a constant throughout all of vi—if you precede a command by a number, it is interpreted as meaning that you want to do something a number of times equal to that number. For example, the command **10h** will move the cursor 10 spaces to the left.

The arrow keys can also be used for navigation, but only if they are mapped correctly on the terminal. In order for them to function properly, the right arrow must send the same key sequence as pressing l would, the left arrow must send the same key sequence as pressing h would, and so on.

Changing Text

When you reach a word to be changed, there are an almost endless number of ways to make the change. In the earlier table, the letter "w" was used to signify a word when discussing navigation. Using similar mnemonics, it can be combined with "c" for change and thus the command becomes **cw**.

This tells the editor that you intend to change the word, so it removes the current word from view, and places the editor in "insert" mode. You now enter a new word, and then press Esc to exit out of insert mode and enter command mode once again.

Note

Whenever you want to exit insert mode, regardless of the method used to place you into it, you always press Esc to return to command mode.

There are a number of combinations that the **change** command can be used in conjunction with. Table 4.6 offers a synopsis of the possibilities.

TABLE 4.6
vi Change Text Combinations

KEY SEQUENCE	RESULT
c$	Change from here to the end of the line
c)	Change from here to the end of the sentence
c^	Change from here to the beginning of the line
c}	Change the remainder of the paragraph
3cw	Change the next three words
r	Replace an individual character
R	Go to "Replace" mode—overwriting exiting text with new text

Notice that so many of the choices in Table 4.6 begin with the current cursor position and making changes from that point to the beginning or end of the line. If you need to change an entire line, regardless of where the cursor resides within the line, you can use the command **cc**. In a similar vein, the command **C** is the same as **c$**; selecting all text from the current cursor position to the end of the line.

Saving Files

After a change has been made, and you are finished with the editor, it is time to save the file. Just like everything in **vi**, there are numerous ways to accomplish this. Most of the ways require entering command mode, and this is accomplished by pressing the Esc key; after which, you usually enter a colon (:) and type another command.

Note

As a matter of history, the use of the colon to precede a command is a carryover from an earlier editor: ex.

You can save the file, under its current name, by typing

```
:w
```

This saves (writes) the file, but leaves you in the editor. To exit the editor, you then enter

```
:q
```

You are then returned to the Linux command-line prompt, having quit the editor. This sequence is useful if you want to write your changes out several times prior to quitting, as you can always enter **:w** and continue with edits.

If you want to write and quit at the same time, however, you can combine the operation into a single command:

```
:wq
```

This will write the file and quit the editor. A shortcut to this operation (which makes no mnemonic sense whatsoever) is to enter **ZZ**, which will also write and quit.

If you want to save the file by a different name (for purposes such as keeping the original intact), you can use the **:w** syntax and follow it by a space and the new name. It is worth pointing out at this point that if you make *any* changes to a file, the default operation of vi is to not let you exit the editor until you save the changes. If you try to leave by using :q, you will be notified that changes have been made with an error message:

```
No write since last change (use ! to override)
```

The error message spells out what must be done to get around the default. If you made changes that you do not want to save—having clobbered too much text to undo, changed your mind, and so on—you can exit the file and leave it in the state of the last save operation with this command:

```
:q!
```

SAVING A PORTION OF A FILE

Not only can you save the entire file, but vi allows you to save only part of a file by specifying the line numbers you want to write. By now, you've probably figured out that every line can be referenced by a number, and this operation requires using this syntax:

```
:first_line, last_linew FileName
```

Pay special attention to the "w" attached to the last line number. This must be there to identity the operation as a write request. Two wildcards can be used for either line number specification:

- $ to signify the last line in the file
- . to signify the current line

Some examples of commands to save only a portion of the file are shown in Table 4.7.

TABLE 4.7
Examples of Saving Portions of a File

KEY SEQUENCE	RESULT
`:.,12w newfile`	Saves lines from where the cursor currently is to line 12 in a file named newfile
`:2, 5w newfile`	Saves lines 2 to 5 in a file named newfile
`:12, $w newfile`	Saves lines from 12 to the end of the file in a file named newfile
`.,+12w newfile`	Saves 12 lines from the current cursor position into the file newfile

Inserting and Deleting

Changing existing text is simple enough if there is already text there. Inserting, however, allows you to add to the text already there, and is the mode you want to go into when starting a new file. When working within a line, you can choose to insert or append, as well as open a new line above or below the current one. Table 4.8 lists the possibilities.

TABLE 4.8
Keys to Enter Input Mode

KEY SEQUENCE	RESULT
a	Inserts text after cursor (append)
A	Inserts text at the end of the current line
i	Inserts text before cursor
o	Opens a new line below the cursor
O	Opens a new line above the cursor
s	Removes the current letter and places you in insert mode—this is known as the "substitute" command
S	Substitute mode for the whole line

Regardless of the method by which you enter insert mode, the means by which you leave this mode is by pressing Esc.

Deleting text is accomplished by pressing x to delete a single character. It can also be preceded by a number to indicate how many characters to delete. For example,

16x

will delete the next 16 characters. To delete the character before the cursor, substitute the X command in place of x.

If you want to delete something other than characters, you can use the **d** (delete) command with a sequence indicating what you want to delete. Table 4.9 lists the possibilities.

TABLE 4.9
Key Sequences for Deletion

KEY SEQUENCE	RESULT
d$	Deletes from here to the end of the line.
d)	Deletes the remainder of the sentence.

KEY SEQUENCE	RESULT
d}	Deletes the remainder of the paragraph.
d0	Deletes from here to the beginning of the line.
db	Deletes the previous word.
dl	Deletes a letter.
7dl	Deletes seven letters.
dw	Deletes a word.
7dw	Deletes four words—dw will not only delete the word, but also deletes the space after the word. To delete only to the end of a word, use de instead.

Navigating Screens

All the discussion thus far has been about changing text that appears on the screen. The vi editor shows 23 lines within a screen. If your file exceeds 23 lines, as a great many will, you have a number of screens that you can work with. For an analogy, think of viewing screens one at a time when using more or less commands.

Table 4.10 shows the methods of navigating between multiple screens.

TABLE 4.10
Key Sequences for Moving Between Screens

KEY SEQUENCE	RESULT
Ctrl+F	Moves forward one screen
Ctrl+B	Moves backward one screen
Ctrl+D	Moves forward one-half screen
Ctrl+U	Moves backward one-half screen
Ctrl+E	Scrolls the screen up one line
Ctrl+Y	Scrolls the screen down one line
H	Moves to the top line of the screen
L	Moves to the last line of the screen
M	Moves to the middle line of the screen

Note

You can use numbers before each of these operations as well. 7H moves the cursor seven lines below the top line on the screen, and 7L moves the cursor seven lines above the last line on the screen.

Searching for Text

Another method of moving through the file besides using navigational keys is to perform a search. You can search the file for string values, and the screen containing the first occurrence of that string will become your current view of the file.

Searches are initiated by pressing the slash key (/) and entering the string value to search for. As you enter the search text sequence, the editor will move through the file looking for a match.

When you have entered the search string, press Enter to signify that you are done. All searches automatically begin at the top of the document. To move the cursor to the next instance, use the **n** command (for next). To move backward through the file, use the **N** command.

Two characters can be used with the search to specify where the located text must reside:

- ∧ to signify that the text must be at the start of the line
- $ to signify that the text must be at the end of the line

For example, to find the string "is" only if these two characters are the last two characters on the line, the search syntax would be

```
/is$
```

You can also use many of the wildcard options present in **grep** and similar utilities:

- \ to ignore the following character's special value
- [] to find multiple values
- \< to find matches at the beginning of a word

If you need to find values and change them, you can do so using the substitute command (**s**), with syntax that resembles **sed**:

```
:first_line, last_line s/old string/new string/
```

For example, to change all occurrences of "speed" to "pace" in lines between the first and thousandth, the command is

```
:1,1000 s/speed/pace/
```

Note

The question mark character (?) can be used to search backward through the file.

Copying Text

Text can be copied into the buffer to be reused or moved from one part of the file to another. As simplistic as it sounds, when you copy text, you leave the original where it is and make a duplicate elsewhere. However, when you move text, you take it from one location in the file and place it in another. Whether you are copying or moving, the **p** command is always the counterpart of the operation; standing for print/put/place, it completes the operation.

Unfortunately, the "c" mnemonic had already been used for change when vi was being created, and there weren't a whole lot of other good choices left. Given that, Bill Joy chose to use **y** for **yank**. Table 4.11 shows a series of key sequences that can be used for copying text.

TABLE 4.11
Key Sequences for Copying Text

KEY SEQUENCE	RESULT
y$	Yanks from here to the end of the line
y)	Yanks the remainder of the sentence
y}	Yanks the remainder of the paragraph
y0	Yanks from here to the beginning of the line
yb	Yanks the previous word or part of a word
yl	Yanks a single letter
7yl	Yanks the next seven letters
yw	Yanks a single word
7yw	Yanks the next seven words
yy	Yanks an entire line
7yy	Yanks seven lines
Y	The same as y$

To do a copy operation, you move to the desired location in the file where the text should go, and then use the **p** command. To do a move operation, delete the text after yanking it, and then move to the desired location and use the **p** command to place the text where you want it.

Other Operations

If there is one single command to commit to memory, it is **u**—the undo command. This command will undo the previous action, and only the previous action. It has a counterpart—**U**—which will undo all previous actions to the current line. It is important to note, however, that U will only buffer changes for one line (the current one); this prevents you from making changes to four lines and then moving to the first and undoing them.

Note

If you mess up four lines and cannot put back in the first line what was changed, your only salvation is to exit the file without saving.

So many of the operations discussed in this section revolve around line numbers—you can move to a particular line by specifying its number, you can save only specific lines, and so on—that it is often helpful to have the lines numbered as you view them. Turning on line numbering in vi is accomplished by first going to command mode with a colon (:)(sometimes called colon mode; this will move the cursor to the bottom of the screen), and then entering the command set number followed by Enter. This will turn on line numbering.

The numbers appear only within the editor, just as if you were viewing them with the nl command, and are not saved out with the file. Incidentally, set number can be abbreviated as set nu. If you only want to see the number of the line you are currently on, you can press Ctrl+G, and the line number (as well as the total number of lines within the file) will appear at the bottom of the screen.

If you need to run an external command while in the editor, you can do so by using the syntax

`:!{command}`

For example, to see a list of files in the current directory while working in vi, the command would be

`:!ls -l`

This will show the listing, then prompt you to press Return (Enter) to go back to the file you are working within.

If you need to copy the contents of another file into this one, you can do so by using the syntax

`:r {filename}`

For example, to bring the contents of a file named first into this file, the command is

`:r first`

This inserts the text from the other file directly into the location in this file where the cursor resides.

Summary

This chapter covered a great deal of material as it examined what you need to know to understand the basics of GNU and Unix commands. All the following chapters assume that you understand the tools and utilities discussed here and will build on them. Table 4.12 lists the metacharacters that appeared in this chapter, as well as their purpose.

TABLE 4.12
Metacharacters Used in GNU and Unix Commands

METACHARACTER	PURPOSE
' '	Cancels the special meaning of anything but the back quote
" "	Cancels the special meaning of most characters
$	Treats the next string as a variable
$()	Allows a command to be treated as a variable
*	Any number of characters
;	Separates dissimilar commands
?	Any single character
[ ]	Any of the enclosed characters
\	Treats the next character literally
` `	Executes the enclosed command
|	Allows one command's output to be the next command's input
<	Input redirection
<<	"Here"
>	Output redirection
>>	Output append

## CHAPTER 5

Working with YaST

One of the primary features differentiating Novell Linux Desktop from other implementations of Linux is its inclusion of YaST (Yet Another Setup Tool). This one-stop tool provides a convenient interface to virtually every aspect of system administration. The latest versions of the Desktop ship with the second version of this tool—YaST2.

Mastering this one tool can save you a great amount of time (and often frustration) as it offers a simple, and convenient, interface to a number of configuration tasks. This chapter looks at a sampling of the administrative tasks that you can do with it.

NOTE

The purpose of this chapter is to walk you through the features of YaST. Complex topics, such as adding users, creating groups, and so on are mentioned in passing in this chapter as the YaST screens are shown, but they are covered in much more depth and detail in subsequent chapters.

Introducing YaST

The YaST tool is available in Novell Linux Desktop as both a command-line interface and an X Window application. The command-line interface, regardless of which version (there are two) of YaST you are running, is an **ncurses** application. When YaST is run as an X Window application, the appearance can differ based on whether you are using the first or second version of the tool—the first is **ncurses** based, and the second (YaST2) is **Qt** based.

NOTE

ncurses and QT are two C libraries containing standard functions that applications can use to perform terminal-oriented or graphical tasks. There are a number of other graphical libraries that people can use, but these are two of the most common.

Novell Linux Desktop 9 ships with YaST2 and still supports **yast** as a link. If you execute the command **yast** from the xterm or terminal command line, you will get the curses/terminal version. If you execute the command **yast2** from the xterm or terminal command line and you are running the X Window System (and the **DISPLAY** environment variable is set), you will get the graphical version. If—on the other hand—you start **yast2** from the command line and you are running from a console login and the DISPLAY environment variable is not set, you will get the curses/terminal version. Last, if you start **yast2** from the command line and you are running from a console login and the **DISPLAY** environment variable is set, you will get the graphical version on the target display.

Most of this discussion focuses on the YaST2 version of the tool because of its ease of use and that's what most people will use in an X Window System environment (which is where most administrators will typically be).

The purpose of this tool is to provide a one-stop interface to most of the tasks an administrator must work with on a regular basis. Although the appearance of the text mode differs from that of the graphical mode, all the choices are available in both interfaces.

NOTE

You should run yast/yast2 as root in order to perform system administration tasks. It is located in the /sbin directory, which is not in the default user's PATH statement.

Figure 5.1 shows the text-mode version of the tool upon startup. (You start it by typing **yast** on the command line.)

From the command line, you can type

yast -h

to see the help information available. You can also type

yast -l

to view a list of all available modules.

In text mode, you can navigate through the menus and choices by using the arrow keys (up and down) and the Tab key to move between boxes (Alt+Tab moves you from window to window). You can also use the spacebar to highlight items and Enter to choose them. You can press **F9** to quit and **F1** to bring up help (as shown in Figure 5.2).

FIGURE 5.1

The startup view of YaST2 in text mode.

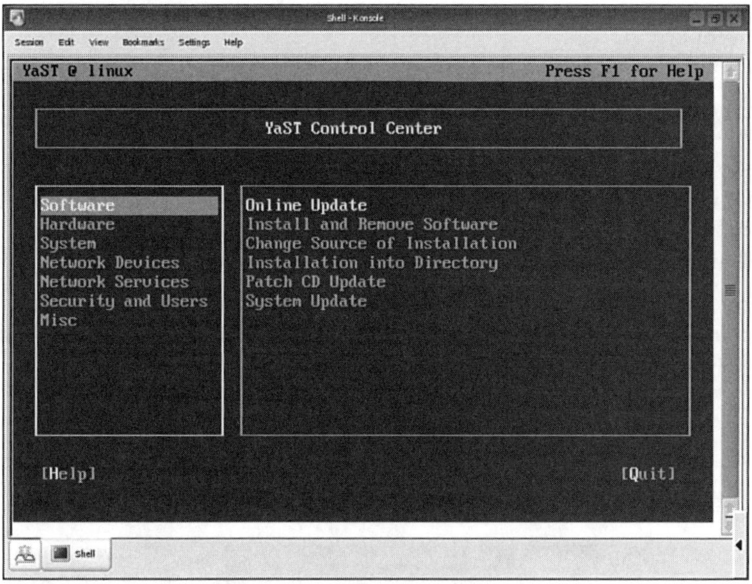

FIGURE 5.2

Help is available in the text mode by pressing **F1**.

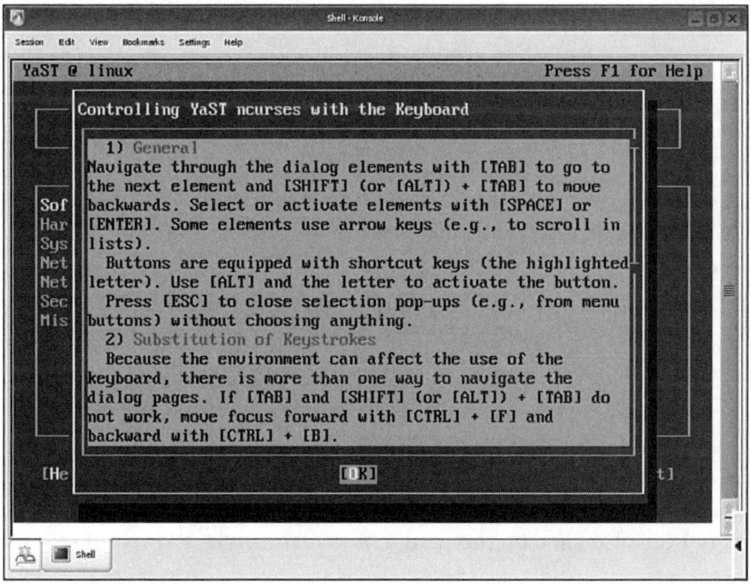

You can start the graphical mode by typing **yast2** at the command line or by simply choosing it from the KDE menu or GNOME menu choices. (In KDE, choose **System** and then **YaST**; in GNOME, choose **System**, and then **Administrator Settings**.) Figure 5.3 shows the startup view of this interface.

TIP

Authentication is handled differently depending on whether you invoke YaST from the command line or menus. For example, if you start it graphically in KDE while a user, you will be prompted for the root password. If you start it graphically by selecting **YaST Modules** from within the Control Center, you will need to authenticate when you execute each privileged YaST module (any of them).

When you run YaST in the former mode, it opens a separate window when you select any YaST module. In the latter mode, it opens each module within the right pane of the existing Control Center window.

FIGURE 5.3
The startup view of YaST2 in graphical mode.

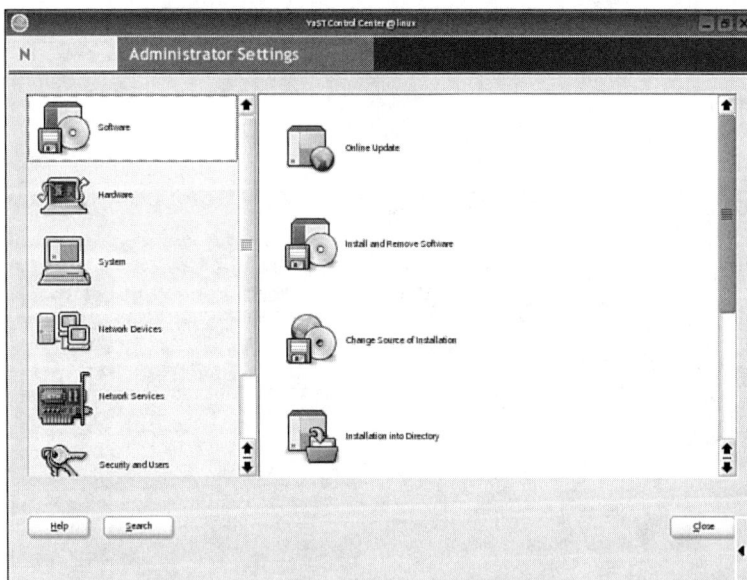

Within the graphical interface, you navigate by using the mouse. You first click on a category within the left frame, and then choose an item from the right frame. You can also click on the Search button and enter a keyword to find.

Working with Software

When you choose Software in the opening left frame of the YaST2 window, as shown in Figure 5.3, a number of choices appear on the right:

- Online Update
- Install and Remove Software
- Change Source of Installation
- Installation into Directory
- Patch CD Update
- System Update

Most of these choices are self-explanatory, and the one you will use most often on a regular basis is Install and Remove Software. When you choose this option, a screen similar to that shown in Figure 5.4 appears.

FIGURE 5.4
You can add and remove software easily.

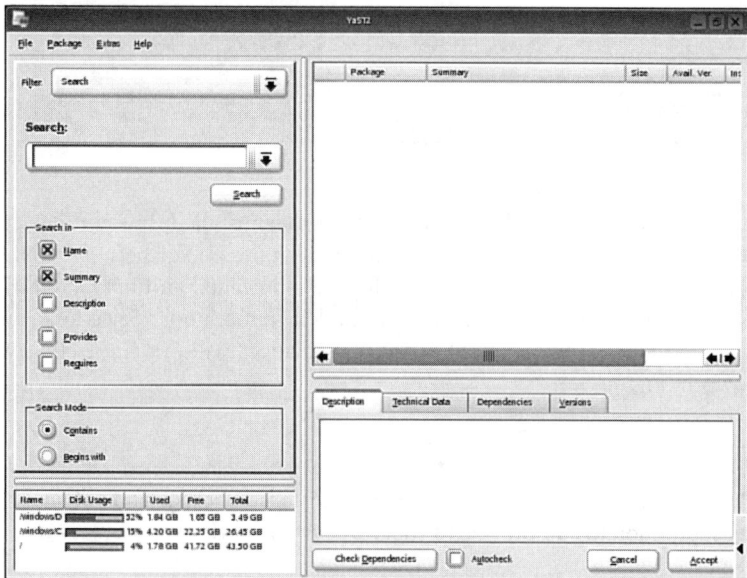

Notice that the Filter drop-down menu allows you to choose what packages you want to see. If you choose **Selections** as your filter, you will see only the installed packages, as shown in Figure 5.5.

FIGURE 5.5
You can easily see what packages are installed.

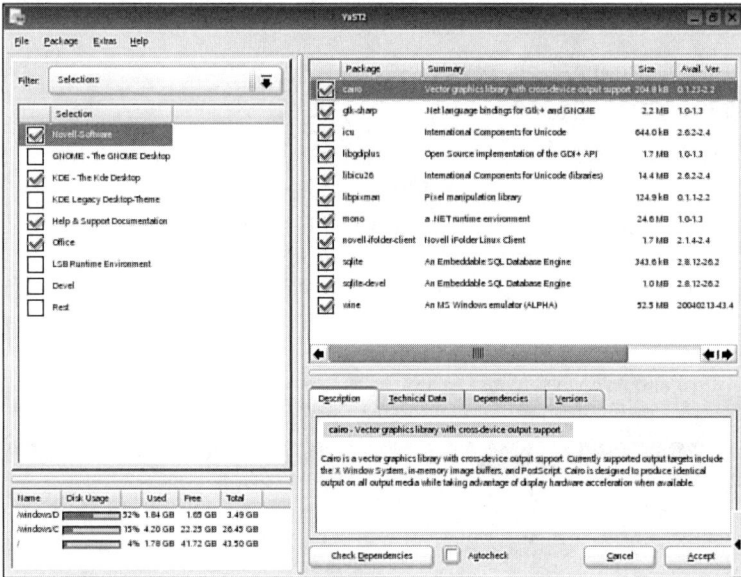

In Figure 5.5, you can see that the KDE Desktop is installed, but not the GNOME one—during installation, you were given the choice between GNOME or KDE at install time. In this example, KDE was installed and not GNOME. To install GNOME, simply check the box in the left frame, under Selections, and click Accept. Quite often, a list of Automatic Changes will present itself as well, as shown in Figure 5.6.

NOTE

This discussion is an example of installing an uninstalled package and not an explicit suggestion to add GNOME to your KDE system, or vice versa, unless you have a need to do so.

After clicking Continue, insert media as prompted. If there is a failure, you will be notified of such, as shown in Figure 5.7, and given the chance to see more details. In most instances, a Retry will solve the problem.

FIGURE 5.6
You will often be prompted to accept Automatic Changes.

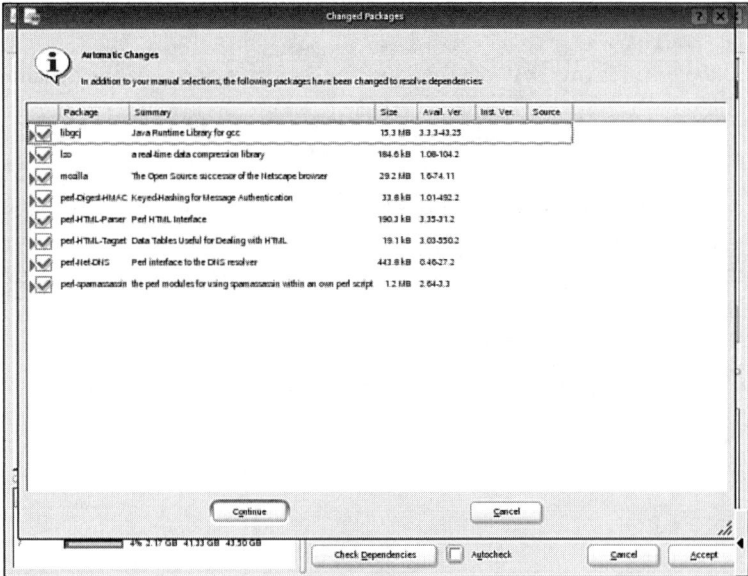

FIGURE 5.7
Errors are reported in either terse or verbose format.

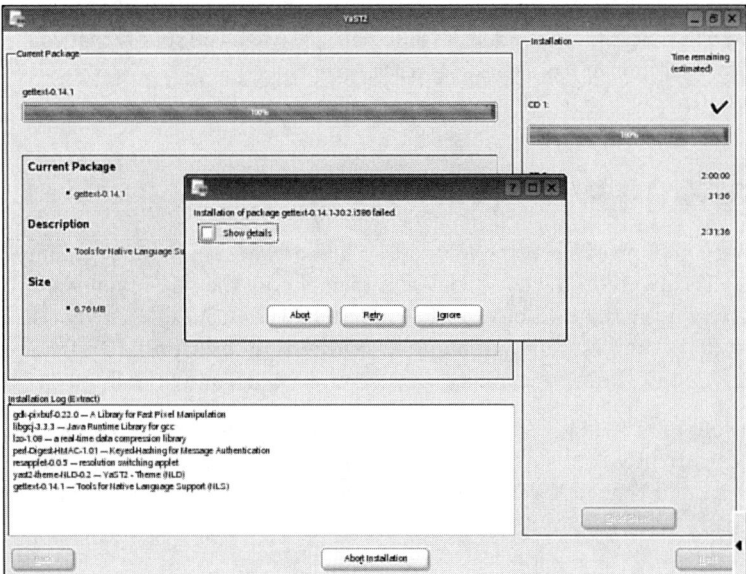

After the software is copied, SuSEconfig runs and finishes the installation before returning you to YaST.

If you choose **Package Groups** in the Filter drop-down menu, you will see all software on the installation media. If you choose **Search**, it searches the list of available packages from the current installation source(s) and lists any packages that match the string you have entered. Last, if you choose **Installation Summary**, you will see all the packages with their status marked.

If you want to install a package listed in your search results that is not currently installed, click on a package until the action you want appears, and then click the **Accept** button. Again, as needed, you will be prompted to insert media.

Working with Hardware

The YaST tool provides a simple interface to hardware configuration. Simply choose **Hardware** in the left frame, and then choose the object you want to configure in the right. Choices include such items as CD-ROM Drives, Disk Controller, Graphics Card and Monitor, Hardware Information, IDE DMA Mode, Joystick, Printer, Scanner, Select Mouse Model, and Sound.

Hardware Information, as the name implies, displays information about all the devices currently configured on your system. Graphics Card and Monitor allows you to change X Window System resolution (a very important and common task). IDE DMA Mode lets you fine-tune how/whether the IDE storage devices on your system use Direct Memory Access. Choosing the correct DMA mode can significantly improve device I/O, whereas choosing the wrong one can significantly hurt performance.

As an example, Figure 5.8 shows the opening screen of the configuration options provided for any printers that are attached to your system in the Printer module.

FIGURE 5.8
You can install a printer through YaST2.

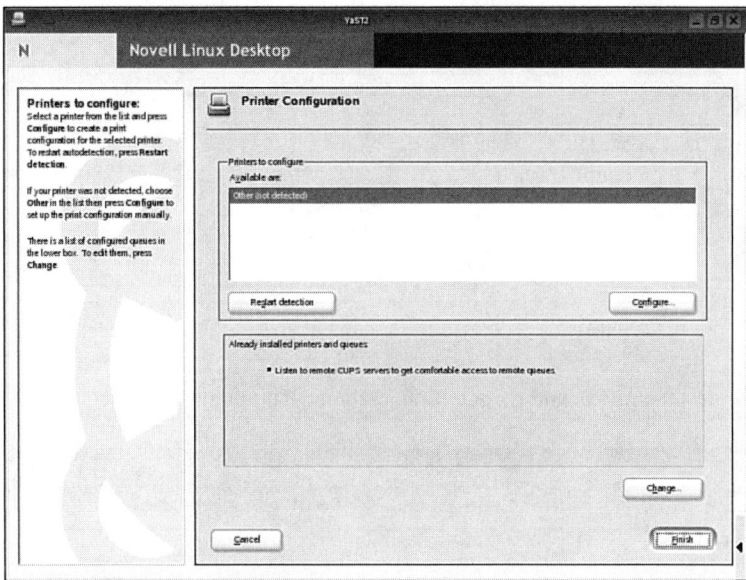

Clicking on the Configure button opens a dialog box offering a plethora of printer types that you can choose from (as shown in Figure 5.9). The easiest type to choose is the Parallel printer, which defaults to /dev/lp0, as shown in Figure 5.10.

NOTE

You can also start YaST with this module loaded by typing **yast2 printer** at the command line.

FIGURE 5.9
You can choose from a number of different printer installations.

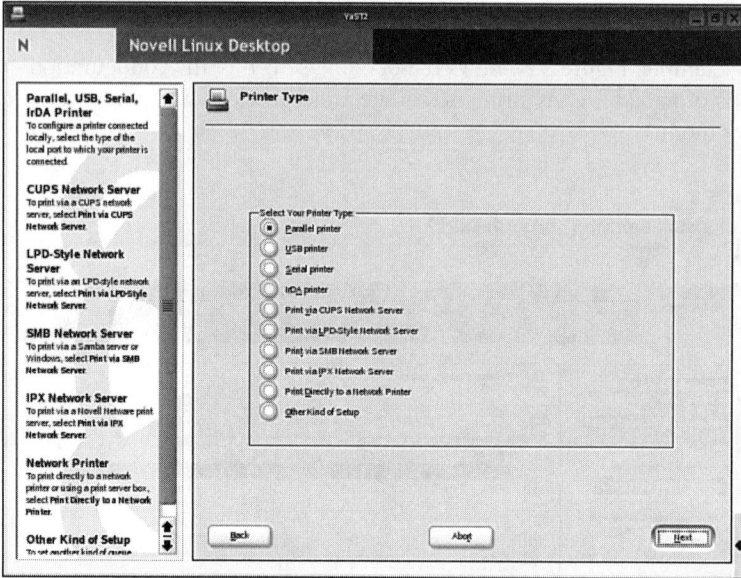

FIGURE 5.10
You can test the printer and change configuration details on the first screen.

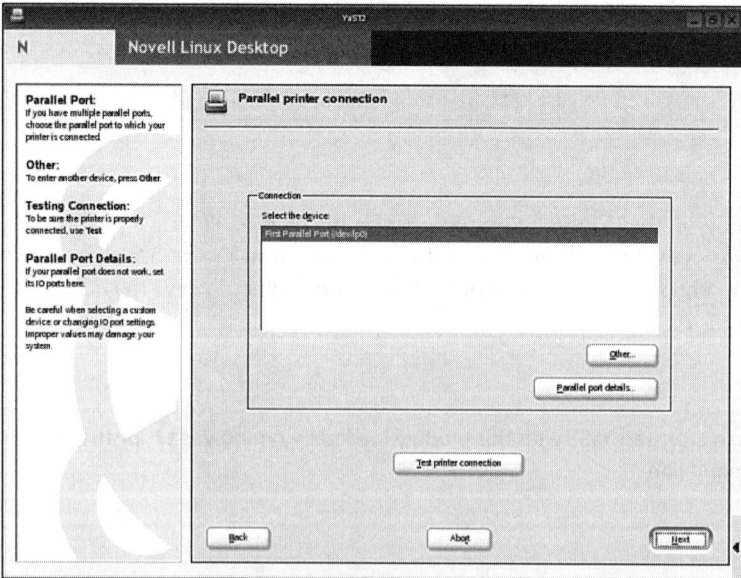

Click **Next** to continue with the configuration, and you are prompted to offer
the queue name and spooler settings. You can also test printing—but only if
Local Filtering is turned off. The Local Filtering feature is turned on (check box
already checked) by default. The three types of things you can send to the
printer to test it are as follows:

- Test Graphical Printing Without Photo (the default)
- Test Graphical Printing with Photo
- Test Text Printing

At the next screen, you can choose the printer model (manufacturer and
model), and then edit the configuration, if needed, on the summary page. This
adds an entry to the printer configuration box, as shown in Figure 5.11.

FIGURE 5.11
The printer configuration now shows the newly added printer.

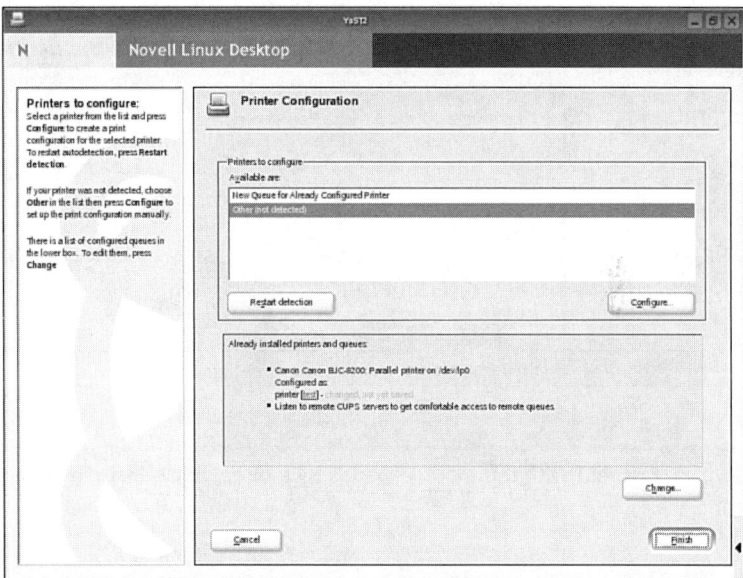

Click **Finish** to complete the addition of the printer, and you are once again
returned to YaST.

NOTE

Before making any changes to any hardware, it is highly recommended that you choose the Hardware Information option. This probes the current configuration and allows you to see the current settings of your devices, as shown in Figure 5.12.

FIGURE 5.12
Hardware Information shows the current settings.

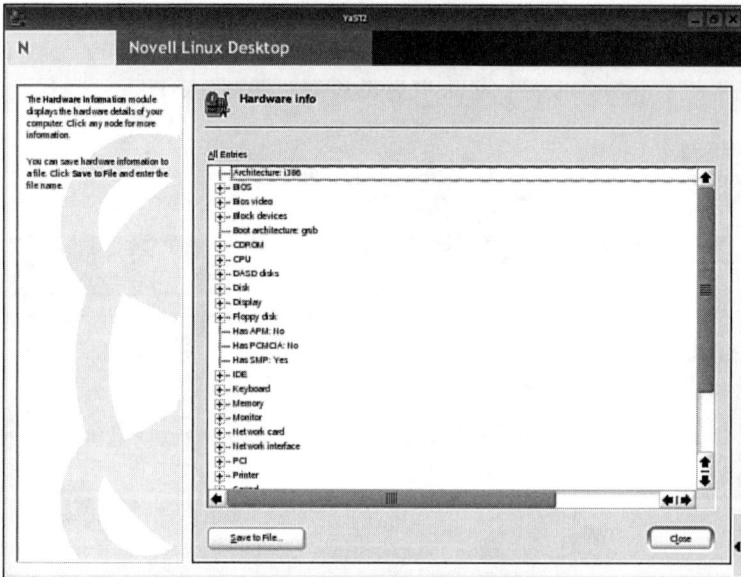

NOTE

You can also start YaST with this module loaded by typing **yast2 hwinfo** at the command line.

Working with System Settings

The choices beneath System offer access to a number tweaks that can help with host configuration. After System is chosen in the left frame, the selections in the right frame become

- /etc/sysconfig Editor—This offers an easy way to access the editor and work with settings for applications, the desktop, or other components.

NOTE

You can also start YaST with this module loaded by typing **yast2 sysconfig** at the command line.

- Boot Loader Configuration—You can choose from GRUB (the default), LILO, or to not use any boot loader.

NOTE

You can also start YaST with this module loaded by typing **yast2 bootloader** at the command line.

- Choose Language—Select a different language for the system.

NOTE

You can also start YaST with this module loaded by typing **yast2 language** at the command line.

- Create a Boot, Rescue, or Module Floppy—As the name implies, you can create an emergency disk for use should a crisis arise.
- Date and Time—Set the system date and time.

NOTE

You can also start YaST with this module loaded by typing **yast2 timezone** at the command line.

- LVM—If the lvm2 package is installed, you can configure volume settings and work with volume groups.

NOTE

You can also start YaST with this module loaded by typing **yast2 lvm_config** at the command line.

- Partitioner—Work directly with the disk partitions.
- Power Management—Choose the energy saving scheme most applicable for this host.

NOTE

You can also start YaST with this module loaded by typing **yast2 power-management** at the command line.

- Powertweak Configuration—You must first install the powertweak package (not installed by default), and then you can fine-tune settings available here.

NOTE

You can also start YaST with this module loaded by typing **yast2 powertweak** at the command line.

- Profile Manager—Using System Configuration Profile Management (SCPM), you can switch between different system profiles as needed. SCPM is disabled during the default installation.

NOTE

You can also start YaST with this module loaded by typing **yast2 profile-manager** at the command line.

- Restore System—Use following a system crash.
- Runlevel Editor—Allows you to change the runlevel settings and can be run in either Simple Mode (the default) or Expert Mode for finer tuning.

NOTE

You can also start YaST with this module loaded by typing **yast2 runlevel** at the command line.

- Select Keyboard Layout—Self-explanatory.
- System Backup—A graphical interface for creating **tar** archives.

NOTE

You can also start YaST with this module loaded by typing **yast2 backup** at the command line.

Working with Networks

To obtain networking configuration information, first choose **Network Devices** in the left pane. Choices in the right pane can include

- DSL
- Fax
- ISDN
- Modem
- Network Card
- Phone Answering Machine

As an example of the options available, choose **Network Card**. This will bring up the screen shown in Figure 5.13.

FIGURE 5.13
Current settings for the network cards.

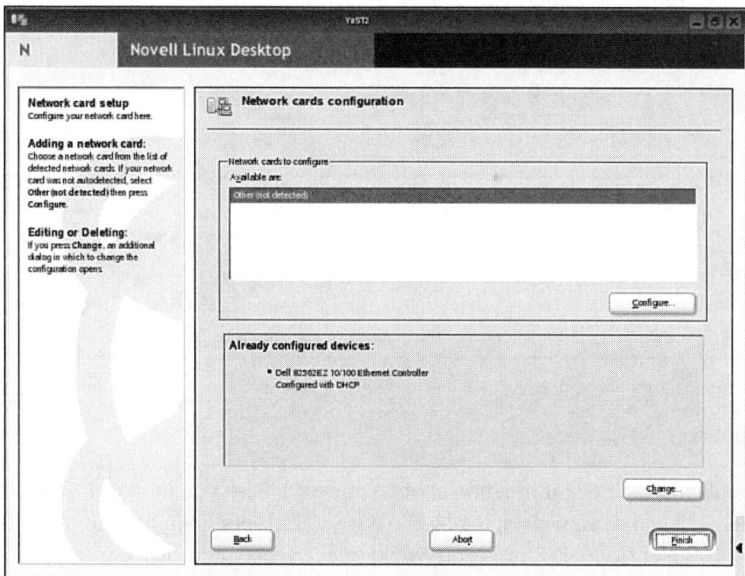

NOTE

You can also start YaST with this module loaded by typing **yast2 lan** at the command line.

Devices already configured will appear in the bottom pane (Change), and new entries can be added at the top (Configure). Choosing **Change** first brings up the screen shown in Figure 5.14. Notice that you can add, edit, and delete from here.

FIGURE 5.14
You can change the network card settings.

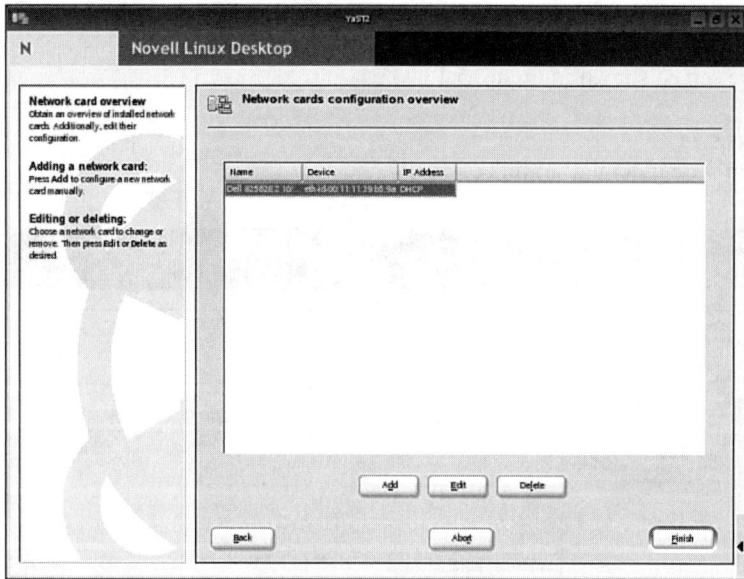

NOTE

Although you can add information about a new card here, you probably have a problem if it wasn't auto-detected by the system. If it were, it would show up in the top pane of Figure 5.13, and you would select it there and click **Configure** to configure it. In the real world, it's pretty rare to add info about a new card on the Change panel.

Choosing a new card (Configure) brings up the manual configuration dialog box shown in Figure 5.15.

FIGURE 5.15
Adding a new card manually.

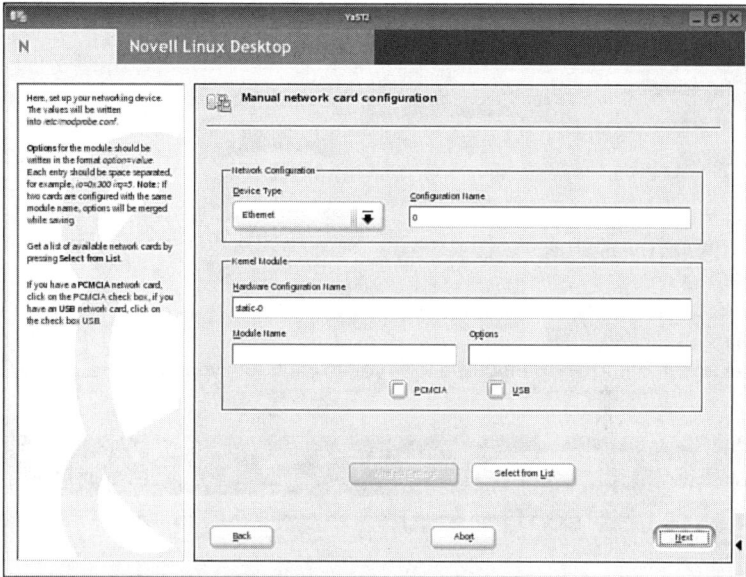

Choices you have to make when configuring a card manually include whether to use DHCP or manually assign an IP address, subnet mask, and other networking values that are discussed in Chapter 11, "Networking."

Working with Network Services

When you click the Network Services option in the left pane of YaST, a number of choices appear on the right. Those choices include

- DNS and Host Name
- Host Names
- Kerberos Client
- LDAP Client
- Mail Transfer Agent
- NFS Client
- NIS Client

- NTP Client
- Network Services (`inetd`)
- Proxy
- Remote Administration
- Routing
- SLP Browser
- TFTP Server

Chief among those choices is the one for Remote Administration, shown in Figure 5.16.

FIGURE 5.16
The Remote Administration module allows you to configure your machine.

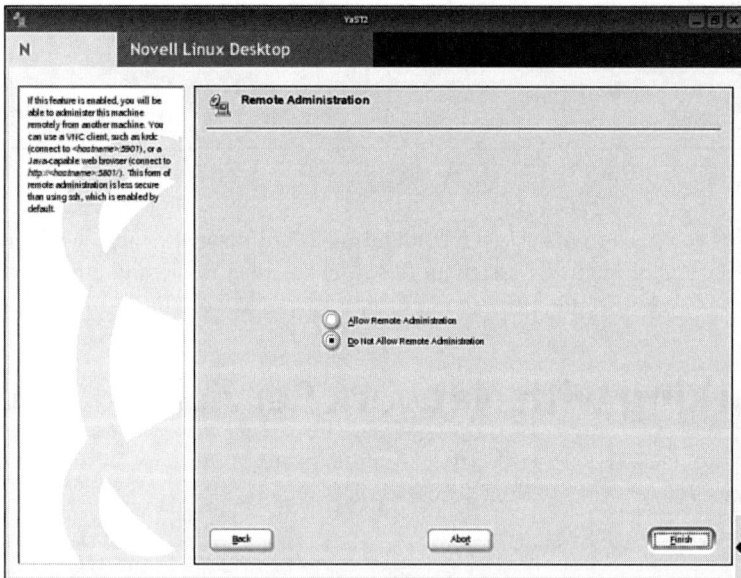

The choices here are remarkably simple—either to allow remote administration or not (the default).

NOTE

You can also start YaST with this module loaded by typing **yast2 remote** at the command line.

If you choose to enable remote administration, the display manager must be restarted. After this is done, the machine can now be accessed and remotely administered.

To administer it remotely, enter the following in a browser (replace *host* with the IP address of your machine): **http://*host*:5801**

A Virtual Network Session (VNS) window will open, and you will be prompted for a username and password. At the prompt for these items, you can click the Administration button instead and YaST will be initiated (requiring you to enter the root password).

NOTE

Should it be necessary to restart your X session, the rcxdm restart command will do the trick for you.

Working with Security and Users

Just as YaST can be used for all other aspects of configuration, it can also provide an interface to your user and security settings.

Working with User Settings

To work with users in the YaST tool, first choose **Security and Users** from the left frame. This brings up a number of choices in the right frame:

- Edit and create groups
- Edit and create users
- Firewall
- Security Settings

Select the **Edit and Create Users** choice, and a screen similar to that shown in Figure 5.17 appears.

FIGURE 5.17
Users and groups can be added and altered from the User and Group
Administration module.

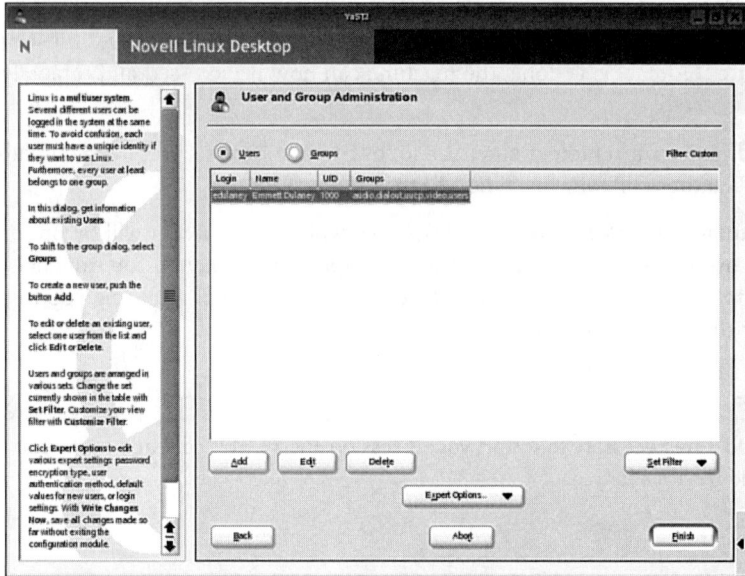

NOTE

You can also start YaST with the user account module loaded by typing **yast2 users** at the command line.

From this menu, you can add, delete, or edit a user. The Expert Options button is used to set defaults that will apply to newly created accounts, and the Set Filter button lets you choose what you want displayed—local users are the default, but you can also choose system users or customize the display.

To edit a user, click the **Edit** button. A dialog similar to that shown in Figure 5.18 appears. Here, you can change any of the existing settings for that user.

If you click Details, you can see and change such values as the user ID, home directory, shell, and so on. Figure 5.19 shows the variables present in the Details settings.

FIGURE 5.18

The Edit button can change any of the parameters set for a user.

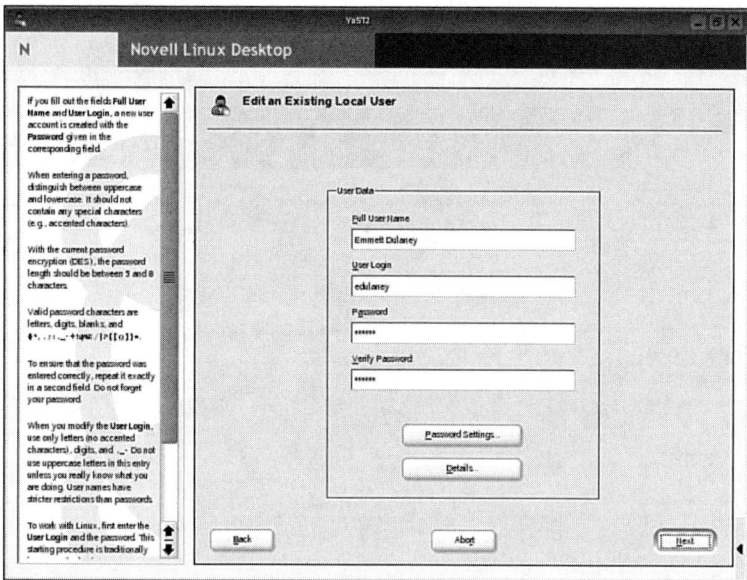

FIGURE 5.19

All values for the user can be changed.

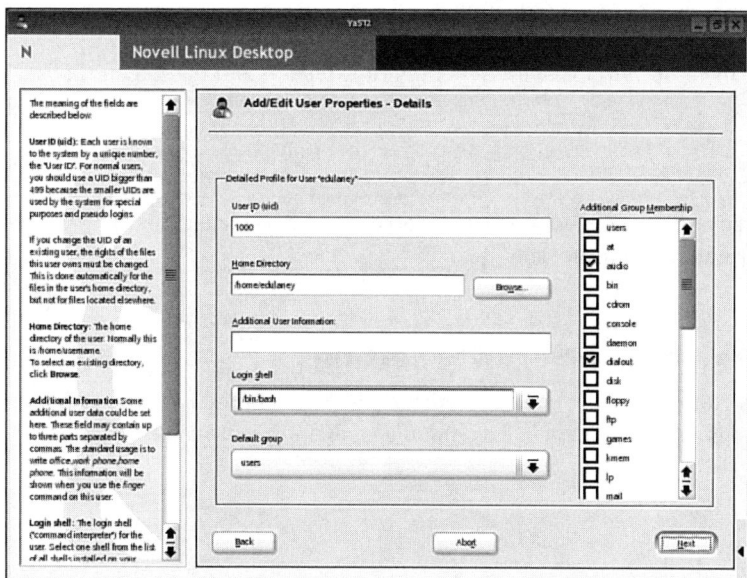

Conversely, clicking on **Password Settings**, shown in Figure 5.18, allows you to set password expiration and other variables as shown in Figure 5.20.

FIGURE 5.20
Password configuration parameters can be displayed and changed.

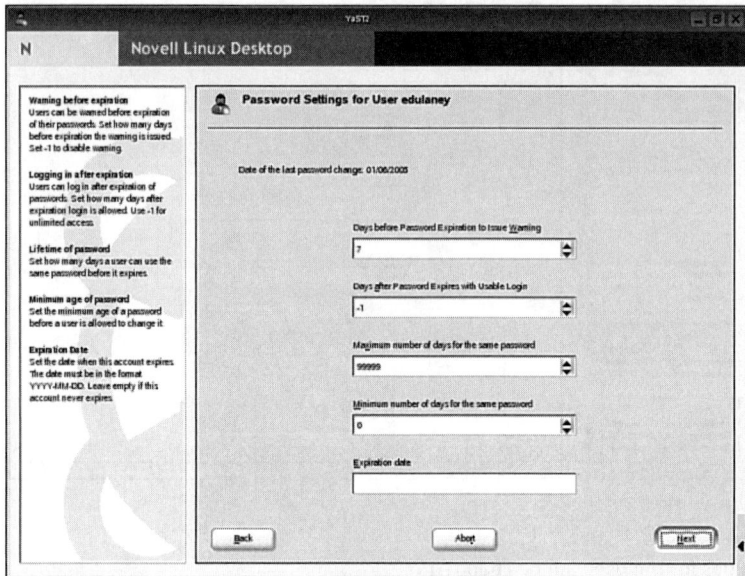

Groups are added and edited in the same way as users. Figure 5.21 shows the main menu for groups, with System groups filtered and the Expert Options expanded.

NOTE

You can also start YaST with the group account module loaded by typing **yast2 groups** at the command line,

Working with Security Settings

To reach this module, choose **Security and Users** in the left pane and **Security Settings** in the right pane. The module shown in Figure 5.22 will appear.

FIGURE 5.21
You can add, edit, and delete groups in the same way as you do with users.

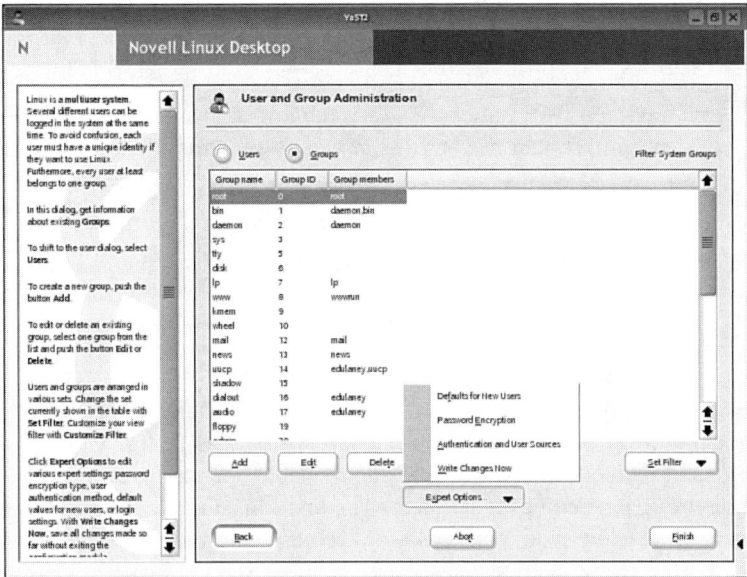

FIGURE 5.22
Security settings within YaST.

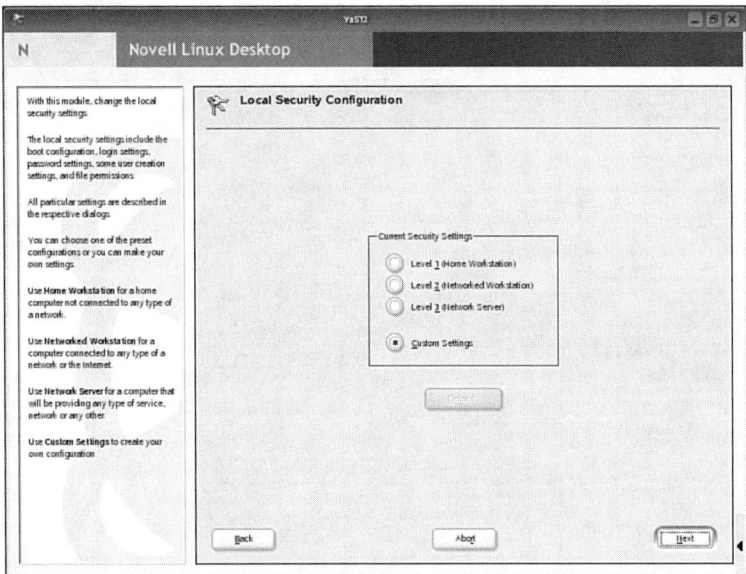

NOTE

You can also start YaST with this module loaded by typing **yast2 security** at the command line.

The four settings that appear on this menu are

- Level 1 (Home Workstation)—This is the lowest level of security that you can apply and should not be used in a business setting.

- Level 2 (Networked Workstation)—This is a moderate level of security and should be considered the minimum setting for a business.

- Level 3 (Network Server)—A high level of security recommended for servers.

- Custom Settings—The default.

You can choose any of the predefined roles and choose **Details** to tweak any individual settings. Alternatively, you can stick with the default of Custom Settings, and then click **Next** to see all the available options. (Next is only available if Custom Settings is selected.) The first screen that appears (shown in Figure 5.23) allows you to set password settings, and the next screen, shown in Figure 5.24, shows boot settings.

FIGURE 5.23
Configure the default password settings.

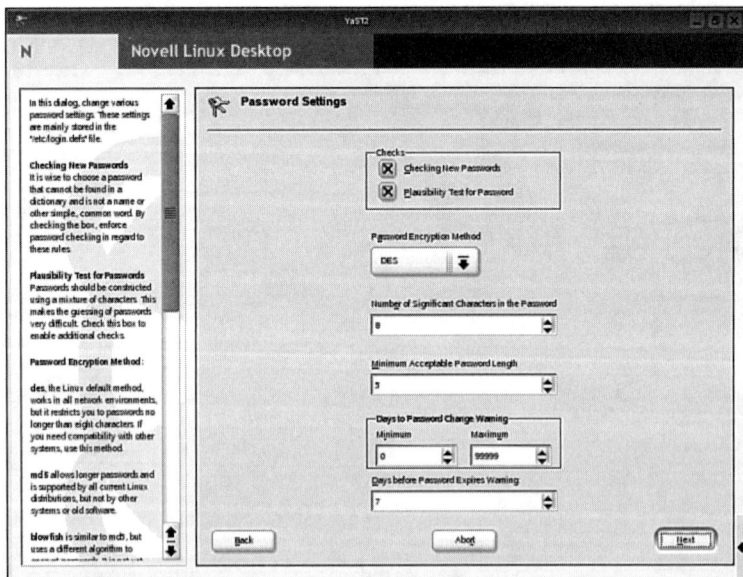

FIGURE 5.24
Configure the default boot settings.

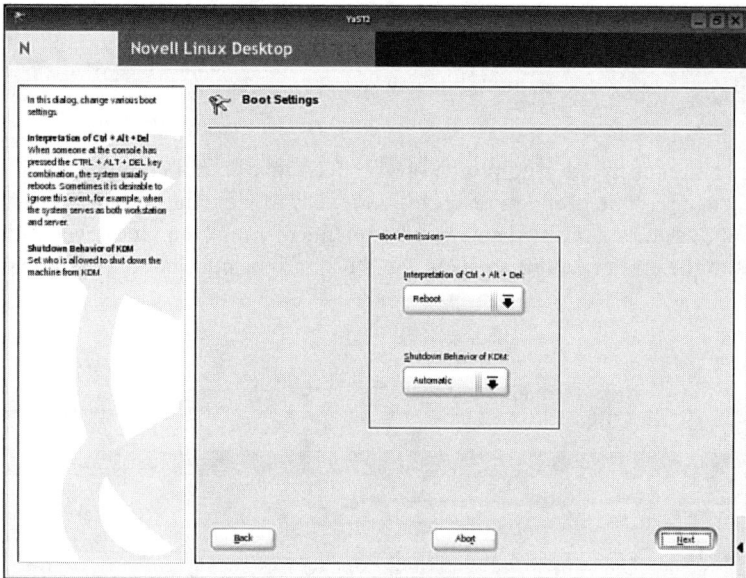

Following boot settings, you configure login settings, and then parameters to affect newly added users and groups. Last, miscellaneous settings allow you to configure the user who runs **updatedb** (either nobody or root) and the settings on file permissions. You can choose from three possible file permission settings:

- Easy—The majority of configuration files can be read by users.
- Secure—Only root can read system files such as **/var/log/messages**.
- Paranoid—Access rights are the most restrictive possible.

You can see the individual settings for each of these levels by going to **/etc** and looking at **permissions.easy**, **permissions.secure**, and **permissions.paranoid**. Around 850 lines are in each file.

The Misc Option

When you choose **Misc** in the opening left frame of the YaST2 window, the following choices appear on the right:

- Autoinstallation
- Load Vendor Driver CD
- Post a Support Query
- View Start-up Log
- View System Log

These choices truly are a potpourri of selections that do not comfortably fit anywhere else. One of the most useful options is to view the system log. When chosen, this automatically displays the contents of **/var/log/** messages and jumps to the end of the file to show the most current information, as shown in Figure 5.25.

FIGURE 5.25
It is easy to view the system log messages.

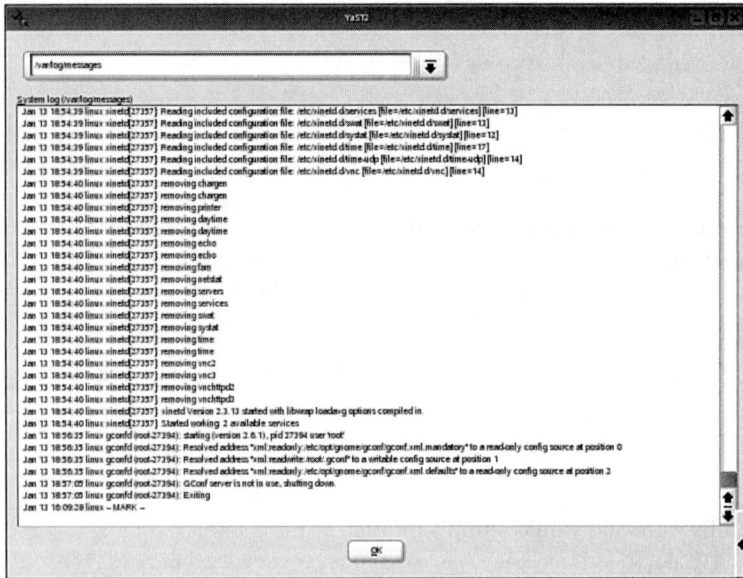

NOTE

You can also start YaST with this module loaded by typing **yast2 view_anymsg '/var/log/messages'** at the command line.

Though messages is the default file shown, the drop-down box at the top left allows you to choose almost any log file and view its contents.

Summary

This chapter focused on the graphical side of Linux and examined how YaST (Yet Another Setup Tool) makes SUSE stand out from the rest of the pack. Using this tool, you can perform most administrative functions without needing to fumble for the command-line syntax in order to accomplish the task.

CHAPTER 6

Working with Devices

This chapter focuses on three main issues: understanding how devices are attached to a host, printing, and creating a boot floppy. Compared with a number of other operating systems, Linux is far more straightforward and configurable in terms of setup than some.

Attaching Devices

When external devices are attached to a host running Novell Linux Desktop, the system will often recognize that device and automatically start the configuration for it, provided that the device is plug-and-play compatible. For example, Figure 6.1 shows the dialog box that appears when a removable USB drive is suddenly attached to the system.

FIGURE 6.1
The USB drive is found.

After choosing Yes, in this case, the contents of the drive are displayed. A new directory is automatically created in /media that is a mountpoint for the drive.

An icon on the lower left of the taskbar (the "system tray" portion of the panel) depicts a computer and the ToolTip identifies it as the SuSE Hardware Tool. When you click on it, suseplugger (shown in Figure 6.2) opens.

FIGURE 6.2
The suseplugger offers a convenient interface to hardware.

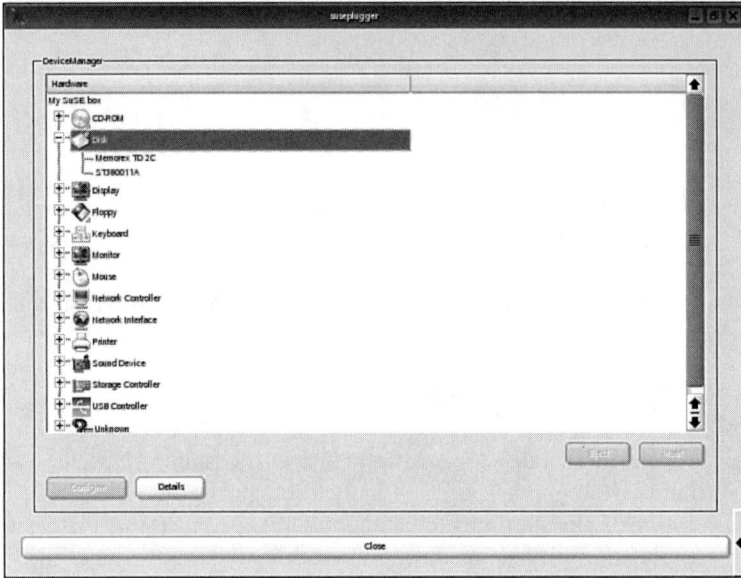

NOTE

In addition to clicking on the icon, you can also access suseplugger by clicking on the giant N, and then choosing System, Desktop Applet, and SuSEPlugger.

In Figure 6.2, you can see the USB controllers at the bottom of the list. Though the USB drive attached in the previous step uses the USB Controller, it is available as a standard system hard disk like any other, and is therefore itself listed in the Disk section at the top. The Disk options have been expanded to show that the USB drive appears here (as Memorex TD 2X). After selecting this entry, you can click on **Details** and see the General information, as well as the Resources information associated with it (see Figure 6.3).

FIGURE 6.3
The Resources information for the drive is quickly accessible.

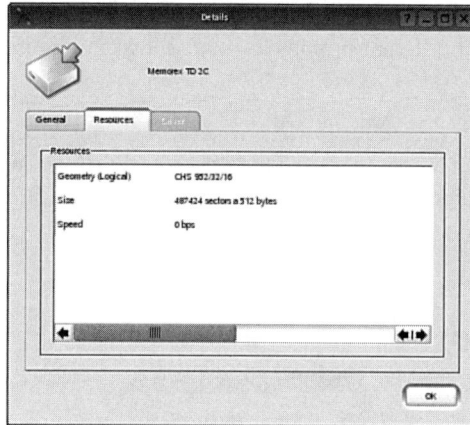

If the device you are working with has a driver associated with it that contains specific information, that tab will also be accessible, and you can see the information associated with it. Figure 6.4, for example, shows the additional information available about the driver for a monitor.

FIGURE 6.4
The Driver tab becomes accessible if information is there.

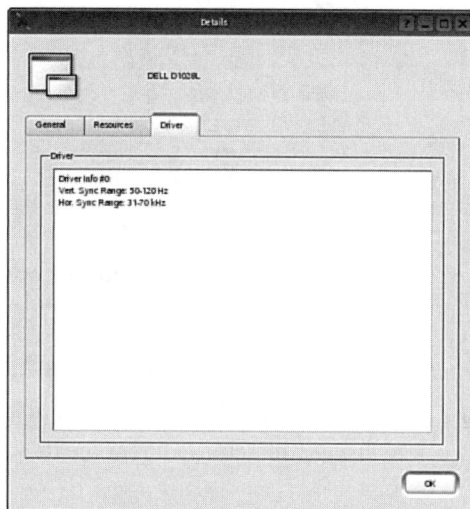

Suseplugger is a great tool for seeing the settings that apply to hardware, but it is limited in its capability to make changes. Even though a Configure button appears at the bottom left, it does not tend to become enabled. If you right-click on the icon for it, and choose **Configure** from the pop-up menu, you can choose a number of different options for it, as shown in Figure 6.5.

NOTE

The Configure button is only enabled if the driver for the device in question can be manually configured.

FIGURE 6.5
The suseplugger utility is configurable.

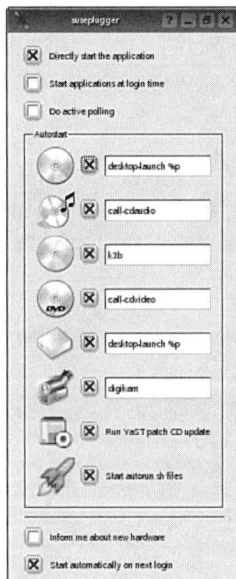

Notice in Figure 6.5, the Inform Me About New Hardware option that can be checked. It is recommended that you enable it. When eliminating removable devices, be certain to stop them first. This can be accomplished by choosing **Eject** in the device manager (which sends a SIGTERM or SIGKILL signal).

Whereas suseplugger is good at showing the values presently there, a number of other tools allow you to change the settings. From the desktop, you can choose **System**, **Configuration**, and choose between YaST (discussed in Chapter 5, "Working with YaST"), and SaX2. SaX2 is used to configure the X Window System server that underlies the graphical subsystems discussed in Chapter 3, "Working with the Desktop Environment," as shown in Figure 6.6.

FIGURE 6.6
The SaX2 utility allows for the configuration of some devices.

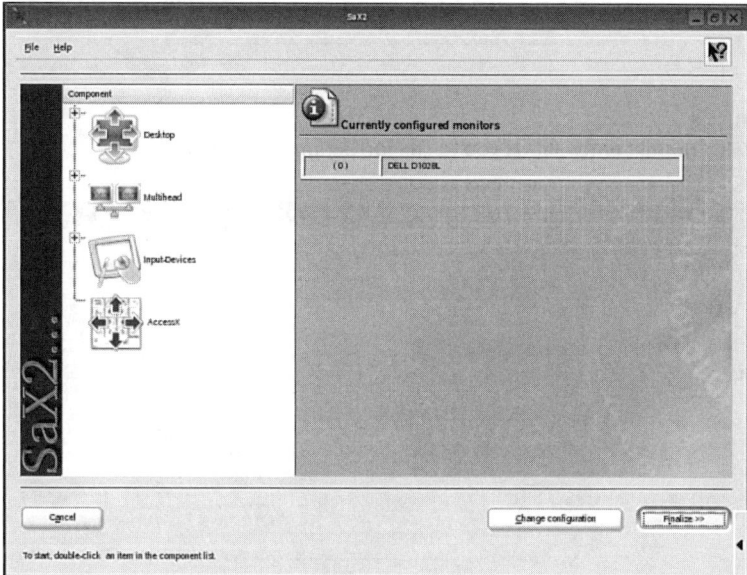

This utility is useful in making changes for any problems with resolution, color, graphics cards, input devices, and so on. For example, to change the resolution, first pick Desktop, followed by Color and Resolution, and then Properties for the monitor. On the Resolutions tab, make the desired change; then click **OK**, **Finish**, and **Finalize**.

When you make any changes in SaX2, you are always prompted to test them before saving them, as shown in Figure 6.7.

After testing your settings, choose **Save**, and you will be informed that the changes will take place the next time the X server starts.

If you are using KDE, you can also choose the KDE Control Center from the Utilities menu and make changes to peripherals from there. The Control Center only enables you to change the settings for peripherals. Figure 6.8 shows the settings available for the keyboard within this interface.

FIGURE 6.7
SaX2 prompts you to test your settings before saving them.

FIGURE 6.8
The KDE Control Center allows you to change peripheral settings.

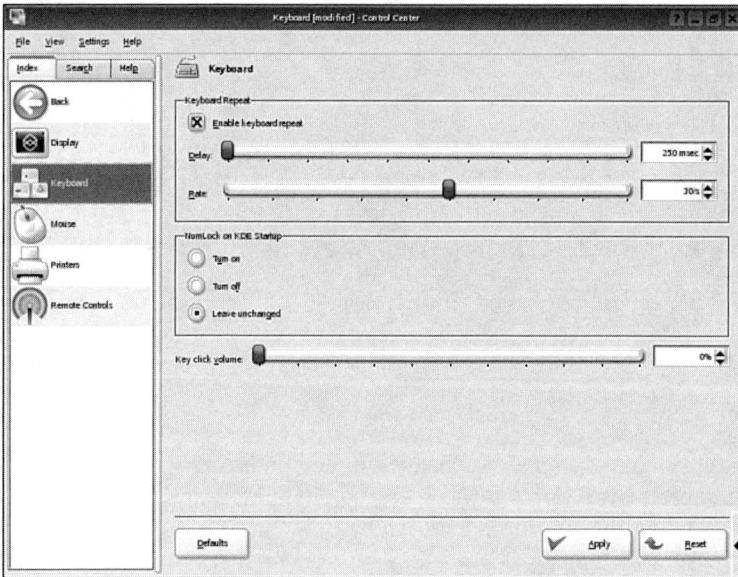

If you are using GNOME, this same information can be found by choosing Personal Settings from the System menu and looking at the entries in the Hardware section, as shown in Figure 6.9.

FIGURE 6.9
The GNOME Personal Settings allows you to change peripheral settings.

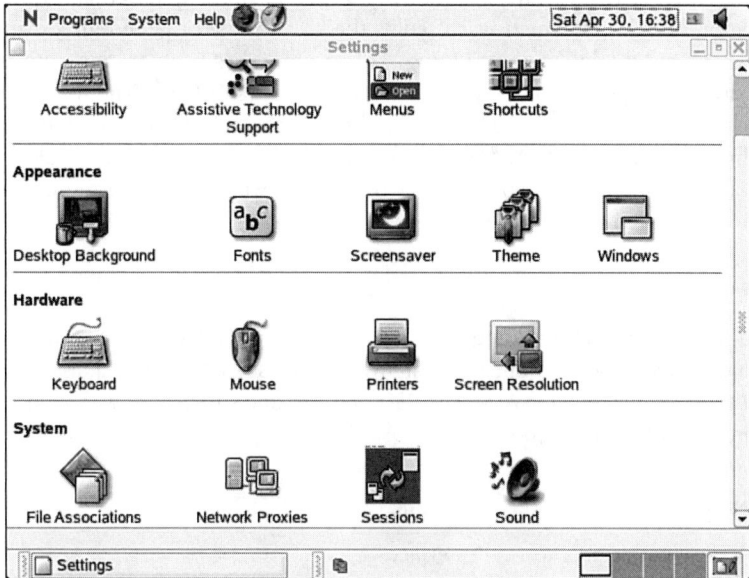

Understanding Printing

Chapter 5 shows how to add a printer, but it does not go into detail on what transpires when you print. Knowing the basics behind printing operations is imperative to being able to diagnose and troubleshoot printing issues.

In this section, we will walk through the basics of printing. We will examine the commands that can be used to administer and work with printers and print jobs. There are several ways in which this can come about, and we will start with the most simple models first and work from there.

NOTE

Before installing any printer, you should verify that it is supported in Linux by checking the printer database at http://www.linuxprinting.org/.

Printing a File

Let's start the discussion by looking at the legacy method of printing and move up from there. Unix systems traditionally used a printing system that required a daemon called **lpd**, which was used as the basis of the original Linux print subsystem and its descendant, LPRng. This daemon has been around, and is virtually unchanged in operation, since the early days of Unix. The first utility written to allow jobs to be submitted to the daemon on AT&T-based Unix was **lp**. This utility still exists and is included in many versions of Linux, but is generally overlooked in favor of **lpr**, which is a newer utility with more logical options and originated with BSD-based Unix versions.

NOTE

This discussion focuses on LPRng. CUPS, an alternative to LPRng (an alternate printing/spooling method for Linux systems), is discussed later in this chapter. The disparities between the AT&T and BSD Unix printing subsystems was a big reason that CUPS came to be.

A user can choose to print a file in one of two ways:

- From within a graphical interface
- From the command line

The simplest syntax to use from the command line is

`lpr {filename}`

So if you wanted to print a file named Saturday, the command would be

`lpr Saturday`

NOTE

You must have a printer setup first for this to work. Otherwise, an error indicating that the scheduler is not responding will always result.

When this command is issued, a number of other processes kick in. If the printer does not exist, the print job will spool to nothing. Assuming that the printer does exist, after the print job is sent to the appropriate queue for a printer, the daemon removes the job from the printer and produces the finished output. As long as the file exists, entries for it remain in the spooler beneath `/var/spool/lpd`.

NOTE

A list of supported printers for Linux can be found at
http://www.linuxprinting.org/. Although their presence in this list is reassuring,
printers do not, technically, need to appear on this list in order to work well with
Linux. Any PCL or PostScript printer, for example, will work with Linux with proper
drivers.

Once properly configured and functioning, the printing service in Linux runs
very smoothly.

Formatting a File

When discussing printing options, one utility to be aware of that is valuable for
formatting is **pr**. The primary purpose of this utility (**/usr/bin/pr**) is always to
convert the contents of a text file before sending the output to a printer.

The output includes a default header with date and time of last modification,
filename, and page numbers. The default header can be overwritten with the -h
option, and the -1 option allows you to specify the number of lines to include
on each page—with the default being 66. Default page width is 72 characters,
but a different value can be specified with the -w option. The -d option can be
used to double-space the output, and -m can be used to print numerous files in
column format.

Moving Up to CUPS

In newer Linux implementations, including Novell Linux Desktop and SUSE,
CUPS (Common Unix Printing System) replaces much of the functionality of
lpr/lpd. CUPS is a superset of **lpr/lpd**, not a subset. It introduces much new
value, such as classes and detailed printer-oriented authentication. From an
operations standpoint, however, there is great similarity:

1. The user submits the print job.
2. The file is spooled—in this case, beneath **/var/spool/cups/**.
3. The **cupsd** daemon formats the data in the spool and sends it to the
   printer.
4. When the job is done printing, the daemon removes the files from the
   queue.

The /etc/cups/cupsd.conf file (or /etc/cups/cupsd.y2 sample file) contains an enormous amount of narrative and comments that fully explain how to configure cups. Although space does not allow printing the file in its entirety here, it is *highly* recommended that you carefully walk through the file on your system and make certain that you understand the options available.

The /etc/init.d/cups stop command is used to stop the service, and the /etc/init.d/cups start command is used to manually start it. (Once configured, it should start automatically at boot using the startup script /etc/init.d/cups.)

Using the Add Printer Wizard

In addition to using YaST (discussed in Chapter 5), you can also choose to install the printer using the Add Printer Wizard in KDE, as shown in Figure 6.10. To access this, click on the (N), and choose **Control Center**. In the Index, choose **Peripherals**, and then **Printers**. Next, select **Add**, and then choose **Add Printer/Class**.

NOTE

You can only add physical printers either when logged in as root or when using tools such as the Control Center in Administrator mode. In order to create systemwide printers, you need to be able to write to files owned by root in /etc/cups and to the spool directories.

Yet another alternative method for configuration is to use kprinter. This is accessed by pressing (N) for the KDE menu, and then choosing **Utilities**, **Printing**, **Printing Manager**. This utility, shown in Figure 6.11, allows you to interact with all aspects of the printing function, including manage jobs. When you choose **Add**, it brings up the same Add Printer Wizard shown in Figure 6.10.

Regardless of the method used to add the printer, a number of things happen when it successfully joins the system:

- A print queue is added to /etc/cups/printers.conf.
- A ppd file for the printer is placed in /etc/cups/ppd for settings.
- The print queue is added to /etc/printcap.

A network printer can be set up just as easily, and it will support SMB (Standard Message Block—for printing from Windows-based clients), IPP (Internet Printing Protocol), and the LPD protocol previously discussed. Most of these options are available to you when choosing the printer type.

FIGURE 6.10
The Add Printer Wizard can also be used to add a printer.

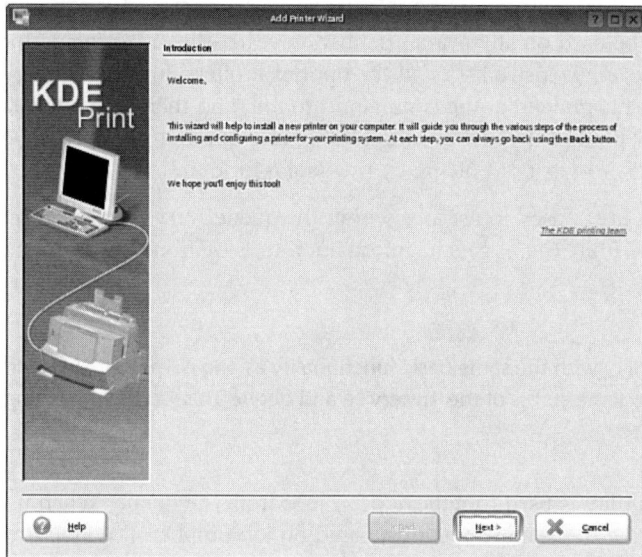

FIGURE 6.11
The Printing Manager provides an interface to all printing functions.

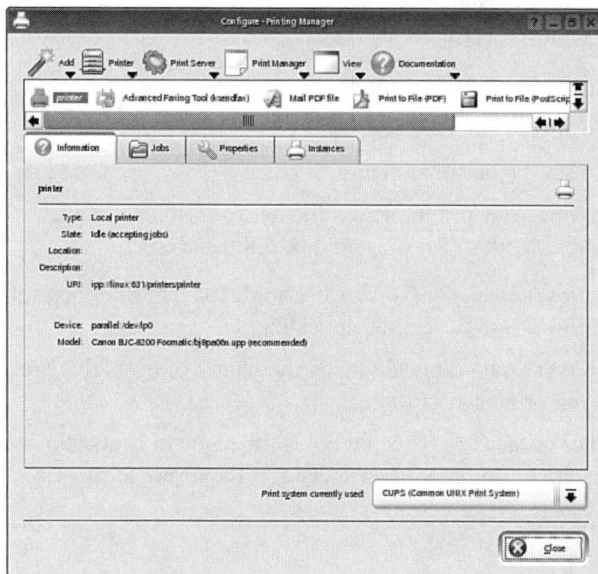

Printing Utilities

A number of utilities exist to work with various components of the printing service. The first to examine is lpc—the line printer control program. This utility can be used on any printer defined in either the **printcap** or **lpd.conf** files. To see an extensive list of all the options it offers, first start lpc by entering the command at the command prompt, and then type **m** for the menu at the lpc> prompt if you are using LPRng, or a question mark (**?**) if you are using CUPS. You exit out of lpc by pressing **q** for quit.

The lpq utility is used to list jobs within the queue. Very similar to the status command within lpc, it gets its information directly from the daemon.

NOTE

An older utility with the same basic functionality as lpq is lpstat. This utility is used to check the status of the lp service and queue. This works with LPRng, but not CUPS.

The lprm utility is used to remove print jobs from the queue. When used, it sends a request to remove the jobs, based on job number. If no job number is given, it attempts to remove the last job you submitted.

The lpadmin utility is used for creating and manipulating printer and class queues—in brief, most of the configuration you can do within YaST from the command line. A complement to this utility is lpoptions, which is used for setting any printer defaults from the command line. Some of the options that can be used with it include

- -d   To set the default printer
- -h   To specify the CUPS server
- -p   To set the destination and instance

If you are sharing your printer across the network, there are a few other files that can be helpful, although they are not utilities as such:

- /etc/cups/cupsd.conf—This file holds the names of hosts that are allowed to access the printer in CUPS.
- /etc/hosts.lpd—This file holds the names of hosts that are allowed to access the printer in LPRng.
- /etc/hosts.equiv—This file holds the name of hosts allowed to access this machine (not just the printer) as if they were local.

To enable and disable printing from the command line, you can use the /usr/bin/enable and /usr/bin/disable commands, respectively. Each command must be followed by the name of the printer for which you are enabling/disabling. If you want the printer to finish what is in its queue but not accept any additional jobs, you can use /usr/sbin/reject followed by the printer name (the opposite of which is /usr/sbin/accept).

NOTE

Under CUPS, enable and disable are symlinks to /usr/sbin/accept.

The CUPS service can be stopped in two ways: using the command /etc/init.d/cups stop or rccups stop. The opposite of these actions is accomplished by using start in place of stop.

TIP

Most of the utilities and commands discussed require you to be root in order to execute them.

The lppasswd utility can be used to add a password to CUPS (for example, for use with the Web Administration tools). If you enter the command by itself at the command line, you will be prompted to enter a password twice. The password you give must be at least six characters long and cannot contain your username; it must also contain at least one letter and number. Options that can be given at the command line are –g to specify a groupname and –a or –x to specify a username. For the Webadmin tools, you need to run the following command:

```
lppasswd -g sys -a root
```

to create the sys group and root user. You will then be prompted for the password to use.

One last item of note is that the file /var/log/cups/error_log is where error messages for the CUPS daemon are written. The access_log shows all access to the service. Both can be useful in troubleshooting situations in which you need to ascertain why a printer is unavailable.

Using the CUPS Web Interface

To access the Web Administration tools, simply access port 631 on the server. These tools allow you to remotely manage the printers and jobs, as well as do administrative tasks such as add/manage classes, manage jobs, and add/manage printers. The server is the system on which the CUPS daemon is running. If you're on that machine, the easiest URL to use is http://localhost:631; whereas from another machine, simply use http://*ip_addrress_of_host*:631.

Figure 6.12 shows the opening screen.

FIGURE 6.12
The opening screen of the CUPS Web interface.

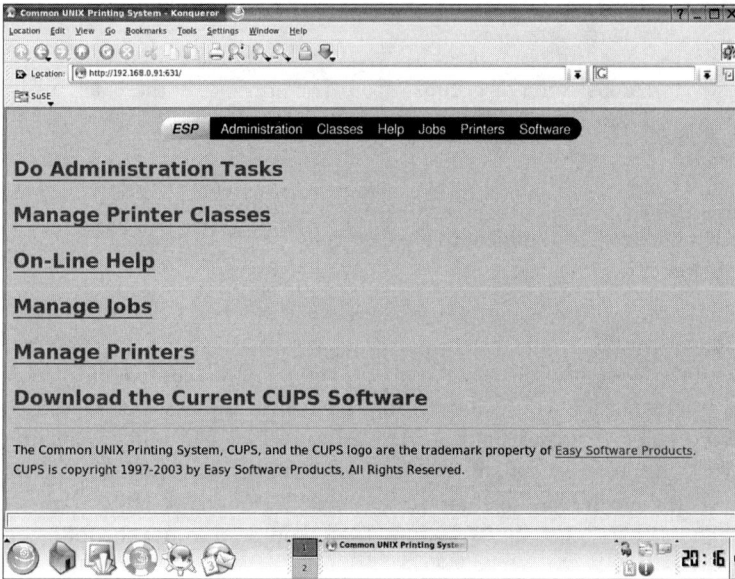

If you choose **Do Administration Tasks**, the choices that present themselves are

- Classes—You can add and manage classes.
- Jobs—You can manage jobs.
- Printers—You can add or manage printers.

To add a new printer, you must supply the name, location, and description on the first dialog box, and then choose the device. Choices for device include all the serial ports, parallel ports, LPD/LPR, and USB, as well as Windows Printer via SAMBA.

As an example, after choosing Windows Printer via SAMBA, you must next supply the Device URI. This can be given a number of ways, including specifying a socket (socket://192.168.0.30:9100), a file, http, or smb path. Figure 6.13 gives an example of two printers, and their URIs, as viewed in the Printers tab.

FIGURE 6.13
The existing printers and their current information.

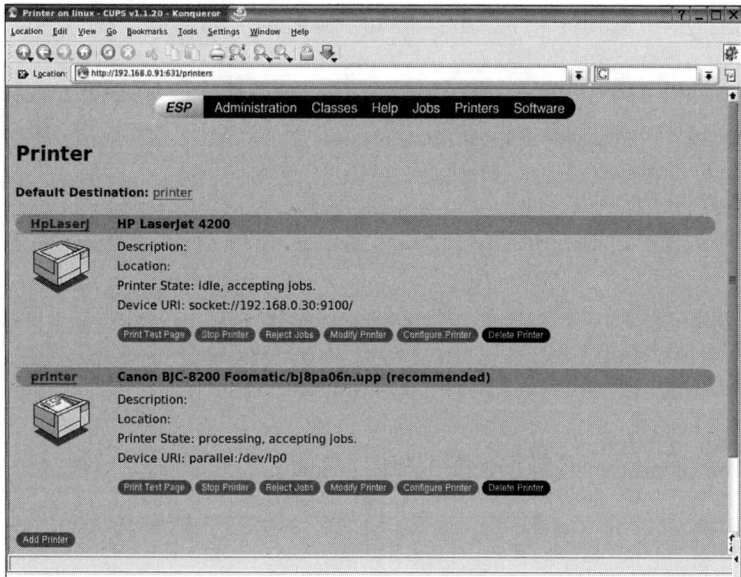

The next step in configuring is to choose the model and driver for the printer. After that, the additional printer is added and can be managed from this Web interface using the choices shown in Figure 6.13. Clicking on the hyperlink for any printer will bring up additional information on that printer and any pending jobs, as shown in Figure 6.14.

Canceling a job is as simple as clicking the corresponding button, and an acknowledgement that it has been accomplished (see Figure 6.15) is returned.

FIGURE 6.14
Additional information is available on each printer.

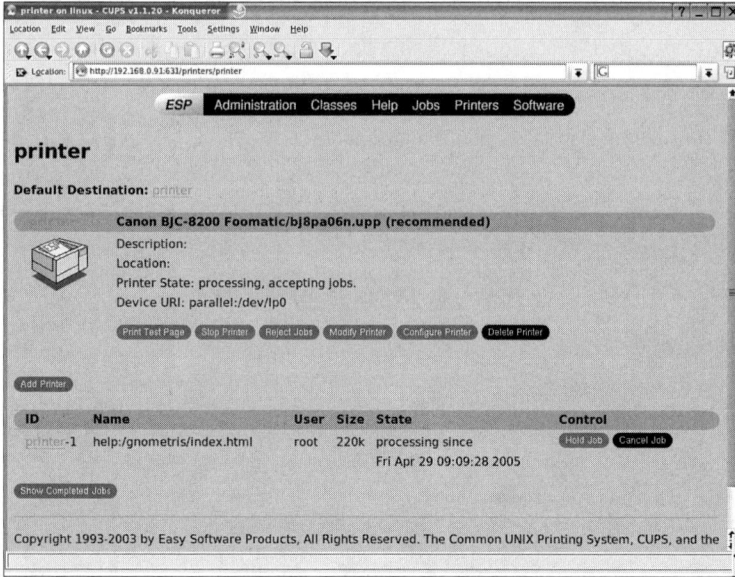

FIGURE 6.15
Jobs can be canceled easily through the Web interface.

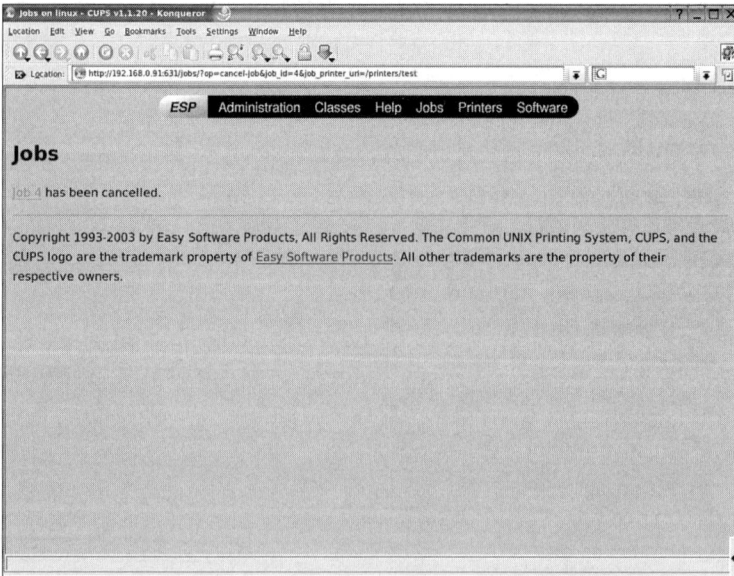

Other items of note within the Web interface are the Help choice, which brings up a list of all the known documentation for printing on this server (see Figure 6.16), and the Software choice. The latter takes you directly to the http://www.cups.org site, where you can find drivers, forums, links, and other related information (see Figure 6.17).

FIGURE 6.16
All printing-related documentation is available through the Web interface.

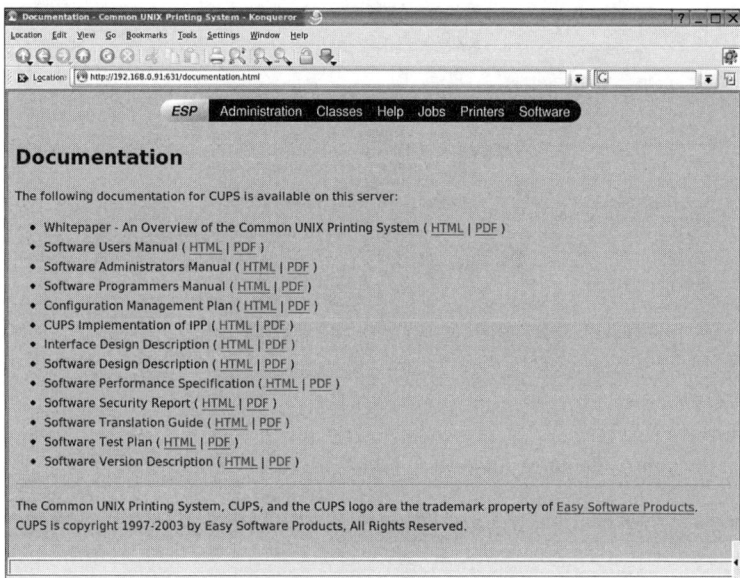

Simplified Administration

Now that the commands and files associated with printing have been given, it is possible to look at the simplified interfaces for administering them. Within KDE, from the (N), you can choose **Control Center**, **Peripherals**, **Printers**, and have access to far more than just the ability to add a printer.

NOTE

As with so many things, you must have root privilege to make changes.

Figure 6.18 shows the options available from the drop-down menu for the Printer, whereas Figure 6.19 shows those for the Print Server.

FIGURE 6.17

Choosing Software takes you to the cups.org site.

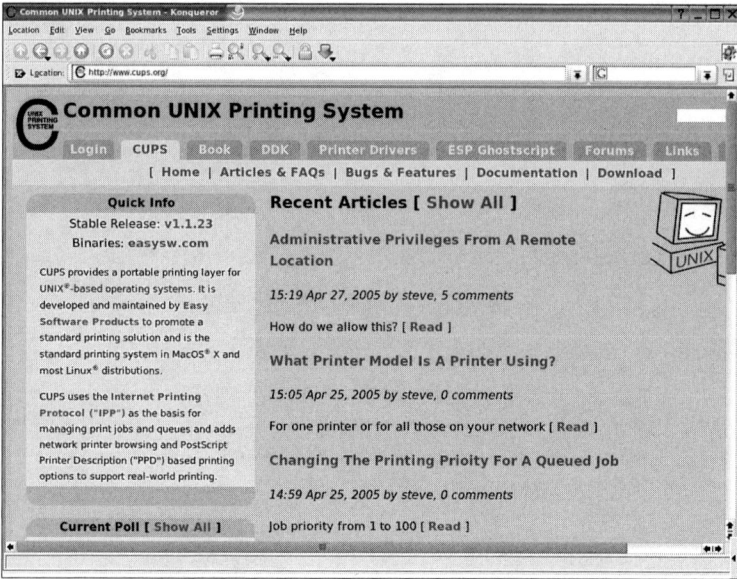

FIGURE 6.18

Within the Control Center, a number of options are available for the printer.

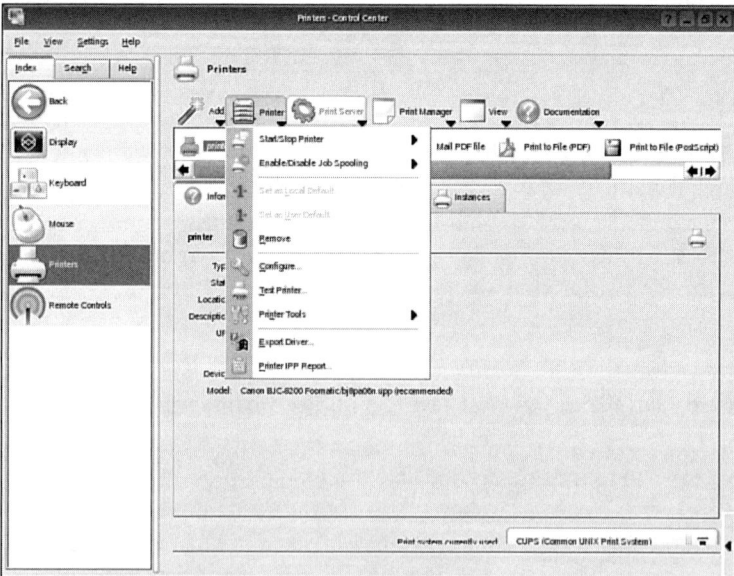

FIGURE 6.19
Within the Control Center, you can also manage the Print Server.

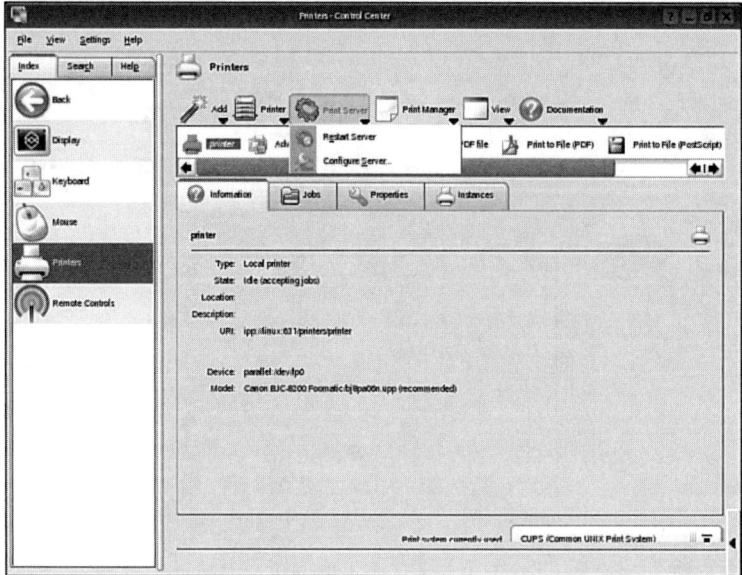

Figure 6.20 shows the options available from the Print Manager drop-down menu, as well as on the Jobs tab.

This utility provides a convenient interface that allows you to manage printing options within a single, handy, tool.

Creating Bootable Floppies

As painful as it is to think about, every system runs a risk of being corrupted to the point at which it is no longer bootable. To prepare for this possibility, you should use YaST to create a set of boot (also known as *rescue*) floppy disks ahead of time.

NOTE

There is an alternative to using the boot floppies. If you have the NLD CDs or DVD, and your system supports bootable drives, you can boot using the DVD or CD1. At the boot screen, select **Rescue System** and press **Enter**. Choose the desired language and press **Enter** and then log in as root when prompted.

FIGURE 6.20
A few options are available for the Print Manager.

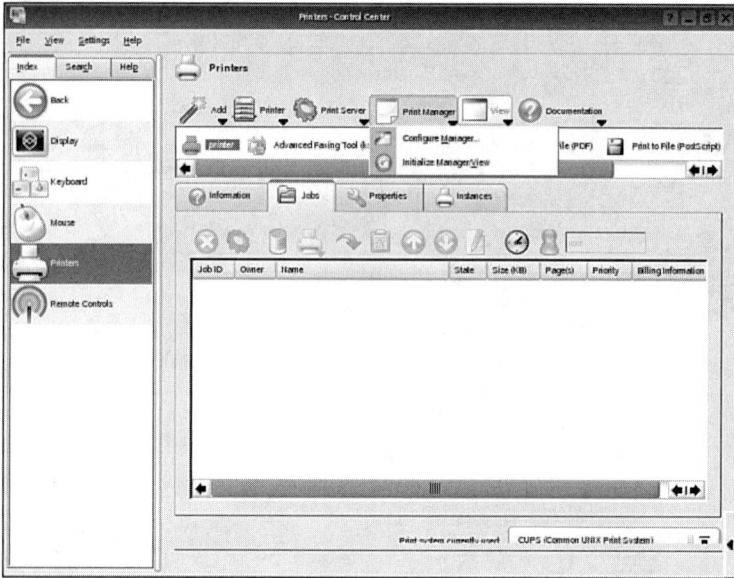

To create the disks, open YaST from the desktop and choose **System, Create a Boot, Rescue, or Module Floppy**, as shown in Figure 6.21.

NOTE

There is an alternative way of starting YaST at the right point. From a terminal window, type `yast2 bootfloppy`.

As Figure 6.22 shows, this module allows you to create a number of different types of floppy disks.

The Standard Boot Floppy options (1, 2, or 3) are used to create the standard boot disks needed to boot an installed system. These disks can be made as a set unto themselves or can be used in conjunction with the rescue floppy.

The Rescue Floppy option is used to create a disk that sets up the environment needed to carry out maintenance tasks such as repairing the file system.

The Module Floppies option is used for holding additional system drivers needed for specific hardware access. (The standard kernel that loads supports only IDE drives.)

FIGURE 6.21
YaST allows you to create the rescue disk.

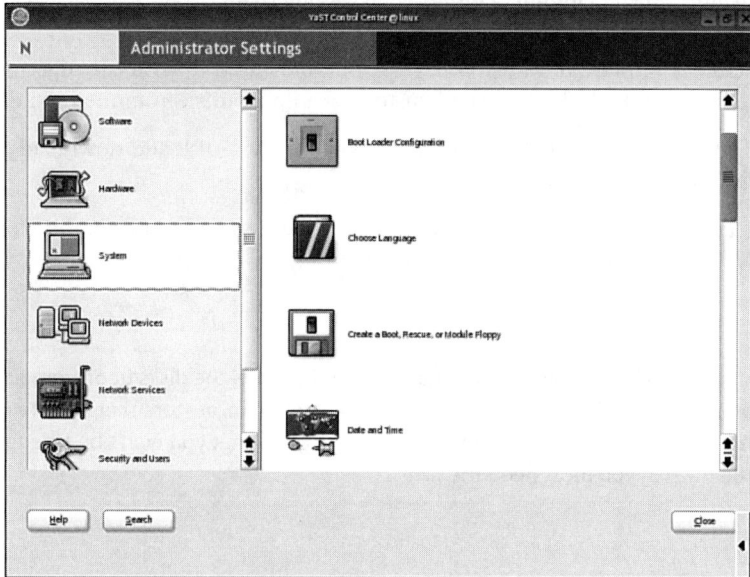

FIGURE 6.22
More than one type of disk set can be created.

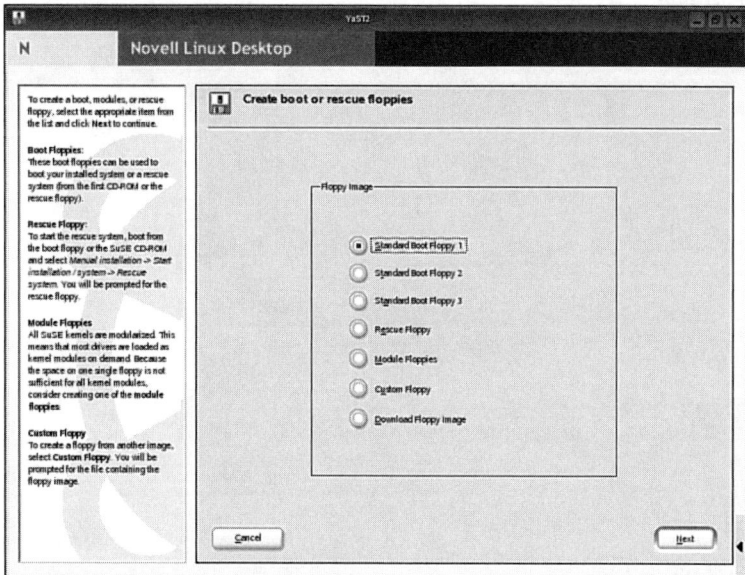

NOTE

There are actually five different module floppies that you choose between on the screen after selecting **Module Floppies** and clicking **Next**.

As the name implies, the Custom Floppy option is used to write any disk image that you might have created custom to a floppy disk from the hard disk.

The Download Floppy Image option lets you specify a URL and download a disk image from the Internet.

To create any of these types of disks, simply choose the option from the menu shown in Figure 6.15 and then follow the prompts.

TIP

One of the most important steps is that you need to label the disks upon completion and put them in a safe place. If you do not label them, or store them where they are protected and easily found, the odds are good that you won't be able to find them when you most need them.

Summary

This chapter focused on the topics you need to know about working with devices, printers, and creating a bootable floppy. The next chapter focuses on the filesystem.

## CHAPTER 7

Working with Filesystems

The filesystem is what allows you to create, access, and work with files. An operating system without a filesystem is like a sandwich without bread—you still have something, but it can hardly be called a sandwich.

Many of the files stored in a filesystem actually hold the utilities, startup scripts, and other binaries (including the kernel) that an operating system requires in order to start, run processes, and so on. Without a filesystem—or at least a disk partition (in embedded devices)—in which to store the kernel, you can't even boot.

This chapter looks at the filesystem and the utilities used to work with it and the associated media. It sets the foundation for the following chapter, which focuses exclusively on how to work with files.

The Standard Disk Layout

During the installation of Novell Linux Desktop, a number of directories are created to hold system files. By default, the file structure depicted in Figure 7.1 is created.

Together, these directories adhere to the Filesystem Hierarchy Standard (FHS), which all implementations of Linux follow. Each of these directories is discussed in the following sections.

FIGURE 7.1

The standard directory layout after installing Novell Linux Desktop.

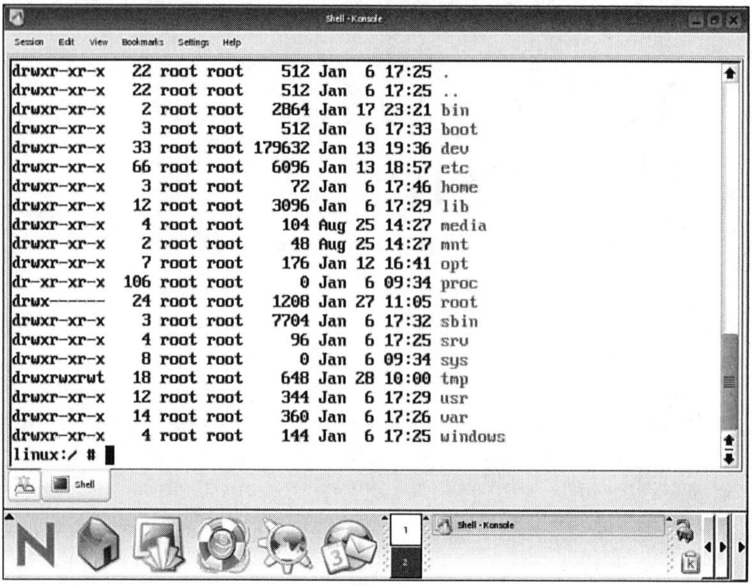

```
                                          Shell · Konsole
Session   Edit   View   Bookmarks   Settings   Help
drwxr-xr-x   22 root root     512 Jan  6 17:25 .
drwxr-xr-x   22 root root     512 Jan  6 17:25 ..
drwxr-xr-x    2 root root    2864 Jan 17 23:21 bin
drwxr-xr-x    3 root root     512 Jan  6 17:33 boot
drwxr-xr-x   33 root root  179632 Jan 13 19:36 dev
drwxr-xr-x   66 root root    6096 Jan 13 18:57 etc
drwxr-xr-x    3 root root      72 Jan  6 17:46 home
drwxr-xr-x   12 root root    3096 Jan  6 17:29 lib
drwxr-xr-x    4 root root     104 Aug 25 14:27 media
drwxr-xr-x    2 root root      48 Aug 25 14:27 mnt
drwxr-xr-x    7 root root     176 Jan 12 16:41 opt
dr-xr-xr-x  106 root root       0 Jan  6 09:34 proc
drwx------   24 root root    1208 Jan 27 11:05 root
drwxr-xr-x    3 root root    7704 Jan  6 17:32 sbin
drwxr-xr-x    4 root root      96 Jan  6 17:25 srv
drwxr-xr-x    8 root root       0 Jan  6 09:34 sys
drwxrwxrwt   18 root root     648 Jan 28 10:00 tmp
drwxr-xr-x   12 root root     344 Jan  6 17:29 usr
drwxr-xr-x   14 root root     360 Jan  6 17:26 var
drwxr-xr-x    4 root root     144 Jan  6 17:25 windows
linux:/ #
```

NOTE

More information about the Filesystem Hierarchy Standard can be found at http://www.pathname.com/fhs/.

The / Directory

Everything begins at the root directory (/). This is the beginning directory of which everything else becomes a subdirectory, or subcomponent beneath the root directory. It does not appear in Figure 7.1, per se, because all the entries that do appear in that figure are subdirectories of it.

When specifying locations and using absolute addressing, you always start with the root directory; it is impossible to go back any further. The single and double period that appear at the top of the listing in Figure 7.1 are shortcuts that appear in each directory. The single period (.) is a shortcut for the directory you are currently in, and the double period (..) is a shortcut for the parent directory of this directory. In the case of /, there is no parent directory for it, but the shortcut appears in the listing anyway.

The bin **Directory**

The **bin** directory holds the binaries (executables) that are essential to using the Linux operating system. A large number of the utilities discussed thus far are located here, including

- cat
- cp
- date
- gzip
- ls
- mkdir
- mv
- ps
- rm
- vi

As a rule of thumb, the executable/binary files located in this directory are available to all users. Binary files that are not critical to the operation of the system or needed by all users are commonly placed in **/usr/bin** instead of here.

TIP

If a disk, partition, or filesystem is corrupted, it won't mount at boot time. In order to repair it, you need some core binaries, which are those stored in /bin and /sbin.

The boot **Directory**

The **boot** directory houses the files needed to boot the system, minus configuration files used by servers to start system services, as well as the kernel. In some implementations, the kernel is stored in the / directory (a holdover from the days of Unix); but in most newer versions, **/boot** is used. This directory contains all the files needed to boot (including the kernel and its configuration file) *except* the individual service configuration files.

THE dev **DIRECTORY**

The **dev** directory holds the device definitions (known as *nodes*). When you drag a file to a graphical icon of the floppy drive on the desktop, it is possible because a definition for the floppy drive is held in the **/dev** directory. A definition file is associated with every device, whether it is a terminal, drive, driver, and so on. Their major and minor numbers tell the system where to address them and which driver to use.

The first character of the permissions on files in this directory is either "b" or "c" to indicate how data is read—by block or by character. Typically devices that require constant interaction such as the mouse, terminal (tty), and such are character-based. Devices that read and write data in blocks—groups of bytes/characters instead of single characters—such as floppy drives, memory (RAM and ROM), CD drives, and such are block based.

Some of the entries you will find beneath here are for the floppy, printer, and terminals. Examples include /dev/tty* for terminals, /dev/pty* for pseudo-terminals used by network processes such as telnet, /dev/lp* for printers, /dev/fd* for floppies, and /dev/hd* for IDE disks.

The etc **Directory**

In everyday language, "etc." is used to mean "and so on." In the Linux world, however, the **etc** directory is used to hold system and service configuration files that are specific to this machine. For example, DS Tech Corporation and Mercury Corporation can both install the same version of Linux on Intel-based machines at their sites. When they do, both will have **root** directories, both will have **/bin** directories with matching sets of utilities in them, and so on.

One major difference between the two machines will be the values that can be found in the /etc directory. The users who log on at DS Tech are not the same as those who can log on at Mercury; thus, information about user accounts are stored in files within **/etc**. The groups are not the same at the two organizations; again, those related files will be stored here. Other files include

- motd—The Message of the Day file for displaying text when logging on
- X11—A directory containing configuration information for the X Window System and graphical applications that use it
- HOSTNAME—The name of the machine
- hosts—A file that maps host names to IP addresses for other machines available through a network
- SuSE-release—The version number of the server

- inittab—The configuration file for startup and the runlevels (the init process)
- profile—The login script for the shell

In a nutshell, the /etc directory holds system configuration files specific to a machine and some configuration files.

The home **Directory**

This directory will hold subdirectories that are the home directories for users. For example, the files and directories created, owned, and used by edulaney are located in /home/edulaney, which is known as his home directory.

Each user's home directory is used to provide him or her with a location where he or she can store files, as well as where individual configuration files can be found and accessed.

Files that are used to configure the environment for the user, such as .profile, .bashrc, and .bash_history are stored in the home directories.

The lib **Directory**

Shared library files needed by binaries (such as those in the /bin directory) are located in the /lib directory and subdirectories beneath it. /lib also holds static libraries used during compilation. Generally, the libraries contain binary functions that other applications can use during execution.

The media **Directory**

The media directory is used for mounting removable media. Two subdirectories are created here by default—cdrom and floppy. Other devices—such as dvd, dvdrecorder, or cdrecorder might appear as well if they are installed.

The mnt Directory

The mnt directory is used to contains mountpoints (directories) for other filesystems or devices that are mounted. The entities that appear in this directory are never on this filesystem, but rather external resources that can be linked to and accessed from here. The external resources can be other filesystems, or devices.

The devices will appear as directories with common names. The tmp subdirectory here is intended to hold temporary files, but the use of /tmp is preferred. External filesystems are loaded—and thus appear beneath this directory—with the mount command and removed with the umount command.

The opt Directory

The opt directory is used to hold optional (add-in) application software. Not all applications install themselves here, but when they do, they create a subdirectory to hold the binaries, libraries, configuration data, and documentation associated with that application using the application name. For example, if an application were named DEF, the directory it should create would be

/opt/DEF

There is no requirement that third-party applications *must* write their values here, but it is traditional from the days of Unix. Some common subdirectories to find here include

- kde3—For the K Desktop Environment variables
- MozillaFirefox and mozilla—For the browser
- gnome—For desktop binaries, libraries, and such needed for this graphical interface
- novell—For NNLS (Novell Nterprise Linux Services) files

The proc Directory

The proc directory is a virtual filesystem. A virtual filesystem is dynamically generated, transient, and created in memory at boot time (re-created each and every time you boot your system). /proc holds information about processes, the kernel, and related system information.

Processes are depicted as directories (see Figure 7.2)—each having permissions and variables associated with it. Other system information is most commonly depicted as files.

FIGURE 7.2
Processes appear beneath /proc as directories.

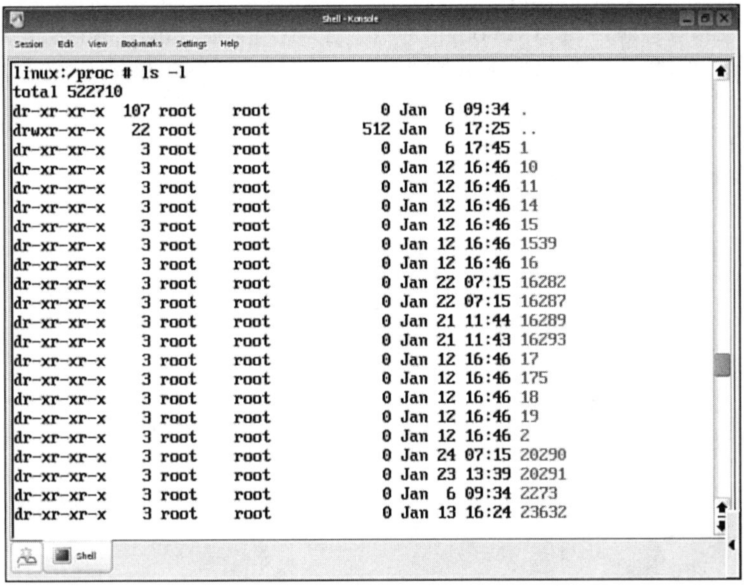

```
linux:/proc # ls -l
total 522710
dr-xr-xr-x  107 root    root       0 Jan  6 09:34 .
drwxr-xr-x   22 root    root     512 Jan  6 17:25 ..
dr-xr-xr-x    3 root    root       0 Jan  6 17:45 1
dr-xr-xr-x    3 root    root       0 Jan 12 16:46 10
dr-xr-xr-x    3 root    root       0 Jan 12 16:46 11
dr-xr-xr-x    3 root    root       0 Jan 12 16:46 14
dr-xr-xr-x    3 root    root       0 Jan 12 16:46 15
dr-xr-xr-x    3 root    root       0 Jan 12 16:46 1539
dr-xr-xr-x    3 root    root       0 Jan 12 16:46 16
dr-xr-xr-x    3 root    root       0 Jan 22 07:15 16282
dr-xr-xr-x    3 root    root       0 Jan 22 07:15 16287
dr-xr-xr-x    3 root    root       0 Jan 21 11:44 16289
dr-xr-xr-x    3 root    root       0 Jan 21 11:43 16293
dr-xr-xr-x    3 root    root       0 Jan 12 16:46 17
dr-xr-xr-x    3 root    root       0 Jan 12 16:46 175
dr-xr-xr-x    3 root    root       0 Jan 12 16:46 18
dr-xr-xr-x    3 root    root       0 Jan 12 16:46 19
dr-xr-xr-x    3 root    root       0 Jan 12 16:46 2
dr-xr-xr-x    3 root    root       0 Jan 24 07:15 20290
dr-xr-xr-x    3 root    root       0 Jan 23 13:39 20291
dr-xr-xr-x    3 root    root       0 Jan  6 09:34 2273
dr-xr-xr-x    3 root    root       0 Jan 13 16:24 23632
```

The `init` process will always have a PID number of 1. Because of this, you can get a quick glance at what is the current state of the system by looking at /proc/1 with the command:

```
$ ls -l /proc/1
```

TIP

To see current system status from information beneath /proc, you can use the following command:

```
procinfo
```

The root **Directory**

The **root** directory is the home directory for the root user. For security purposes, it is beneath the / directory rather than being a subdirectory of /home. For true security, it is further recommended that you move this directory to another location and rename it to a less obvious (and inviting) name.

The sbin **Directory**

The /bin directory holds standard executables that most users utilize; the /sbin directory holds binary executables for system administration. As a point of reference, the 's' in /sbin originally stood for statically linked, but is now more generally interpreted as 'superuser' since this directory holds applications that are typically only run by the superuser or used for booting the system.

The following list shows some of the files located beneath this directory:

- dump
- fdisk
- fsck
- halt
- ifconfig
- init
- mkfs
- poweroff
- reboot
- SuSEconfig
- shutdown
- yast2

NOTE

SuSEconfig uses files found in /etc/sysconfig/).

The srv **Directory**

The /srv directory holds the files for the services that are available on the server—each in a separate subdirectory. Typical entries found here include a directory for the www (for Apache) and ftp services.

The sys **Directory**

This is a virtual entity that is the mountpoint for a sysfs filesystem used by 2.6-based Linux systems to provide information about the devices and interfaces attached to the system. It is analogous to /proc in that /proc holds process information and /sys holds system information.

By changing into the **/sys/bus** and **sys/devices** directories, you can find files that identify the entities connected with the system.

The tmp **Directory**

As the name implies, the **tmp** directory is used to hold temporary files. Nothing that is to be kept other than for a short time should be placed here as many systems clean (delete) all entries in this directory on either shutdown or startup.

Examples of files that exist beneath **/tmp** are shadow copies of files opened for editing, any application's temporary files (stored between operations), and so on.

The usr **Directory**

Originally an acronym for "user-specific resources," **usr** is now an enormous directory with a large number of subdirectories. Subdirectories beginning with X are used to define the X Windows environment. The **bin** subdirectory, as has been the case each time the same name has been encountered, contains user binary (executable) files. The files placed here include

- cut
- diff
- file
- grep
- killall
- nl
- passwd
- wc

NOTE

As a general rule, necessary utilities for all users are stored in /bin, whereas ones that are helpful to have (but not critical) are stored in /usr/bin. Those for the system administrative tasks are stored in /sbin.

NOTE

Not all the subdirectories beneath /usr are necessary, and they will differ slightly based on the type of installation chosen.

The `include` directory holds C program header files, whereas `lib` offers more libraries for the C-based programs. The `local` directory is a temporary holding facility used during installation, and the subdirectories beneath it should be empty.

The `sbin` directory (yet again) holds system-specific binaries. Most of the utilities found in this subdirectory are related to managing the system from the standpoint of adding users and groups, as well as working with networking. These are noncritical utilities in that the system could function without them, and an administrator could manage without them as well; it would be more difficult, but certainly possible.

The `share` directory holds information specific to the machine for certain utilities, and it holds the man directories for manual pages. Last, the `src` directory contains the operating system source code.

The var **Directory**

The name **var** is derived from the word *variable*, and the data contained beneath this directory is fluctuating in nature. Typically, a number of subdirectories here are used to hold dynamic files, such as spools, logs, and so on.

The main directories to know among these are

- `lock`—Holds files that represent locks on files elsewhere on the system and per-service directories under **/var/lock/subsys** that hold locks for those subsystems.
- `log`—Used for log files such as those created by login and logout (`wtmp`), who is currently using the system (`utmp`), and those for mail, the spooler, and so on.
- `run`—Files associated with the various processes running on the system. These contain the process ID of running processes and make it easy to terminate or restart those processes by using the scripts in **/etc/init.d**.
- `spool`—Spooled data waiting for processing (such as printing).

Other Directories

Other directories can, or may, be created and exist beneath the / directory. Those listed in the preceding sections are always present, and the ones that follow may be present:

- `install`—As the name implies, it holds information about the installation, such as scripts, errors, and so on.

- **lost+found**—On a perfect system, this directory should be empty. When corruption occurs, however, any unreferenced files that cannot be relinked into the filesystem are put in this directory so that they are not lost and system administrators have a chance to examine and rename them.

- **windows**—If you install NLD on a system that already has Microsoft Windows installed on it, and do not remove the other operating system, it will be recognized in the root directory as **/windows**.

The Hard Disk Layout

Partitioning your hard disk divides a single disk into one or more logical sections or drives. The partition itself is a set of contiguous sectors on the disk that are treated as an independent disk. The partition table is the index on the disk that describes how the sections of the disk relate to the actual partitions.

A long-standing argument exists about the need for multiple partitions. Most DOS and Windows users are used to having their entire hard disk, regardless of the size, represented as one disk. Although this might seem convenient for some users, it is not desirable in the Unix or Linux world.

By using multiple partitions, you can encapsulate your data and limit filesystem corruption to a single filesystem. This limits the potential data loss. You can also increase disk efficiency. Depending on the purpose of your system, you can format different filesystems with different block sizes. If you have a lot of smaller files, you want smaller blocks.

NOTE

You can also format different partitions using different filesystems—for performance reasons or in order to facilitate data sharing with other operating systems such as Windows.

Multiple partitions are also useful to limit data growth. This ensures that users who require extra disk space do not crash the system by consuming all available root filesystem space.

Some constraints must be considered when planning your disk layout:

- To prevent data loss and corruption, partitions must not overlap.
- To maximize usage of the disk, there should be no gaps between partitions.

- You do not have to fully partition your disk.

- Partitions cannot be moved, resized, or copied without the use of special software.

When working with the disk drives, you must remember the naming convention used. All devices in a Linux system are represented as device files. These files are named with specific conventions to make it easier to identify the associated device.

IDE hard disks are identified with the name **/dev/hd** followed by the letter "a," "b," "c," or "d." The letter identifies the drive as the first disk on the first IDE controller (a) or the second disk on the second IDE controller (d).

SCSI disks are identified in a similar manner, except the device name is **/dev/sd** followed by a letter. These names, **/dev/sda**, refer to the entire disk.

After the drive has been partitioned, a number is added to the device name. Primary partitions are numbered 1–4, and extended or logical partitions are numbered 5 and higher.

The partition table was originally written in the disk boot sector, and as this was a predefined size, there was a limit to four partition table entries. These are now referred to as *primary partitions*. One primary partition can be subdivided into logical partitions. The partition used to hold the logical partitions is called an extended partition. Various versions of Linux can impose limits on the number of partitions on a drive.

Partitions must be labeled to identify the format of the data that will be subsequently written on them. This is important for mounting the partition or performing filesystem repairs. Each filesystem has a code associated with it, and is used by **fdisk** to specify the filesystem type.

Some of the valid filesystem types are listed in Table 7.1.

NOTE

You can obtain a current list of the filesystems available by using the fdisk utility, and choosing m, and then l, or using the following command:
fdisk -l /dev/whatever

This is discussed further in the "Working with Hard Disks" section later in this chapter.

TABLE 7.1
Some of the Valid Filesystem Types

CODE	FILESYSTEM TYPE
5	Extended
6	FAT16
7	HPFS
82	Linux Swap
83	Linux Native
85	Linux Extended
86	NTFS
1b	Windows 95 FAT32

At the very least, your Linux system will require the following:

- A boot partition
- A swap partition

You can also have any other primary or extended partitions as desired. It is recommended that you use a primary partition for the boot partition. This eases recovery in case of problems later, as only a small amount of data is lost.

While running, Linux will swap pages of memory out to disk when the contents have not been used for some time. This is much slower than adding more physical memory. If you find your system is swapping a lot, it is time to add more memory.

As discussed earlier, if necessary you can fit everything, including your swap file, in a single partition. However, this does limit how the filesystem is managed and the growth of the data within the filesystem. For example, if your user mailboxes are on the root filesystem and it fills up, the system will effectively hang.

NOTE

All Linux distributions, including NLD, use swap partitions by default. You can use swap files, but they're a last resort without adding disks to systems with no free partitions.

Despite the ability to run everything in one partition, this is not good practice. The filesystems listed in Table 7.2 are good candidates to be placed in their own partition.

TABLE 7.2
Filesystems Needing Partitions

FILESYSTEM NAME	PRIMARY/EXTENDED	DESCRIPTION
/boot	Primary	This is where your kernel images are located. It is usually best that this partition be the first on the disk.
/root	Primary	This is your root filesystem.
/usr	Extended	Most application data is stored here, including system binaries, documentation, and the kernel sources.
/home	Extended	This is where home directories for the users on the system are located. Depending on the number of users you have and the amount of disk space required, you might need multiple home directory partitions.
/var	Extended	This is a spool partition, containing files for log and error messages, Usenet news, mailboxes, and so on.
/tmp	Extended	This is a temporary storage place for files that are being processed. Compilers and many applications create many files in this area. Often these files are short-lived, but they can sometimes be very large.

Working with Hard Disks

In order to use a hard disk with Linux (and every operating system), at least one partition must exist on the disk. A partition is a portion of the disk (some or all) that has been properly formatted for storing data. Although there must be a minimum of one primary partition on the hard drive, there can be up to a total of four if a DOS-style partition table is used (the default), and each partition must be formatted before use. A partition must be a primary partition in order for the operating system to be capable of booting from it.

TIP

The fact that a partition exists does not mean that it has to be usable. It must be formatted in order to be used.

If you want, a primary partition (only one) can be further subdivided into extended partitions (known as logical drives). Again using DOS-style partitions, up to four logical drives can be created from a primary partition, but none of them are bootable by the operating system.

NOTE

The maximum number of partitions you can have if all are primary is four. The maximum number of partitions you can have if mixing and matching primary and extended is three primary partitions and four logical drives (for a grand total of seven).

In actuality, the theoretical limit on SCSI disks is 15 partitions, and on IDE it is 63. The limitations mentioned previously are enforced with the DOS-style partition table used as a default.

All partitions must be referenced in the /dev directory, and the first partition on the first disk is either

- hda1—The first disk on the primary IDE controller (the first disk on the secondary IDE controller is hdc)
- sda1—For SCSI

The name of the device can always be broken into the four fields that each character stands for:

1. The type of drive: h for IDE, or s for SCSI.
2. The type of device: d for disk.
3. The number of the disk expressed in alphabetic format: a for the first, b for the second, and so on. Bear in mind that this is on a per-controller basis.
4. The number of the partition. Numbers 1–4 are set aside for use on primary partitions, whether or not you have that many, and the logical drives start numbering with 5.

If you run out of room in the partition (or have not configured such), a swap file will always be created for the same purpose, but the use of the partition is preferred. You do not want to run a Linux system without swap space unless you have many gigabytes of memory; even then, you might encounter problems. Swap files are used, for example, if you add memory to a machine but don't have free disk space to assign to additional swap partitions. If necessary, swap files should be created on primary partitions for performance reasons.

NOTE

Linux can work with either swap files or swap partitions, but partitions provide more system efficiency.

Creating Partitions

Disks are partitioned for you during installation, and you should really only need to create additional partitions if you add new disks to your system. The primary tool to use in creating disk partitions is `fdisk`. The `fdisk` utility will divide the disk into partitions and write the partition table in sector 0 (known as the superblock). When run without parameters, `fdisk` brings up a menu of choices with which you can interact. You can avoid the menu, however, and run `fdisk` with these options:

- `-l` to just list the partition tables
- `-v` to print the version of `fdisk` only

`fdisk` does not have a default device and displays a usage message if you try to start it without specifying a device. Also, you would never specify a partition to `fdisk` (hda1)—you can only specify devices because it is a disk partitioner.

After the utility has started, entering **m** provides for help in the form of a menu:

```
a    toggle a bootable flag
b    edit bsd disklabel
c    toggle the dos compatibility flag
d    delete a partition
l    list known partition types
m    print this menu
n    add a new partition
o    crate a new empty DOS partition table
p    print the partition table
q    quit without saving changes
s    create a new empty Sun disklabel
```

```
t    change a partition's system id
u    change display/entry units
v    verify the partition table
w    write table to disk and exit
x    extra functionality (experts only)
```

The following examples illustrate what can be done with this utility, moving from simple actions to more complex. First, to see the partition table, give the **p** command (this gives you the same result as you would have gotten by using the command **fdisk -1**). The result looks like this:

Disk /dev/hda: 20.4 GB, 20416757760 bytes
255 heads, 63 sectors/track, 2482 cylinders
Units = cylinders of 16065 * 512 = 8225280 bytes

Device Boot	Start	End	Blocks	Id	System
/dev/hda1	1	50	401593+	82	Linux swap
/dev/hda2 *	51	2482	19535040	83	Linux

The information here shows that there are two partitions (1–2) on a single IDE disk (**hda**). The second partition is bootable, and the first partition is the swap partition.

To modify the system, you would first enter the **d** command to delete the partition. A prompt ask which partition number (1–4), and you would give the appropriate number, which would then appear to be gone. It is only really "gone" when you write your changes to disk using **w**.

TIP

Given that changes are not done until you write your changes, you can always experiment and exit without breaking anything as long as you do not write the changes to disk.

To create a new partition, enter the **n** command. An additional prompt requesting additional information appears:

```
e    extended
p    primary partition (1-4)
```

If you have already created other partitions, the prompts might not appear. **fdisk** will only allow you to execute commands that are possible given the current disk and partitioning setup.

To change a third partition to a swap file, if one existed, the sequence would be

```
Command (m for help): t
Partition number (1-4): 3
Hex code (type L to list codes): 82
Changed system type of partition 3 to 82 (Linux swap)
```

To change an existing swap file to a Linux partition, run the procedure shown in the preceding snippet for it, and make the change to **83**. Typing **L** at the hex code prompt will show all the possible filesystem types (as will just pressing l at the main **fdisk** menu). Refer to Table 7.1 earlier in the chapter for a list of the types.

After all changes have been made, you can quit **fdisk**, and then format any partitions you need to. If you write the changes, an alert will appear indicating that the partition table has been altered, and the disks will be synchronized. You should reboot your system to ensure that the table is properly updated.

NOTE

You can make dozens of changes with **fdisk** and lose them all if you use **q** to quit the tool. If you want to save the changes you've made, you must write them with **w**.

Creating Filesystems

Formatting of the partitions is accomplished with the **mkfs** (as in Make Filesystem) utility or **mkreiserfs**. **mkfs** is actually a wrapper program that drives other, filesystem-specific utilities named **mkfs.ext2** (default), **mkfs.reiserfs**, and so on. The -t option tells it which of these to execute. **mkfs**, by default, creates **ext2** partitions, and **mkreiserfs** only creates **reiserfs** partitions.

Because of these actions, you should use options with this utility to indicate the type of filesystem to make (-t), the device, size, and any options you want. For example, to format the newly created fourth partition for DOS, the command would be

```
$ mkfs -t msdos /dev/hda4 3040632
```

Be extremely careful when using **fdisk** and **mkfs**, as both have the capability to render a system inoperable if incorrect parameters are used.

NOTE

The `mkfs` utility can be used to format floppy disks as well as hard drives, but the utility `fdformat` is much simpler to use for the former.

As stated previously, you can choose from a number of different filesystems that are supported in Linux. Regardless of the number, you can create two types of local, physical filesystems: traditional and journaling. Journaling filesystems are those that keep track of their pending actions and store them in a log file to ensure integrity and get the loss of data due to crashes. Journaling filesystems include ReiserFS (the NLD default), and `ext3`.

Traditional filesystems include `ext2`, `vfat`, and so on. You would only use `vfat` or `msdos` filesystems on systems where you are dual-booting Windows or embedded systems that only know about `msdos`.

TIP

As a general rule for Novell Linux Desktop, use `reiserfs`—what the system uses by default—unless you have a compelling reason to go with something else.

Virtual filesystems are hybrids that are only created by the system, with the exception of loopback filesystems (which are totally different from `tmpfs` and `sysfs` filesystems). Virtual filesystems are re-created each time the system boots and are used internally by the system for process, resource, shared memory, and hardware management and interfacing.

TIP

Current memory usage can be seen easily with the command:

`cat /proc/meminfo`

TIP

You can also see the amount of free and used memory in the system with this command:

`free`

To see the output in MB, use this command:

`free -m`

Maintaining Filesystem Integrity

After the filesystem has been created, you can gather information about it and perform troubleshooting using three tools: **df**, **du**, and **fsck**. The first two display information only, and do not allow you to make any changes, and the latter can be a lifesaver in bringing a down system back up and operational once more.

NOTE

df and du are user tools, whereas fsck is only used by system administrators and must be run as root in order to do anything useful.

The **df** utility shows the amount of free disk across filesystems. A number of options/parameters can be used with the utility as well:

- -a—All (include those that have 0 block)
- -h—Display in "human-readable" form
- -l—Local filesystems only
- -m—List in MBs
- -t—Only show those filesystems of a particular type
- -T—Show the filesystem type

For example, the default output, and results with specified options, look like this:

```
$ df
Filesystem              1k-blocks          Used Available Use% Mounted on
/dev/hda1                1980969         573405   1305178  31% /
/dev/hda3                5871498           5212   5562198   0% /home
$
$ df -T
Filesystem      Type    1k-blocks          Used Available Use% Mounted on
/dev/hda1       ext2     1980969         573408   1305175  31% /
/dev/hda3       ext2     5871498           5212   5562198   0% /home
$
$ df -h
Filesystem              Size   Used Avail Use% Mounted on
/dev/hda1               1.9G   560M  1.2G  31% /
/dev/hda3               5.6G   5.1M  5.3G   0% /home
$
```

TIP

Quite often, administrators will combine the preceding two options to see "human readable" form, including the filesystem type:

```
df -hT
```

```
$ df -a
Filesystem          1k-blocks       Used Available Use% Mounted on
/dev/hda1            1980969       573406   1305177  31% /
/dev/hda3            5871498         5212   5562198   0% /home
devpts                     0            0         0   -  /dev/pts
/proc                      0            0         0   -  /proc
noname:(pid12019)          0            0         0   -  /auto
$
$ df -am
Filesystem          1M-blocks       Used Available Use% Mounted on
/dev/hda1                1934        560      1275  31% /
/dev/hda3                5734          5      5432   0% /home
devpts                      0          0         0   -  /dev/pts
/proc                       0          0         0   -  /proc
noname:(pid12019)           0          0         0   -  /auto
$
```

The "ext2" listed for filesystem type stands for Second Extended Filesystem and is the default used by many versions of Linux. ReiserFS is the default created during the installation of Novell Linux Desktop.

Whereas the df utility deals with partitions, the du utility shows disk usage by files and directories. From df, you can see that 560MB of hda1 is used, but you have no way of knowing by what. The du utility is the next step, showing how much space each item is using beginning at whatever starting location you specify. For example, starting in the /root directory (the home directory of the root user), the utility will show the amount of space used by the subdirectories.

If the -a option is used, files are listed and not just directories. Other options that work with the du utility are

- -b—To display the list in bytes
- -c—To show a grand total
- -h—"Human readable" output
- -k—To display the list in KBs
- -l—To show the number of links
- -m—To display the list in MBs
- -s—To only show totals
- -x—To only show directories on this (not different) filesystems

TIP

One common way of using du is du -s ., which summarizes disk usage in the current directory.

The grand utility in this category is **fsck**, the filesystem check utility. Not only will it check the filesystem, but also if errors are encountered, it can be used to correct them. The utility uses entries in the **/etc/fstab** file to tell it which filesystems to check during startup if configured to run automatically. The -A option also tells the utility to use this file.

TIP

fsck uses the sixth field in each /etc/fstab entry to identify the sequence in which filesystems are checked when a Linux system boots. If this field contains a '0,' the filesystem will not be checked.

NOTE

The /etc/fstab file is always read by fsck and related utilities but never written to. As an administrator, you need to update the file—placing each filesystem on its own line—when you want to make modifications to the operation of system utilities.

When you run **fsck**, it acts as a wrapper program and runs the appropriate filesystem-specific utility based on the filesystem type information in /etc/fstab.

NOTE

Filesystems should be unmounted before fscking them

Running **fsck-A** in NLD generates the dialog shown in Figure 7.3.

The first pass looks, among other things, at inodes. An inode is a table entry that contains information about a single file or directory or disk space allocated to a file or directory. There are thousands of inodes on each partition, and the inodes are filesystem specific. For example, each filesystem has inodes numbered 1, 2, 3, and so on.

FIGURE 7.3
Any value entered other than "Yes" is interpreted as no, and the utility ceases
to execute.

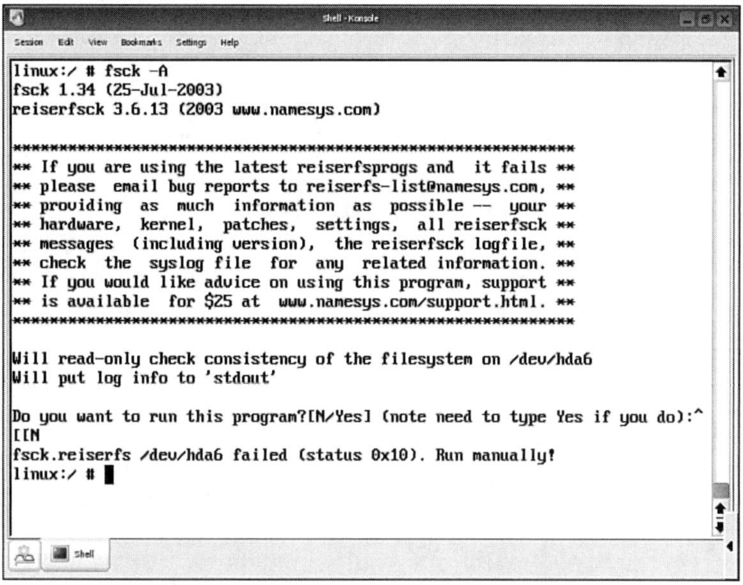

```
linux:/ # fsck -A
fsck 1.34 (25-Jul-2003)
reiserfsck 3.6.13 (2003 www.namesys.com)

**************************************************************
** If you are using the latest reiserfsprogs and  it fails **
** please  email bug reports to reiserfs-list@namesys.com, **
** providing  as  much  information  as  possible -- your  **
** hardware,  kernel,  patches,  settings,  all reiserfsck **
** messages  (including version),  the reiserfsck logfile, **
** check  the  syslog file  for  any  related information. **
** If you would like advice on using this program, support **
** is available  for $25 at  www.namesys.com/support.html. **
**************************************************************

Will read-only check consistency of the filesystem on /dev/hda6
Will put log info to 'stdout'

Do you want to run this program?[N/Yes] (note need to type Yes if you do):^
[[N
fsck.reiserfs /dev/hda6 failed (status 0x10). Run manually!
linux:/ #
```

Every item that appears in a directory listing has an inode associated with it,
and directories also have associated inodes. The inode holds the following
types of information:

1. A unique inode number
2. The type of entry that it is (file, directory, pipe, and so on)
3. Permissions on the file in numerical format
4. The physical size of the file
5. The number of links to the entry
6. The owner of the file
7. The group owning the file
8. Times of creation, modification, and access
9. A pointer to the actual location of the data on the disk

The inode numbers begin with 1 and increment from there, causing files copied during installation to have small numbers and recently created files to have much larger numbers. When files and directories are deleted, their associated inode number is marked as usable once more.

NOTE

Many inodes can be associated with a single file if it is large. Also, some filesystems store file data less than 4k in an inode to simplify allocation.

When corruption occurs, files are dumped to the /lost+found directory, using their inode number as names. Files placed in /lost+found are files that do not appear to have been deleted, but which are not linked into any directory on the current filesystem. To see the inode numbers associated with files, you can use the -i option with ls:

```
$ ls -l
drwx---- 5      root root          1024 Sep 22 23:57 Desktop
-rw-r-r- 1      root root            81 Sep 23 00:25 monday
-rw-r-r- 1      root root           152 Sep 23 00:26 tuesday
-rw-r-r- 1      root root            38 Sep 23 00:26 wednesday
$
$ ls -li
18471 drwx---- 5     root root          1024 Sep 22 23:57 Desktop
18535 -rw-r-r- 1     root root            81 Sep 23 00:25 monday
18536 -rw-r-r- 1     root root           152 Sep 23 00:26 tuesday
18537 -rw-r-r- 1     root root            38 Sep 23 00:26 wednesday
$
```

If a file is moved, it maintains the same inode. If a file is copied, the original file maintains the same inode, but the new entry must have a new inode associated with it:

```
$ mv monday friday
$ ls -li
18471 drwx---- 5     root root          1024 Sep 22 23:57 Desktop
18535 -rw-r-r- 1     root root            81 Sep 23 00:25 friday
18536 -rw-r-r- 1     root root           152 Sep 23 00:26 tuesday
18537 -rw-r-r- 1     root root            38 Sep 23 00:26 wednesday
$ cp friday monday
$ ls -li
18471 drwx---- 5     root root          1024 Sep 22 23:57 Desktop
18535 -rw-r-r- 1     root root            81 Sep 23 00:25 friday
18538 -rw-r-r- 1     root root            81 Sep 23 00:38 monday
18536 -rw-r-r- 1     root root           152 Sep 23 00:26 tuesday
18537 -rw-r-r- 1     root root            38 Sep 23 00:26 wednesday
$
```

Mounting and Unmounting

There will always be a local filesystem, for it is upon that filesystem that Linux is installed. If the filesystem is large enough to hold everything you interact with, that is all you need. In most cases, however, the local filesystem is not sufficient to hold everything you need. If you run out of space on your system, you can add another disk, partition it, and mount those partitions to enable your system to access the new space.

The **mount** command is used without parameters to show what filesystems are currently mounted (available). An example of the output would be

```
/dev/hda1 on / type ext2 (rw)
/dev/hda3 on /home type ext2 (rw)
devpts on /dev/pts type devpts (rw, gid=5,mode=620)
/proc on /proc type proc (rw)
noname: (pid11973) on /auto type nfs (rw)
```

This reads from the dynamic file **/etc/mtab** and relays the device, the mount point, the type of filesystem, and the permissions. (**rw** is read/write.) In addition to read/write, filesystems can be mounted as read-only (**ro**), not allowing users (**nouser**), only able to run binaries (**exec**) or not (**noexec**), not capable of setting user ID upon execution (**nosuid**), or controllable by all users (**user**), and interpret special devices on the filesystem (**dev**).

The entries listed in the preceding output, and that are there by default, appear in the **/etc/fstab** file—mentioned earlier in regard to the **fsck** utility. If there are additional filesystems you want to always mount, you should add their entries to this file. The command **mount -a** will read the **fstab** file and mount/remount all entries found within.

If you do not want filesystems always mounted, you can dynamically load other filesystems using the device name with the **mount** utility.

For example, to mount the CD drive, the command is

```
$ mount /mnt/cdrom
```

And the entry added to **mount** looks like this:

```
/dev/hdc on /mnt/cdrom type iso9660 (ro,noexec,nosuid,nodev)
```

The **/mnt** directory contains mount points, which are just Linux directories with meaningful names such as for the CD-ROM drive and floppy drives. Options that can be used with the **mount** command are

- -a to read through the /etc/fstab file and mount all entries.

- -f to see if a filesystem can be mounted (but not mount it). An error message returned means that it cannot be found, and no error message means that it was found in /etc/fstab or /etc/mtab.

- -n prevents the /etc/mtab file from being dynamically updated when a filesystem is added.

- -r mounts the filesystem as read-only.

- -t allows you to specify the type of the filesystem being mounted.

- -w mounts the filesystem as read/write (the default).

The opposite of mounting a filesystem when it is needed is unmounting it when it no longer is needed. This is accomplished with the **umount** utility. To unload the CD drive when no longer needed, the command would be

```
$ umount /mnt/cdrom
```

Options that can be used with the **umount** utility are

- -a—Unload every entry in /etc/mtab.

- -n—Unload but not update /etc/mtab.

- -r—If the unload fails, remount it as read-only.

- -t—Unload all entries of a specific file type.

NOTE

In most cases, the only filesystems that you would unmount while a system is active are network filesystems or those associated with removable storage.

Hard Disks and YaST

NLD allows you to use the YaST (Yet Another Setup Tool) utility to interact with disks and perform creation and partitioning tasks graphically. Figure 7.4 shows the System submenu and the choices it presents.

Choose Partitioner, and the warning shown in Figure 7.5 appears. Heed this warning carefully for it fully means what it says—you can do irreversible damage if you are not careful.

FIGURE 7.4
The System submenu offers the disk-related choices in YaST.

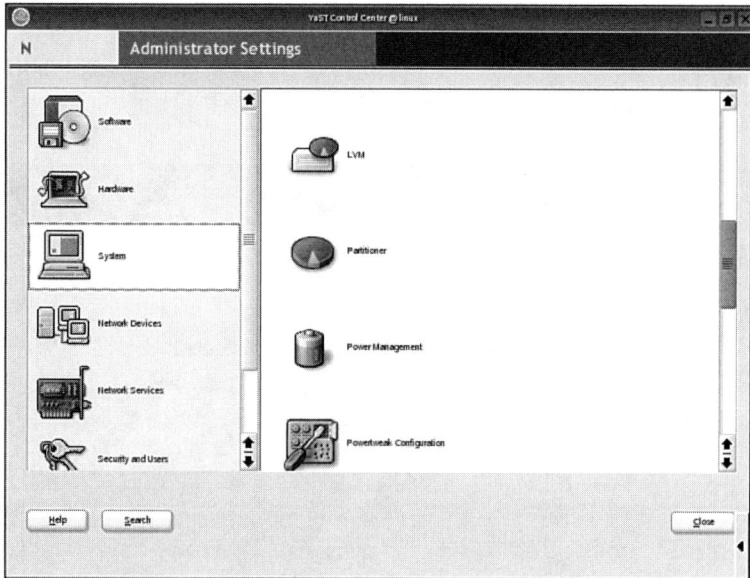

FIGURE 7.5
Know what you are doing before changing partition information.

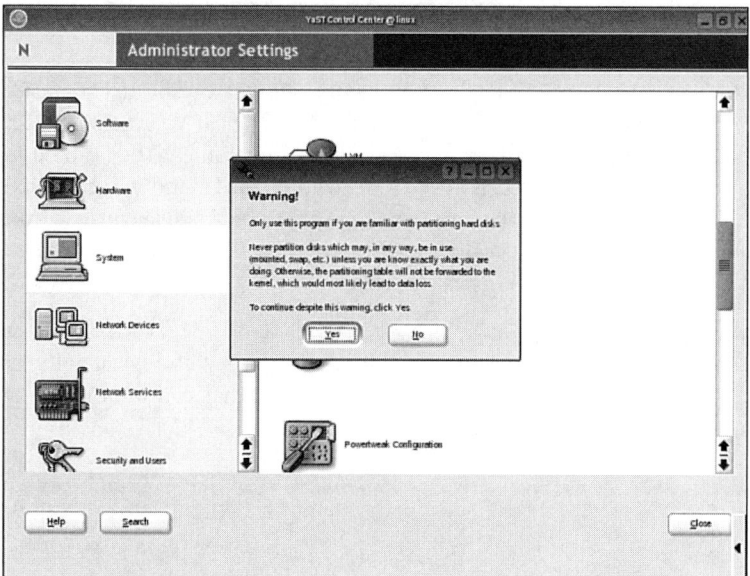

After you choose Yes, the partition table shown in Figure 7.6 appears. The actual partition table that is displayed depends on the disks and partitions in use on your system. You will see something like this figure, but not this figure per se.

FIGURE 7.6
The Partitioner shows the devices installed.

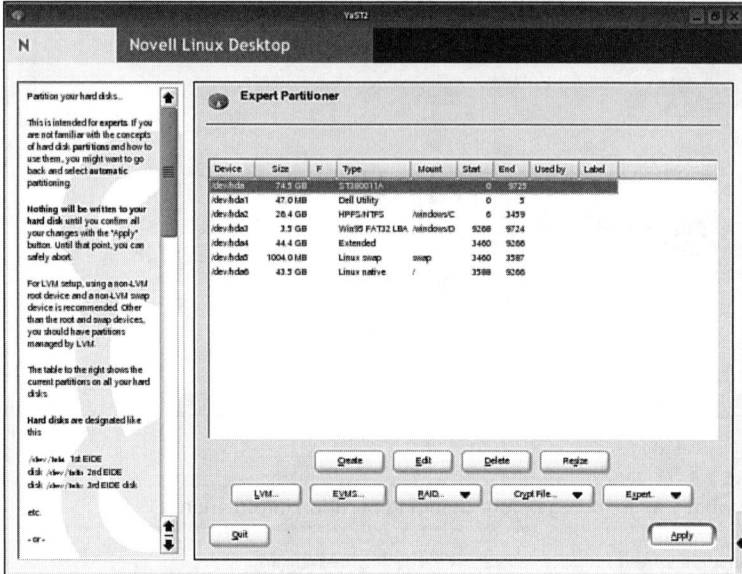

Most of the choices are self-explanatory—you can create, edit, delete, resize, and so on. Of particular note is the LVM choice—Logical Volume Management. Logical volumes offer great benefit over traditional volumes. They can be managed with sensible names such as **DATA** (instead of **sda1**), and you can combine multiple hard disks/partitions into what appears to be a single entity (a volume group). After this group is created, you can increase it by adding more hard disks as needed (up to 256 logical volumes).

You use LVM by creating Native Linux partitions (type 83) on which you create physical volumes. You then associate physical volumes with logical volumes and format them according to the type of filesystem that you want to use on them. You can then mount and use them.

You should only do this—especially from YaST (choose **LVM** from the System submenu of YaST instead of choosing Partitioner)—when you have added new disks to a system. You cannot use this to change an existing system without destroying any existing data on partitions.

After making any changes, you must always choose to apply them before exiting in order to save your changes.

Summary

This chapter focused on the topics you need to know about how to partition, format, mount, unmount, and check partitions. The chapter also covered the Filesystem Hierarchy Standard (FHS) and the standard layout of the Linux filesystem. The next chapter builds on these concepts and walks through the operations that can be done with files.

## CHAPTER 8

Working with Files

This chapter focuses on working with files and builds upon the discussion of the Linux filesystem in the previous chapter. The topics addressed here include how to create files, change their characteristics, modify permissions on them, and remove them.

Working with File Permissions and Ownership

Permissions determine who can and cannot access files and directories, as well as what type of access the permission holders have. The first 10 characters of an `ls -l` listing of any entity resemble the following:

```
-rwxrwxrwx
```

The first character identifies the type of entity: "-" for a standard file, "d" for a directory, "b" for a block device (such as a tape drive), "c" for a character device, "l" for a link, or "p" for a pipe.

The remaining nine characters can be broken into three groups, as shown in Figure 8.1.

FIGURE 8.1
Permissions divide into three sections.

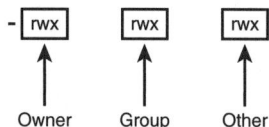

When a user attempts to access a file, the first check is to determine if the user is the owner of the file. If so, the first set of permissions apply. If the user is not the owner, a check is completed to see if the user is a member of the group owning the file. If she is a member of the group, the second set of permissions applies. If she is not the owner of the file, and not a member of the owning group, the third set of permissions applies.

Standard Permissions

The available permissions that can be assigned to an entity—either owner, group, or other—are

- r—To read a file. This is the only permission needed to copy a file as well. When applied to a directory, it grants the ability to read (see) the files within the directory.

- w—To write a file. Writing allows you to change the contents, modify, and overwrite files. When this permission is applied to a directory, you can delete and move files within the directory (even if you don't specifically have write permission to an individual file).

- x—To execute the file if it contains scripts or can otherwise be run by the system. On a directory, it allows you to change to a specific directory. When applied in conjunction with read on a directory, it allows you to search the directory.

- -(dash)—Indicates the absence of a permission. For example, r-x would indicate that the user can read and execute, but cannot write.

Thus, to summarize the 10 fields in the permissions, they are

1. What type of entity (file, directory, and so on)
2. Whether the owner can read
3. Whether the owner can write
4. Whether the owner can execute
5. Whether the group can read
6. Whether the group can write
7. Whether the group can execute
8. Whether others (not group or owner) can read
9. Whether others can write
10. Whether others can execute

Numerical values can be associated with these permissions as well:

Permission	Numerical Value
r	4
w	2
x	1
–	0

The numerical values make it possible to add a set of permissions and make them easier to understand. For example, if a file has permissions for the user of **rwx**, the numerical value becomes 4(r)+2(w)+1(x)=7. The full set of permissions for the file can be computed as shown in Figure 8.2.

FIGURE 8.2
Numerical values for the file's permissions.

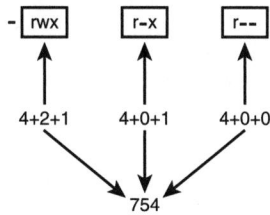

Table 8.1 extrapolates on the numerical conversion and outlines some of the 100+ possible values for a file's permissions.

TABLE 8.1
Examples of Permission Values for Files

NUMERICAL VALUE	PERMISSIONS
1	----x
2	---w-
3	---wx
4	--r-
5	--r-x
6	--rw-
7	--rwx

TABLE 8.1
Continued

NUMERICAL VALUE	PERMISSIONS
10	---x--
11	---x-x
22	--w-w-
33	--wx-wx
55	--r-xr-x
77	--rwxrwx
100	-x---
101	-x---x
111	-x-x-x
222	-w-w-w-
311	-wx-x-x
322	-wx-w-w-
400	r----
444	r-r-r-
511	r-x-x-x
544	r-xr-r-
644	rw-r-r-
666	rw-rw-rw-
755	rwxr-xr-x
777	rwxrwxrwx

The default permissions for all newly created files are 666 (rw-rw-rw-), and for directories 777 (rwxrwxrwx). This number is altered, however, by the presence of a variable known as umask. The umask variable is equal to a number that is subtracted from the default permissions to arrive at the permissions that apply per user.

NOTE

The umask on Novell Desktop Linux systems is set to 022 in /etc/profile by default.

To see the value of **umask**, simply enter the command at a prompt:

```
$ umask
0022
$
```

With a **umask** value of 0022, the permissions assigned to new files now become 644 (rw-r-r–), and for directories 755 (**rwxr-xr-x**), as shown in Figure 8.3.

FIGURE 8.3
Computing default permissions on newly created entities after subtracting the value of umask.

```
            Files:                  Directories:
            666 -rw-rw-rw-          777 drwxrwxrwx
            -022 -----w--w-         -022 -----w--w-
            ===========            ===========
            644 -rw-r--r--          755  drwxr-xr-x
```

You can change the value of **umask** by specifying a different value on the command line (**umask 15**, for example), and this value will be used for the session. The variable is defined in the login information, and will revert to its normal value at the beginning of each session.

Note

While possible, administrators rarely want to set the umask temporarily. It is more common to put an updated value in the .profile or .bashrc.

Tip

If you are sharing files using Unix groups, it is common to set the umask to 0002 so that the file is group writable.

Changing Values

To change permissions on a file or directory, you can use the **chmod** utility. The utility will accept either numeric or symbolic arguments. For example, to change the permissions of a file to allow all to read and write to it, you could write this:

```
$ ls -l turbo
-rw-r–r– 1  root    root                 14  Sep 6 22:42  turbo
```

```
$ chmod 666 turbo
$ ls -l turbo
-rw-rw-rw-  1  root    root              14  Sep 6 22:42  turbo
$
```

In symbolic format, "u" signifies user, "g" is group, and "o" is other. You can choose to add to existing permissions:

```
$ ls -l turbo
-rw-r-r-  1  root    root              14  Sep 6 22:42  turbo
$ chmod go+w turbo
$ ls -l turbo
-rw-rw-rw-  1  root    root              14  Sep 6 22:42  turbo
$
```

Or, you can specify exact permissions:

```
$ ls -l turbo
-rw-r-r-  1  root    root              14  Sep 6 22:42  turbo
$ chmod ugo=rw turbo
$ ls -l turbo
-rw-rw-rw-  1  root    root              14  Sep 6 22:42  turbo
$
```

The plus sign (+) is used to add to the existing permissions, whereas the minus sign(-) removes from existing permissions. The equal sign (=) ignores existing permissions and sets the value to whatever is specified. A -c option causes chmod to echo the names of files that are changed, whereas -f cancels the display of any error messages.

In conjunction with chmod, the chown utility can be used to change the owner of the entity. The syntax is

```
chown {new user} {entity}
```

Thus, to change the owner of a file, the sequence would be

```
# ls -l turbo
-rw-rw-rw-  1  root    root              14  Sep 6 22:42  turbo
# chown edulaney turbo
# ls -l turbo
-rw-rw-rw-  1  edulaney   root           14  Sep 6 22:42  turbo
#
```

Note

Changing the owner does not change permissions or any other values, just as changing permissions did not change the owner, and so on. Only the root user can change the file's ownership.

If you are changing a directory and want to recursively change all the entities beneath it, you can use the -R option.

A cousin of the other two utilities, **chgrp**, can be used to change the group associated with the entity. Once again, the -R option is available to recursively change all the files and subdirectories beneath a directory as well. The root user can make any group changes she wants, as long as she is the owner of the file and belongs to the group she is making the changes to.

If you are the root user and changing both the owner and group at the same time, you can use **chown** and separate the two values by a colon:

```
# ls -l turbo
-rw-rw-rw-  1 edulaney    root            14  Sep 6 22:42  turbo
# chown kristen:business turbo
# ls -l turbo
-rw-rw-rw-  1 kristen     business        14  Sep 6 22:42  turbo
#
```

The command will fail if either the owner or the group are not in existence. You can also use **chown** to change only the group by using only the second part of the argument:

```
# ls -l turbo
-rw-rw-rw-  1 kristen     business        14  Sep 6 22:42  turbo
# chown :users turbo
# ls -l turbo
-rw-rw-rw-  1 kristen     users           14  Sep 6 22:42  turbo
#
```

Access Control Lists

The permissions used throughout the operating system to secure files and directories can be loosely thought of as Access Control Lists (ACLs) for they define what can be done with each entity. ACLs give per-user and per-group control over file/directory access and modification and liberate system administrators from having to create and manage a million special-purpose groups.

Note

Linux ACLs are conceptually similar to NetWare ACL files.

Using the **getfacl** utility to Get File ACL information, you see the exact same information, only it is displayed slightly differently:

```
$ getfacl turbo
# file: turbo
```

```
# owner: kristen
# group: users
user::rw-
group:rw-
other::rw-
```

```
$
```

This utility can be used for files and directories and allows the use of wildcards and regular expressions.

Working in conjunction with `getfacl` is `setfacl`, which is used to Set File ACL information, and is thus a substitute for `chmod`. The following example sets the permissions on the `turbo` file equal to those on a file named `slowmotion`:

```
$ getfacl slowmotion
# file: slowmotion
# owner: kristen
# group: users
user::rw-
group:r-
other::r-
```

```
$ getfacl slowmotion | setfacl -set-file=- turbo
$ getfacl turbo
# file: turbo
# owner: kristen
# group: users
user::rw-
group:r-
other::r-
```

```
$
```

The benefit of `setfacl` over `chmod` is that it does a number of options—like that shown in the example—which are available only in it.

Special Permissions

Three special permissions are used in rare circumstances. Read, write, and execute are always used (or their absence expressed), but sometimes you need to do a bit more with a file or directory. The three special permissions are

- Set User ID (SUID)
- Set Group ID (SGID)
- Sticky bit

These permissions are discussed in the following sections.

SUID

The Set User ID permission is used when you have an executable file that a normal user would not be able to run, but must. For example, only the root user should be able to do function **xyz** (start backups, do restores, log in to other devices, and so on) because of the security ramifications, but what if you need the users to run a shell script to perform this action because you don't have time to do it personally?

You can create the shell script as root and set the SUID permission such that whoever runs the script will become root only within the framework of that script. Before and after the script, they are themselves, but the script runs as root.

The numerical permission of SUID is **4000**, and it is added to the value of other permissions. When applied, it changes the "x" that would appear in the execute field for the owner's permission set to an "s":

```
$ ls -l turbo2
-rwxrwxrwx  1  root   root            542  Sep 9 20:02  turbo2
$ chmod 4777 turbo2
$ ls -l turbo2
-rwsrwxrwx  1  root   root            542  Sep 9 20:02  turbo2
$
```

Remember, the value of using this permission is that the process runs as the owner of the person who created it (root in this case) and not as the person executing it. To do the same operation in symbolic format, the command would be

```
chmod u+s turbo2
```

SGID

Similar in nature to SUID, the Set Group ID permission is used when you need the person executing the file to be a member of the group owning the file (and not the owner). This changes the "x" in the group permission to an "s," and the numerical value is **2000**:

```
$ ls -l turbo2
-rwxrwxrwx  1  root   root            542  Sep 9 20:02  turbo2
$ chmod 2777 turbo2
$ ls -l turbo2
-rwxrwsrwx  1  root   root            542  Sep 9 20:02  turbo2
$
```

To use the symbolic syntax, the command would be

```
chmod g+s turbo2
```

STICKY BIT

The last permission does not work as the other special permissions do. With a numeric value of **1000**, its operations differ when applied to a directory versus a file. When applied to a directory, it prevents users from deleting files from folders that grant them the write permission *unless* they are the owner of the file. By default, any user who has write permission to a directory can delete files within that directory even if the user doesn't have write permission to that file.

When the sticky bit permission is applied to a file, the file becomes "sticky" (hence the name). The first time the file is run or accessed and loaded into memory, it stays loaded into memory or swap space so that it can run faster than if it had to be read from the drive.

If the file is not executable, the last permission bit ("x" for the other category) becomes "T." If the file is an executable file or a directory, the last bit becomes a "t."

Copying and Moving Files and Directories

System administration would be so much easier if nothing ever moved or changed. Unfortunately, it is very rare for anything to stay static anymore, and changes take place at a nonstop pace. Linux offers two powerful utilities for copying and moving files: cp and mv, respectively.

cp

cp works with both files and directories and can move multiple entities at a time using wildcards. After the name of the utility, you must specify the source, followed by the target. The simplest use of all can be illustrated as follows:

```
$ ls -l fileone onefile
ls: onefile: No such file or directory
-rw-r--r--   1    root     root     85    Aug 22 10:26    fileone
$
$ cp fileone onefile
$ ls -l fileone onefile
-rw-r--r--   1    root       root    85    Aug 22 10:26    fileone
-rw-r--r--   1    edulaney   users   85    Aug 30 16:18    onefile
$
```

Notice that the original entry (source) remains unchanged, but now there is a second entry (target) as well. On the second entry, the contents are identical, but the date and time are those of the present (when **cp** was executed), not those of the source. Notice as well that the owner and group of the new file became that of the user executing the command. This is the same action that would take place if you were creating the target file completely from scratch.

Note

To be able to copy a file—create a new entity equal in content to another—you need only read permission to the source.

The -p option can be used to force as many of the old variables to remain the same. It preserves what it can in terms of attributes:

```
$ ls -l fileone nextfile
ls: nextfile: No such file or directory
-rw-r-r-    1    root    root    85    Aug 22 10:26    fileone
$
$ cp -p fileone nextfile
$ ls -l fileone nextfile
-rw-r-r-    1    root       root     85    Aug 22 10:26    fileone
-rw-r-r-    1    edulaney   users    85    Aug 22 10:26    nextfile
$
```

Notice that the date and time associated with the source were kept, but the owner and group still must change.

When you do a copy operation, the utility first checks to see if the source file exists. If it does, whatever file is specified as the target is created (with a size of zero), and the contents of the source are copied. The emphasis here is on the fact that the target is always created—regardless of whether it existed before or not. Here's an illustration:

```
$ ls -l fileone filetwo
-rw-r-r-    1    root    root    85      Aug 22 10:26    fileone
-rw-r-r-    1    root    root    16432   Aug 28 13:43    filetwo
$
$ cp fileone filetwo
$ ls -l fileone filetwo
-rw-r-r-    1    root       root     85    Aug 22 10:26    fileone
-rw-r-r-    1    edulaney   users    85    Aug 30 16:18    filetwo
$
```

The original contents of `filetwo` have been lost, except for any backup tape versions, as `filetwo` is *created* to be a copy of `fileone`. There is a `-i` (as in inquire) option, which can be used to always ask if you really want to erase the contents of the target file if it already exists:

Tip

A copy operation always overwrites any existing target file, as long as you have permissions/ACLs to do so.

```
$ ls -l fileone filetwo
-rw-r-r-    1    root    root    85     Aug 22 10:26     fileone
-rw-r-r-    1    root    root    16432    Aug 28 13:43     filetwo
$
$ cp -i fileone filetwo
cp: overwrite 'filetwo'?
```

At the prompt, you can enter "**y**" to perform the operation, or anything else to stop it.

You can copy a number of files from one directory to another so long as the last item on the command line is a valid directory path into which the files will be copied:

```
$ ls -l /usr/home/sdulaney
-rw-r-r-    1    root    root    85     Aug 22 10:26     exit
$
$ cd /usr/home/examples
$ ls -l s* q*
-rw-r-r-    1    root    root    585     Aug 23 12:16     questions
-rw-r-r-    1    root    root    1985    Aug 24 15:17     samples
-rw-r-r-    1    root    root    8501    Aug 25 18:30     snapshot01.gif
$ cp s* q* /usr/home/sdulaney
$ cd ../sdulaney
$ ls -l
-rw-r-r-    1    root    root    85     Aug 22 10:26     exit
-rw-r-r-    1    root    root    585     Aug 31 22:50     questions
-rw-r-r-    1    root    root    1985    Aug 31 22:50     samples
-rw-r-r-    1    root    root    8501    Aug 31 22:50     snapshot01.gif
$
```

To copy an entire directory from one location to another, use the `-r` or `-R` option to recursively move the directory as well as any subdirectories and files beneath it. Other options that can be used include `-f` to force a copy without any prompting (the opposite, so to speak, of `-i`); `-u` to copy only when the source file is more recent (updated) than the target; and `-v` for verbose mode (show all operations, rather than perform them silently).

Last, the -P option tells **cp** not to follow symlinks. The -p option clones ownership, permissions, and time stamps on copied files rather than using the user's default permissions and the current time.

mv

The **move** utility (**mv**) can be used for several operations. At the risk of being overly simplistic, this includes the ability to

- Rename a file
- Rename a directory
- Move a file from one directory to another
- Move a subdirectory from one directory to another
- Move an entity to another partition or media

The simplest operation is to rename a file in its current directory:

```
$ ls -l file*
-rw-r-r-    1   root    root    85      Aug 22 10:26    fileone
-rw-r-r-    1   root    root    16432       Aug 28 13:43    filetwo
$
$ mv fileone filethree
$ ls -l file*
-rw-r-r-    1   root    root    85      Aug 22 10:26    filethree
-rw-r-r-    1   root    root    16432       Aug 28 13:43    filetwo
$
```

The dates, permissions, and everything else associated with **fileone** stay with **filethree**. This is because when a file is moved within the same directory (or even on the same partition), all that changes is the information about the name—no physical operation takes place; only the descriptor is changed. The move has become a simple rename operation.

Note

As simplistic as it might sound, always remember that when you copy a file, you leave the original intact and create something that did not exist before—thus a new set of attributes is created for the new entity. When you move a file, however, the default action is a rename—you are changing only the name of the original entity and not creating anything new.

One way to put it in perspective is that if you copy a file that is 9MB in size, it will take longer than if you copy a file that is 9 bytes in size. With move being used as a rename, it will take the same amount of time to do the operation regardless of the size of the file.

As with the copy operation, if you attempt to move a file to a name that already exists, the contents of the target are lost. Here's an illustration:

```
$ ls -l file*
-rw-r--r--    1    root     root     85     Aug 22 10:26    fileone
-rw-r--r--    1    root     root     16432     Aug 28 13:43    filetwo
$ mv fileone filetwo
$ ls -l file*
-rw-r--r--    1    root     root     85     Aug 22 10:26    filetwo
$
```

The -i option (as in inquiry or interactive) can be used to prompt before overwriting, and the opposite of it is -f (for force), which is the default operation. The -u option will only do the move if the source file is newer, and -v turns on verbose mode. The -b option makes a backup of the target file, if it exists, with a tilde as the last character—essentially performing a pseudo-copy operation:

```
$ ls -l help*
-rw-r--r--    1    root     root     85     Aug 22 10:26    helpfile
$ mv -b helpfile helpfiletwo
$ ls -l help*
-rw-r--r--    1    root     root     85     Aug 22 10:26    helpfiletwo
$
$ ls -l file*
-rw-r--r--    1    root     root     85     Aug 22 10:26    fileone
-rw-r--r--    1    root     root     16432     Aug 28 13:43    filetwo
$ mv -b fileone filetwo
$ ls -l file*
-rw-r--r--    1    root     root     85     Aug 22 10:26    filetwo
-rw-r--r--    1    root     root     16432     Aug 28 13:43    filetwo~
$
```

In the first instance, there wasn't an existing file with the target name present, so the -b option was ignored. In the second instance, a file by the name of the target was in existence, so the original target file is renamed with a tilde (~) as the last character.

Note

The -b option can also be used with cp to perform the same action during a copy as it does with mv.

Removing Files and Directories

When files are no longer needed, they can be removed from the system with the **rm** (remove) command. Be careful using this command, for Linux offers no undelete command or function like those found in other operating systems.

```
$ ls -l file*
-rw-r-r-    1    root    root    85      Aug 22 10:26    fileone
-rw-r-r-    1    root    root    16432       Aug 28 13:43    filetwo
$ rm fileone
$ ls -l file*
-rw-r-r-    1    root    root    16432       Aug 28 13:43    filetwo
$
```

When used with the -i option, a prompt appears before each file to be deleted. Pressing Y deletes the file, and any other character skips the file.

```
$ ls -l t*
-rw-r-r-    1    root    root    85      Aug 22 10:26    today
-rw-r-r-    1    root    root    16432       Aug 28 13:43    tuesday
$ rm -i t*
rm: remove 'today'?
```

The -f option forces deletion, and -v puts the utility in verbose mode. The -r or -R option recursively delete directories (including subdirectories and files beneath). In order to delete a file, you much have write permissions within the directory in which it resides.

Note

Write permission is only required on the directory from which you are deleting the file—not on the file itself.

A safer utility, **rmdir**, can be used to delete directories that have nothing beneath them. It will only delete empty directories and cannot be used for directories that have files or subdirectories beneath them. The only option that can be used with **rmdir** is -p to remove parent directories (if empty).

```
$ ls -R kdulaney
kdulaney:
docs

kdulaney/docs:
```

```
attempt
$
$ rmdir kdulaney
rmdir: kdulaney: Directory not empty
$
```

Because there is a file (**attempt**) within **kdulaney/docs**, and a subdirectory (**docs**) beneath **kdulaney**, the directory **kdulaney** cannot be deleted with the rmdir utility. There are three possible ways to accomplish the task:

1. Use the rm -r command.
2. Delete **attempt** with rm, and then delete **docs** with rmdir, and—finally— delete **kdulaney** with rmdir.
3. Delete **attempt** with rm, and then delete **kdulaney/docs** with rmdir -p.

Note

Because rmdir can only delete empty directories, it is naturally a safer utility to use than rm for cleaning a system.

Making Directories

Now that you've learned how to copy, move, and delete directories, the only order of business left is to make a directory, which you can do by using the mkdir command. Used without options, it creates a child directory (subdirectory) in the current directory. There are two options that work with it as well:

- -m—To specify permissions other than the default for the new directory.
- -p—To create the full path to a target directory. It can create any number of parent directories necessary to create the specified directory.

Here are some examples of the utility:

```
$ pwd
/usr/home
$ mkdir edulaney
$
```

This created the subdirectory **edulaney** beneath **/usr/home(/usr/home/edulaney)**.

```
$ pwd
/usr/home
```

```
$ mkdir kdulaney/docs
mkdir: cannot make directory 'kdulaney/docs': No such file or directory
$
$ mkdir -p kdulaney/docs
$ cd kdulaney
$ cd docs
$
```

In the first attempt, the utility fails as you cannot create multiple directories by default. If you use the -p option, however, the multiple directories are created.

Working with Links

The purpose of a link is to allow one file to be referenced by more than one name. There are any number of reasons why you would want or need to do this, for example:

- For historic purposes—Assume that you want to combine all the vendor information into a single file. In the past, marketing has always had a file in which similar information was kept and called **vendor**, whereas accounting kept information in a file called **contacts**, and admin information was called **references**. When you create the single file, you can make it available by all three names so that all parties can find it as they formerly did.

- To make the nonlocal look local—Assume that there is a template that all users are to use when making system modification requests. This file can exist in the root user's home directory (**/root**), and a link created within each user's home directory (**/home/user**) to make it appear as if it exists within her directory.

The utility to create links is **ln**. When you create a link, you are merely creating another pointer to an already existing entity; because this is the case, only one inode is used, not two. Because there is only one copy, you are also saving disk space.

Note

When you link to a file to give others access, you must make certain that they have appropriate permissions to access the file, or you are defeating your purpose.

Note

Two types of links can be created: hard and symbolic. Both are examined in the following sections.

Hard Links

The simplest of the two link types is the hard link. It is created by default with `ln`, and its use can be illustrated as follows:

```
$ ls -l
drwx---- 5    root root    1024 Sep 22 23:57    Desktop
-rw-r-r- 1    root root      81 Sep 23 00:25    friday
-rw-r-r- 1    root root      81 Sep 23 00:38    monday
-rw-r-r- 1    root root     152 Sep 23 00:26    tuesday
-rw-r-r- 1    root root      38 Sep 23 00:26    wednesday
$
$ ln monday thursday
$ ls -l
drwx---- 5    root root    1024 Sep 22 23:57    Desktop
-rw-r-r- 1    root root      81 Sep 23 00:25    friday
-rw-r-r- 2    root root      81 Sep 23 00:38    monday
-rw-r-r- 2    root root      81 Sep 23 00:38    thursday
-rw-r-r- 1    root root     152 Sep 23 00:26    tuesday
-rw-r-r- 1    root root      38 Sep 23 00:26    wednesday
$
```

Notice that the attributes related to the time of the new entry (**thursday**) remained the same as those associated with **monday** and did not assume the current time—as would be done with a copy operation. This is because there is only one file, even though there are now two ways of referencing it. The second column from the left indicates the link count for files: the number of ways this same set of data can be referenced. The link count has incremented from 1 to 2.

Another way to verify that it is the same data is to view the inodes. Every entity must have its own inode, as was discussed earlier. If, however, you have only one set of data and multiple ways of accessing it, all the access methods (names) will share the same inode:

```
$ ls -i
18471 Desktop      18538 monday      18536 tuesday
18535 friday       18538 thursday    18537 wednesday
$
```

As you add links to the data, the link count will increment, and as you remove links, the link count will decrement. The data that the links point to will remain on the system as long as anything at all points to it. For example, the file thursday was linked to monday. If monday is now deleted, thursday will still remain, but the link count will decrement to 1: Linux does not care which file was created first. It's only when the link count drops to 0 that the data will no longer exist on the system.

Note

To put it into perspective, when you create a file, its initial filename serves as a link to the data that the file contains and there is a link count of 1. When you remove the link (delete the file), the count becomes 0 and the data goes away.

When the contents of the files are viewed, there is no indication that they are links of each other.

To prove the link exists, however, any modification made to either file is made to both because they both reference the same data. This can be readily illustrated:

```
$ ls -l
drwx---- 5    root root          1024 Sep 22 23:57    Desktop
-rw-r-r- 1    root root            81 Sep 23 00:25    friday
-rw-r-r- 2    root root            81 Sep 23 00:38    monday
-rw-r-r- 2    root root            81 Sep 23 00:38    thursday
-rw-r-r- 1    root root           152 Sep 23 00:26    tuesday
-rw-r-r- 1    root root            38 Sep 23 00:26    wednesday
$
$ cat >> monday
Ingredients include carbonated water, high fructose corn syrup
and/or sugar, citric acid, and natural flavoring.
{press Ctrl+D}
$
$ ls -l
drwx---- 5    root root          1024 Sep 22 23:57    Desktop
-rw-r-r- 1    root root            81 Sep 23 00:25    friday
-rw-r-r- 2    root root           194 Sep 24 15:09    monday
-rw-r-r- 2    root root           194 Sep 24 15:09    thursday
-rw-r-r- 1    root root           152 Sep 23 00:26    tuesday
-rw-r-r- 1    root root            38 Sep 23 00:26    wednesday
$
```

The same effect of a change to one entity being made to both would apply to permissions, owner, group, and so on. Hard links cannot be across filesystems, and must always be local. Users can create links to files, but not to directories; however, the root user can also create links to directories with the -F or -d options.

Note

Links cannot cross filesystems because they refer to inodes, which are filesystem specific.

Symbolic Links

To make a symbolic link, you must use the -s option with ln. A symbolic link is what one might equate with "shortcuts" in the Windows operating systems: small files that point to another file. The primary purpose for a symbolic link is to get around the shortcomings of hard links. As such, they allow users to link to directories and allow links to cross filesystems.

To illustrate how a symbolic link is created, consider the following example:

```
$ ls -l
drwx---- 5     root root    1024 Sep 22 23:57    Desktop
-rw-r-r- 1     root root      81 Sep 23 00:25    friday
-rw-r-r- 2     root root     194 Sep 24 15:09    monday
-rw-r-r- 2     root root     194 Sep 24 15:09    thursday
-rw-r-r- 1     root root     152 Sep 23 00:26    tuesday
-rw-r-r- 1     root root      38 Sep 23 00:26    wednesday
$
$ ln -s friday saturday
$ ls -l
drwx---- 5     root root    1024 Sep 22 23:57    Desktop
-rw-r-r- 1     root root      81 Sep 23 00:25    friday
-rw-r-r- 2     root root     194 Sep 24 15:09    monday
lrwxrwxrwx 1 root root         6 Sep 24 15:49    saturday -> fri-
day
-rw-r-r- 2     root root     194 Sep 24 15:09    thursday
-rw-r-r- 1     root root     152 Sep 23 00:26    tuesday
-rw-r-r- 1     root root      38 Sep 23 00:26    wednesday
$
```

There are several items to note about this transaction:

- The link count on friday did not change.
- The new file will always have the first column equal to "lrwxrwxrwx" to indicate that it is a link.
- The date and time on the new file are not equal to the old file, but instead are the current date and time—this is because a new file has been created (with its own inode).

- To the right of the file name is a graphical indication of the file really being referenced.

- The new file has a size associated with it, but the size is equal to the pointer only.

The last point is worth dwelling on for a moment. The file `friday` has a size of **81**, and `saturday` has a size of **6**. This is completely transparent to the user as any operation done on `saturday` is sent to `friday` instead. To illustrate

```
$ cat friday
this is the way that one and one
will equal two
and two and two
will equal four
$
$ cat saturday
this is the way that one and one
will equal two
and two and two
will equal four
$
$ wc friday
      4    18     81 friday
$ wc saturday
      4    18     81 saturday
$
```

In other words, `saturday` is just a symbolic (name) representation of `friday`. Whatever action you attempt to do is sent to the first file through the pointer held in the second. This can lead to unexpected results: Because the file is a pointer, it can be pointing to something that no longer exists or is currently unavailable (remember, they can span filesystems). Consider the following sequence of events in which the file being pointed to is removed:

```
$ rm friday
$ ls -l
drwx---- 5    root root              1024 Sep 22 23:57    Desktop
-rw-r-r- 2    root root               194 Sep 24 15:09    monday
lrwxrwxrwx 1 root root                  6 Sep 24 15:49    saturday -> fri-
day
-rw-r-r- 2    root root               194 Sep 24 15:09    thursday
-rw-r-r- 1    root root               152 Sep 23 00:26    tuesday
-rw-r-r- 1    root root                38 Sep 23 00:26    Wednesday
$ wc saturday
wc: saturday: No such file or directory
$
```

This can lead to frustration and aggravation on the part of users, for the error messages will tell them that **saturday** does not exist, whereas every listing of the directory will show that it does. As an administrator, it is imperative for you to understand that the file does exist, but it is a pointer to a file that no longer does.

When you view symbolic links in most graphical utilities, their names are italicized and a small box holding an arrow is added to the bottom left of the icon.

A large number of the system files are links to other items. For example, the /dev directory holds a plethora of symbolic links to devices that can be accessed via different names and in different locations.

Finding Files on Your System

With all the files on the system, and all the different directories and subdirectories that exist, finding something you are looking for can sometimes be a daunting task. Thankfully, a number of utilities in Linux can help ease this burden. In this section, we will look at a few of the unique utilities and examine how you can use them to help find what you are looking for.

The utilities to be examined, in order, are

- which
- whereis
- find

The which command looks through the directories listed in your PATH statement. When it finds a match in a directory for a name you give, it stops immediately and reports what it found. How is this useful? Suppose that there are 14 versions of **grep** on your system; which will tell you the first one it finds via the path search, and thus the one that is executed when you use the command.

The following simple example illustrates this:

```
$ which grep
/usr/bin/grep
$
```

Whereas the which utility only shows the first instance of a command in your path, the whereis utility shows them all, including man pages, and anywhere else it appears.

If you had to think of an analogy for the **find** utility, it would be to the Swiss army knife in the real world, or to **grep** on steroids in the operating system world. This tool is capable of looking at all entries in the filesystem and displaying results that meet criteria given. In many ways, it is the vast possibilities of the "criteria" you can specify that allow this tool to be so powerful. The syntax is simply

```
find [starting point] [criteria]
```

The default starting point is the present working directory, but can be specified to be anything. Whatever starting point is used, the search will recursively move from there to all of its subdirectories.

The criteria can be any of the options shown in Table 8.2.

TABLE 8.2
Parameters for **find**

OPTION	PURPOSE
-atime *days*	Tests true if the file was accessed within the number of days specified.
-ctime *days*	Tests true if the file was changed within the number of days specified.
-exec *command*	Executes a command. You must specify that the command is for a group "{}" and continuing on "\;."
-group *name*	Tests true if the file belongs to the specified group.
-inum *number*	Tests true if the file has that inode number.
-links *number*	Tests true if the number of links is equal to the specified number.
-mount	Only looks on the local filesystem.
-mtime *days*	Tests true only if the file was modified within the number of days specified.
-name *file*	True only if matching the name given.
-perm *permission*	True if matching the given permissions.
-print	Prints the names of matching files.
-size *number*	True if matching the number of blocks or characters.
-type *type*	True if matching the specified type (d=directory, f=file, b=block file, c=character file).
-user *name*	True only if owned by the named user.

For example, to find all files on the system, beginning with the root directory, that are named **grep**, you would use these specifications:

```
$ find / -name "grep"
/usr/bin/grep
$
```

Notice that the -**print** option did not need to be specified: This is the default action. Notice also, that unlike **locate**, it found an exact match and not just entries that had the four letters somewhere in the name. If you want to find matches that are portions of words, you need to use the asterisk (*) wildcard (find / -name "*grep*").

When you find the match, you can perform an action on it, such as obtaining a long listing:

```
$ find / -name "grep" -exec ls -l {} \;
-rwxr-xr-x 1 root     root      70652  Aug 11 1999 /usr/bin/grep
$
```

Note

Be very careful with the -exec option, as you can specify anything following it—including move, remove, and so on. The option -ok can be used in place of -exec to force a prompt before every action is taken.

To find which files have been accessed, use the -**atime** option. If the number following is preceded by a plus sign (+), it returns entries in which the access day was more than the number given. If the number following is preceded by a minus sign (-),it returns entries in which the access day was less than the number given. For example, to find files beneath the current directory that have not been accessed for 10 days or more, specify **+10**:

```
$ find . -atime +10
```

To find files that have been accessed within the last two days, specify **-2**:

```
$ find . -atime -2
```

To find only directories beneath the current directory, specify **d**:

```
$ find . -type d
```

To find all files associated with user **edulaney**, use the following command:

```
$ find / -user edulaney
```

The result will include directories and files that are visible and hidden.

Three Utilities of Note

There are three utilities with specific purposes that can be very useful to an administrator in specific circumstances: **xargs**, **tee**, and **touch**. Each of these is covered in the following sections.

xargs

To understand the power of the **xargs** utility, consider the **find** utility, which is limited in the results it can return to values within the filesystem structure. The only real text within the structure is the name of the entity and not the data itself. (The pointer points to that.) To illustrate, suppose that the user **edulaney** put out a memo several months back on acceptable use of the company refrigerator in the break room. Since then, user **edulaney** has quit the company and several new employees (who would benefit from knowing this policy) have joined. You want to find the file and reprint it.

About the closest you can get to accomplishing this with **find** (and its results) would be

```
$ find / -user edulaney -type f -exec grep -i refrigerator {} \;
stored in the refrigerator overnight will be thrown out
$
```

The **type f** option must be used, or else errors will occur every time **grep** tries to search a directory. In this case, the line from the file is found, but there is no way of knowing what file it is contained in. The command

```
find / -user edulaney -type f -exec grep -i refrigerator {} \; -print
```

will show the filename for any matches of the **grep** clause, but only after the results of the **grep** finish.

Enter the **xargs** utility: Analogous to a pipe, it feeds output from one command directly into another. Arguments coming into it are passed through with no changes, and turned into input into the next command. Thus, the command can be modified to

```
$ find / -user edulaney -type f | xargs grep -i refrigerator
/home/edulaney/fileone:stored in the refrigerator overnight will be
thrown out
$
```

The desired file is indicated, and can now be found and printed for the new employees.

Food for thought: If `xargs` works like a pipe, why wouldn't the following command suffice?

```
$ find / -user edulaney -type f | grep -i refrigerator
```

Answer: Because the `grep` operation would take place on the names of the files, not the content of the files. The `xargs` utility pipes the entire name (thus the contents) into the next command in succession (`grep`, in this case), not just the resulting filename.

tee

There is a miscellaneous utility that really stands alone and does not fit well with any section: **tee**. This utility, as the name implies, sends output in two directions. The default for most processes is to write their output to the screen. Using redirection (>), you can divert the output to a file, but what if you want to do both?

The **tee** utility enables output to go to the screen *and* to a file as well. The utility must always be followed by the name of the file that you want **output** to write to, for example:

```
$ ps -f | tee example
UID         PID  PPID  C STIME TTY          TIME CMD
root      19605 19603  0 Aug10 pts/0     00:00:34 bash
root      30089 19605  0 Aug20 pts/0     00:00:00 vi fileone
root      30425 19605  0 Aug20 pts/0     00:00:00 paste -d fileone
filetwo?
root      32040 19605  0 Aug22 pts/0     00:00:00 cat
root       1183 19605  0 Aug23 pts/0     00:00:00 awk -F: questions
root      30778 19605  0 14:25 pts/0     00:00:00 ps -f
$
$ cat example
UID         PID  PPID  C STIME TTY          TIME CMD
root      19605 19603  0 Aug10 pts/0     00:00:34 bash
root      30089 19605  0 Aug20 pts/0     00:00:00 vi fileone
root      30425 19605  0 Aug20 pts/0     00:00:00 paste -d fileone
filetwo?
root      32040 19605  0 Aug22 pts/0     00:00:00 cat
root       1183 19605  0 Aug23 pts/0     00:00:00 awk -F: questions
root      30778 19605  0 14:25 pts/0     00:00:00 ps -f
$
```

As illustrated, the output appears on the screen and is written to the file as well. This can be an extremely useful utility whenever a file is needed and you also want to view the output.

Note

tee only copies standard output. It will not copy standard error.

touch

Essentially three dates are associated with a file or entry: creation, modification, and access. Using the **touch** utility, you can change the access and modification time associated with a file:

```
$ ls -l brio
-rw-r-r-    1    root    root    28    Aug 22 10:26    brio
$ touch brio
$ ls -l brio
-rw-r-r-    1    root    root    28    Aug 30 16:01    brio
$
```

A few options can be used with the **touch** utility as well, as summarized in the following table:

Option	Purpose
-a	Only changes the access time
-m	Only changes the modification time
-r	Uses the time/date associated with a reference file to make the change instead of the current time/date

An example of the latter would be

```
$ ls -l tuesday wednesday
-rw-r-r-    1    root    root    85    Aug 22 10:26    tuesday
-rw-r-r-    1    root    root    85    Aug 29 13:08    wednesday
$ touch tuesday -r wednesday
$ ls -l tuesday wednesday
-rw-r-r-    1    root    root    85    Aug 29 13:08    tuesday
-rw-r-r-    1    root    root    85    Aug 29 13:08    wednesday
$
```

Note

If you use the touch utility with the name of a file that does not exist, it will create the file with the current date and time and a size of 0.

Summary

This chapter focused on the topics you need to work with files. The next chapter turns the focus to booting and initializing the system—a precursor to system administration.

## CHAPTER 9

Booting and Runlevels

In this chapter, you'll learn about the boot process employed by Novell Linux Desktop. You will also see the steps involved when a user logs on to the system, as well as the full cycle from boot to daily operation. After looking at that process, each of the elements will be examined individually.

Walking Through a Normal Boot

Assuming that there are no problems with the system, the following steps walk through the boot process from start to finish:

1. When any machine is started, it first does a Power On Self Test (POST) to verify that internal parts and processes are working. This occurs regardless of any operating system.

2. The boot loader for the operating system begins. With Novell Linux Desktop, that is GRUB. By default, it waits eight seconds (configurable in **/boot/grub/menu.list**) for you to press a key and identify another operating system or choice you want to boot, as shown in Figure 9.1. If no key is pressed, the default of Linux is loaded.

NOTE

If you have an operating system other than NLD also installed, the choice will appear in the menu along with the three choices shown in Figure 9.1. If NLD is the only operating system installed, you should only see these three choices.

FIGURE 9.1
The boot menu displays.

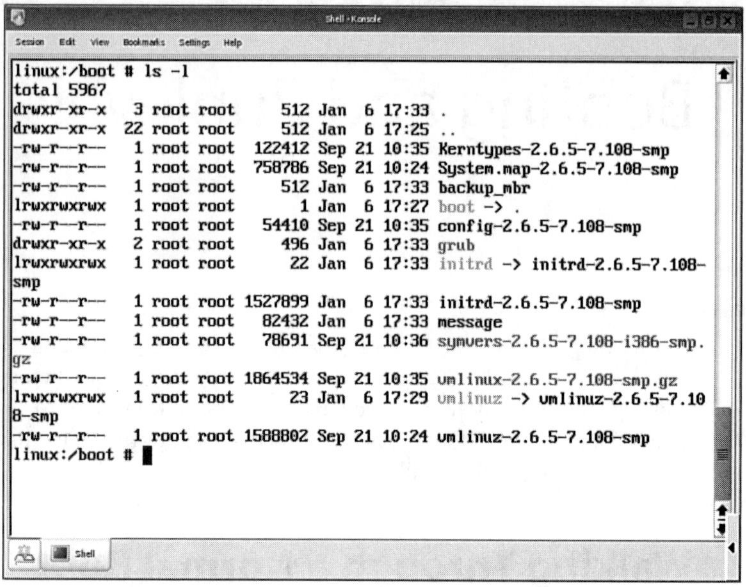

```
                                    Shell - Konsole                          _ □ X
  Session   Edit   View   Bookmarks   Settings   Help
  linux:/boot # ls -l
  total 5967
  drwxr-xr-x   3 root root     512 Jan  6 17:33 .
  drwxr-xr-x  22 root root     512 Jan  6 17:25 ..
  -rw-r--r--   1 root root  122412 Sep 21 10:35 Kerntypes-2.6.5-7.108-smp
  -rw-r--r--   1 root root  758786 Sep 21 10:24 System.map-2.6.5-7.108-smp
  -rw-r--r--   1 root root     512 Jan  6 17:33 backup_mbr
  lrwxrwxrwx   1 root root       1 Jan  6 17:27 boot -> .
  -rw-r--r--   1 root root   54410 Sep 21 10:35 config-2.6.5-7.108-smp
  drwxr-xr-x   2 root root     496 Jan  6 17:33 grub
  lrwxrwxrwx   1 root root      22 Jan  6 17:33 initrd -> initrd-2.6.5-7.108-
  smp
  -rw-r--r--   1 root root 1527899 Jan  6 17:33 initrd-2.6.5-7.108-smp
  -rw-r--r--   1 root root   82432 Jan  6 17:33 message
  -rw-r--r--   1 root root   78691 Sep 21 10:36 symvers-2.6.5-7.108-i386-smp.
  gz
  -rw-r--r--   1 root root 1864534 Sep 21 10:35 vmlinux-2.6.5-7.108-smp.gz
  lrwxrwxrwx   1 root root      23 Jan  6 17:29 vmlinuz -> vmlinuz-2.6.5-7.10
  8-smp
  -rw-r--r--   1 root root 1588802 Sep 21 10:24 vmlinuz-2.6.5-7.108-smp
  linux:/boot # █
```

```
  🔧  ▣ Shell
```

3. The screen changes to a splash screen, as shown in Figure 9.2. You can press F2 to see more verbose information as the kernel is loaded from the hard drive, or floppy drive, or other specified location into memory. By default, it is located within the **/boot** directory and exists in compressed state; as it loads into memory, it uncompresses. Figure 9.3 shows the contents of this directory; the version number of the build is easy to identify based on the filenames.

4. The kernel is booted, and messages are written to /var/log/messages.

5. Modules, default and other, specified /etc/modprobe.conf are loaded. It is sometimes necessary to tweak this file if devices are not recognized correctly or you want a specific behavior configured.

6. The kernel passes control over to the **init** daemon, which begins reading the /etc/inittab file. Because of this, the **init** daemon will always have a process ID of 1 and be the parent of many other daemons.

7. Normally, a check of the filesystem (**fsck**) is carried out and the local filesystem is mounted. Other operations can include mounting remote filesystems, cleaning up temporary files, and so on.

FIGURE 9.2
The splash screen indicates that NLD is loading.

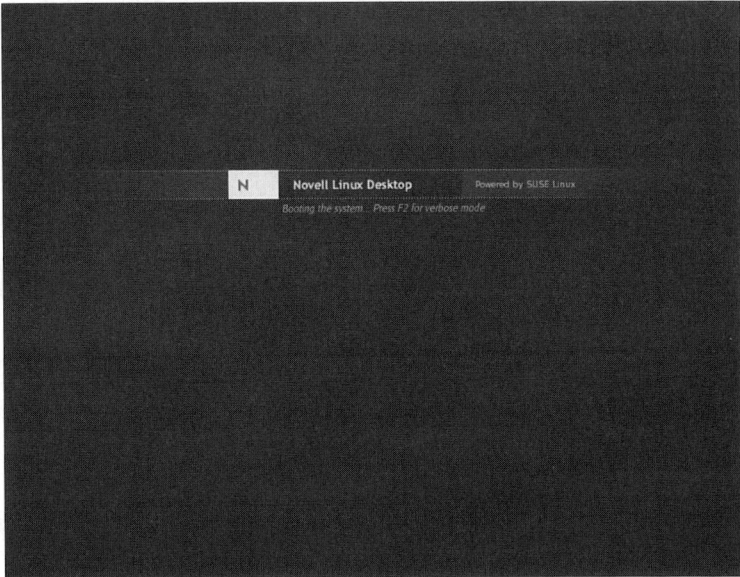

FIGURE 9.3
The contents of the /boot directory.

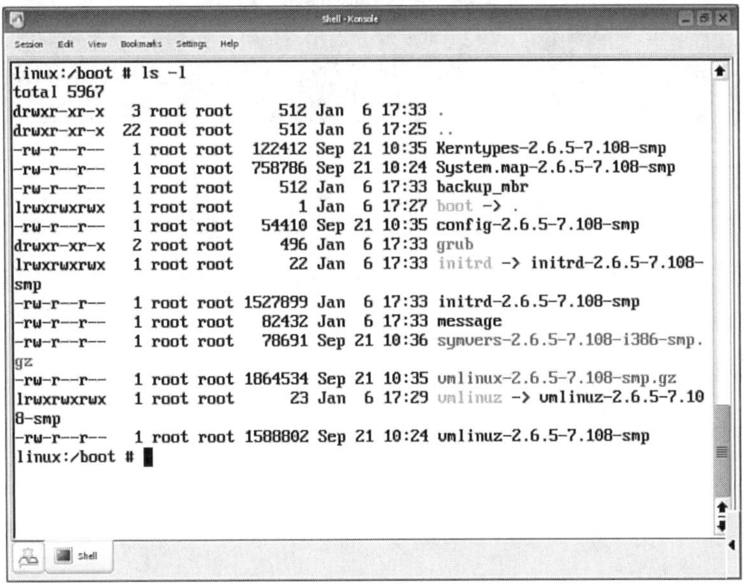

8. The system begins changing to the runlevel specified (as shown in Figure 9.4) by the `initdefault` parameter in `inittab` (runlevel 5 is the default—which is full multiuser mode with **network** and **xdm**.) In so doing, it runs scripts (startup files associated with the current runlevel) beneath the `/etc/rc.d` directory (in this case, those in `/etc/rc.d/rc5.d`) and usually starts other processes/daemons such as a print server, **cron**, **sendmail**, and so on.

FIGURE 9.4
The OS loading completes.

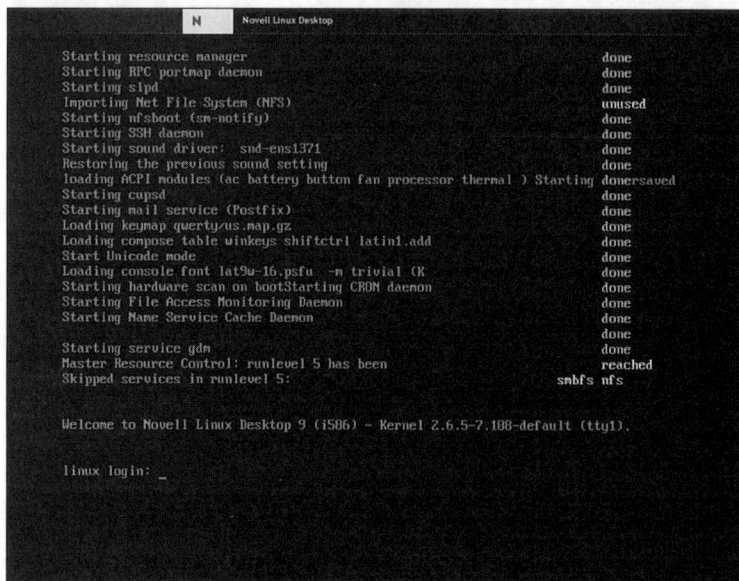

9. The terminals become active for login as a **getty** is initiated for each, as shown in Figure 9.5. The boot process of the system itself is now finished.

Note

If you are solely logging in using xdm, you will never see the terminal login prompts unless you explicitly go to a different virtual console.

FIGURE 9.5
The `inittab` specifies a `getty` to start for each terminal session.

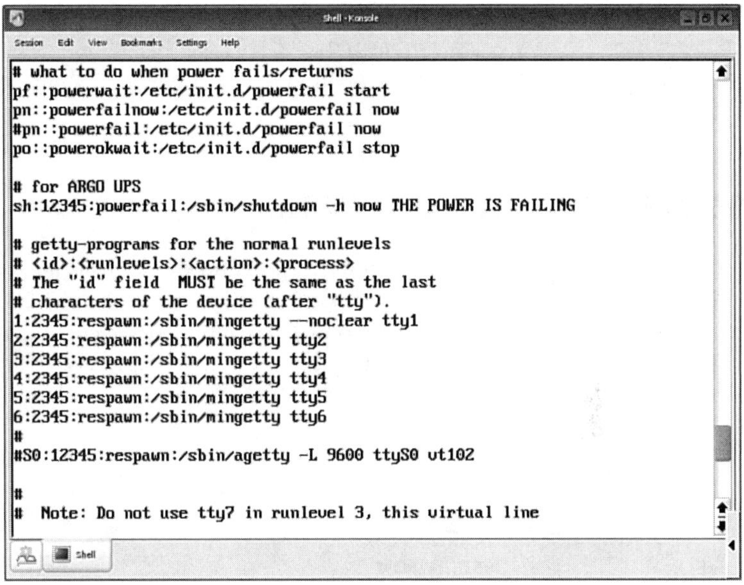

After the system is up, the user(s) can now use it. There is a getty process running on each terminal that can log in that does not currently have a user using it; this is the program responsible for printing the login prompt (get a tty) for the user's login name when he attempts to log in.

To log in, a user must use a valid login name as assigned by the system administrator. Most often, the login name is the user's initials, first name, last name, or some combination derived from the initials or names. The user must also give a password for the login name, and the `/bin/login` utility accepts the password entered by the user and encrypts it using the same mechanism used by the `passwd` command to put the password in the `/etc/passwd` file.

If the encrypted values match, the password is correct. Otherwise, the password entered by the user is incorrect. The `login` command cannot decrypt the password after it has been encrypted. When the password is entered properly, the system updates the accounting and status information in `/var/run/utmp` and `/var/log/wtmp`.

The /etc/profile shell script is run to set up the recurring variables for all users, and then the system runs files related to the shell in the /etc/profile.d directory. Following this, the system runs per-login configuration files and runs the user's local login and bash startup files. If there are customization files within the home directory (such as .bashrc for BASH or .login for C shell), they are executed next; the user's initial environment is configured, and the shell starts executing.

Understanding Runlevels

Now that we've walked through a standard boot, it is time to look at the key elements that were discussed—the first of which is the concept of runlevels. In a great many operating systems, there are only two runlevels—functioning and turned off (halted). In Linux, however, there are seven different levels of functionality at which the operating system can run. These levels are shown in Table 9.1.

TABLE 9.1
Runlevels for Novell Linux Desktop

RUNLEVEL	DESCRIPTION
0	The system is down.
1	Only one user is allowed in.
2	Multiple users are allowed in, but without NFS.
3	Multiple users and NFS.
4	Is not used by default.
5	Full multiuser environment with networking and X.
6	Reboot.

The following paragraphs elaborate on each of the states a bit.

At level 0, the system is in a shutdown state requiring a manual reboot. This can be called a halt, or powerdown, as well as a shutdown. When changing to this level, files are synchronized with the disk and the system is left in a state in which it is safe to power it off.

Level 1 puts the system in single-user mode, and is also known as administrative mode. This allows only one user (only the root user) to access the system and prevents anyone else from getting in. Often, it restricts the login to only one terminal as well: the one defined as the console. This is the level to use when rebuilding the kernel and doing similar tasks.

Level 2 is multiple-user mode—allowing more than one user to log in at a time. This is the level at which background processes (daemons) start up and additional file systems (root is always mounted), if present, are mounted. Network services are not enabled, and NFS is not running.

Level 3, also known as network mode, is exactly the same as level 2 only with networking or NFS enabled. Another way to think of it is as a non-graphical multiuser mode (identical to runlevel 5, but without the X Window System). When you choose Failsafe at the boot menu (shown in Figure 9.1), this is the mode you enter, as shown in Figure 9.6.

FIGURE 9.6
Booting to Failsafe brings the system up in Runlevel 3.

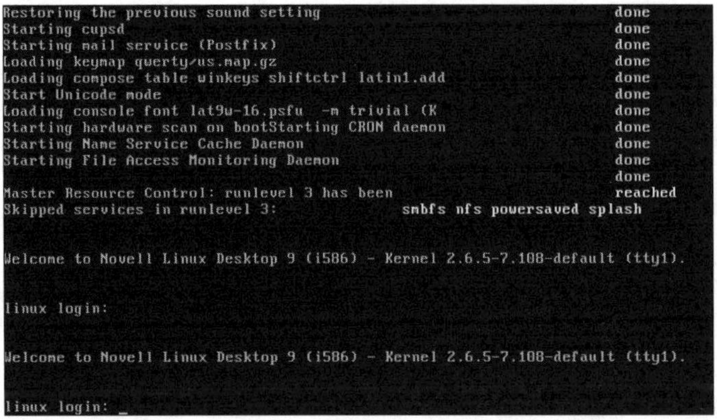

```
Restoring the previous sound setting                                 done
Starting cupsd                                                       done
Starting mail service (Postfix)                                      done
Loading keymap qwerty/us.map.gz                                      done
Loading compose table winkeys shiftctrl latin1.add                   done
Start Unicode mode                                                   done
Loading console font lat9w-16.psfu  -m trivial (K                    done
Starting hardware scan on bootStarting CRON daemon                   done
Starting Name Service Cache Daemon                                   done
Starting File Access Monitoring Daemon                               done
                                                                     done
Master Resource Control: runlevel 3 has been                      reached
Skipped services in runlevel 3:          smbfs nfs powersaved splash

Welcome to Novell Linux Desktop 9 (i586) - Kernel 2.6.5-7.108-default (tty1).


linux login:

Welcome to Novell Linux Desktop 9 (i586) - Kernel 2.6.5-7.108-default (tty1).


linux login: _
```

Level 4 is left to each vendor to define what he wants to define it as, if anything.

Level 5 is traditionally thought of as a graphical multiuser mode. Here, the command prompt is available, and users are allowed to log in and out of the X environment.

Level 6 represents a shutdown and automatic reboot: the same result as changing to runlevel 0 and then rebooting the machine. It can be called a "warm boot" because power is never removed from the components, whereas runlevel 0 represents a "cold boot" because power must be turned off and then restored.

Note

An easy way to summarize the runlevels is that 2, 3, and 5 are operational states of the computer—it is up and running, and users are allowed to conduct business. All other runlevels involve some sort of maintenance or shutdown operation preventing users from processing, with the exception of 4, which differs across implementations.

Typing the command **runlevel** at a prompt will show two values: the previous runlevel and the current runlevel. For example,

```
$ runlevel
N 5
$
```

In this case, the current runlevel is 5, and the "N" means that there was no previous level (None). These values are derived by examining the /var/run/utmp log file, which keeps track of all changes. If this file is corrupt, or the values cannot be found within it, the only value returned is "**unknown**."

Changing Runlevels

An easy way to change the runlevel to shutdown or reboot from within the GUI is to choose Logout from the KDE menu. This brings up the prompt shown in Figure 9.7.

Two commands can be used to change the runlevel at which the machine is currently operating from the command line: **shutdown** and **init**. Both utilities reside in the /sbin directory. As a general rule, **shutdown** is always used to reduce the current runlevel to 0 or 1, whereas **init** can be used to raise it after performing administrative operations.

init must be followed by a number (0–6) or the letters "S" or "s." The numbers identify which runlevel to change to, and the "S" and "s" signify single-user mode. To change to runlevel 2, the command would be

```
init 2
```

Note

The **telinit** utility works the same as **init** and can be used in place of it. It is just a link to **init**.

FIGURE 9.7
You can choose to reboot or shutdown the system from the GUI.

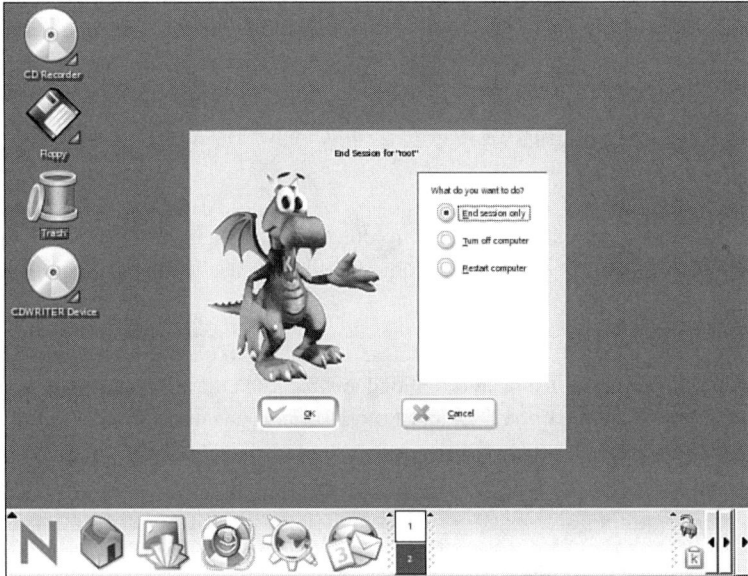

The **shutdown** utility offers a few more options. It informs all users currently logged in that the system is changing state and allows a time (delay) to be specified before the change takes place. Options that work with the utility are

- **-F** to force **fsck** to run after the reboot (the default)
- **-f** to prevent **fsck** from running after the reboot, thus creating a fast reboot
- **-h** to halt after shutdown (level 0)
- **-k** to send out a warning to all users but not really change state
- **-r** to reboot after shutdown (level 6)
- **-t** to specify the number of seconds before the change begins

If no parameters are specified, the default runlevel shutdown attempts to go to is level 0. An example of using the utility would be

```
$ shutdown -h -t 3 now
```

This forces a change to runlevel 0 (-h) three seconds (-t) from the current time (now). Notice that a time must always be specified. If any other text followed the time, it would be interpreted as the warning message to send out to users.

Note

You can also notify users by using the `write` command to send a message to individual users or `wall` to write to all users and tell them of the upcoming shutdown.

Finally, if you want to stop a shutdown after you have summoned it, but before it has begun, you can call **shutdown** once more with the -c (cancel) option.

Note

By default, only the root user can run `shutdown`. You can create a file in the /etc directory named `shutdown.allow` to list other users you want to be able to run the command.

Three minor utilities also exist:

- `halt` (which is similar to **shutdown -h**)
- `reboot` (which links to `halt`)
- `poweroff` (which also links to `halt`)

Regardless of which command you use to shut the system down, you must use one of them to properly halt processes and close files. If you do not properly shut the system down, there is an excellent chance of corruption occurring within the filesystem.

The `inittab` **File**

The main file for determining what takes place at different runlevels is the /etc/`inittab` (initialization table) file. This text file is colon delimited and divided into four fields. The first field is a short ID, and the second identifies the runlevel at which the action is to take place. (Blank means all.) The third field is the action to take place, and the last (fourth) field is the command to execute.

The following file is a representative of what every **inittab** file looks like:

```
#
# /etc/inittab
#
# Copyright  1996-2002 SuSE Linux AG, Nuernberg, Germany.  All rights
reserved.
#
# Author: Florian La Roche, 1996
# Please send feedback to http://www.suse.de/feedback
#
# This is the main configuration file of /sbin/init, which
# is executed by the kernel on startup. It describes what
# scripts are used for the different run-levels.
#
# All scripts for runlevel changes are in /etc/init.d/.
#
# This file may be modified by SuSEconfig unless CHECK_INITTAB
# in /etc/sysconfig/suseconfig is set to "no"
#


# The default runlevel is defined here
id:5:initdefault:

# First script to be executed, if not booting in emergency (-b) mode
si::bootwait:/etc/init.d/boot

# /etc/init.d/rc takes care of runlevel handling
#
# runlevel 0  is  System halt   (Do not use this for initdefault!)
# runlevel 1  is  Single user mode
# runlevel 2  is  Local multiuser without remote network (e.g. NFS)
# runlevel 3  is  Full multiuser with network
# runlevel 4  is  Not used
# runlevel 5  is  Full multiuser with network and xdm
# runlevel 6  is  System reboot (Do not use this for initdefault!)
#
l0:0:wait:/etc/init.d/rc 0
l1:1:wait:/etc/init.d/rc 1
l2:2:wait:/etc/init.d/rc 2
l3:3:wait:/etc/init.d/rc 3
#l4:4:wait:/etc/init.d/rc 4
l5:5:wait:/etc/init.d/rc 5
l6:6:wait:/etc/init.d/rc 6

# what to do in single-user mode
ls:S:wait:/etc/init.d/rc S
```

```
~~:S:respawn:/sbin/sulogin

# what to do when CTRL-ALT-DEL is pressed
ca::ctrlaltdel:/sbin/shutdown -r -t 4 now

# special keyboard request (Alt-UpArrow)
# look into the kbd-0.90 docs for this
kb::kbrequest:/bin/echo "Keyboard Request - edit /etc/inittab to let
this work."

# what to do when power fails/returns
pf::powerwait:/etc/init.d/powerfail start
pn::powerfailnow:/etc/init.d/powerfail now
#pn::powerfail:/etc/init.d/powerfail now
po::powerokwait:/etc/init.d/powerfail stop

# for ARGO UPS
sh:12345:powerfail:/sbin/shutdown -h now THE POWER IS FAILING

# getty-programs for the normal runlevels
# <id>:<runlevels>:<action>:<process>
# The "id" field  MUST be the same as the last
# characters of the device (after "tty").
1:2345:respawn:/sbin/mingetty -noclear tty1
2:2345:respawn:/sbin/mingetty tty2
3:2345:respawn:/sbin/mingetty tty3
4:2345:respawn:/sbin/mingetty tty4
5:2345:respawn:/sbin/mingetty tty5
6:2345:respawn:/sbin/mingetty tty6
#
#S0:12345:respawn:/sbin/agetty -L 9600 ttyS0 vt102

#
#   Note: Do not use tty7 in runlevel 3, this virtual line
#   is occupied by the programm xdm.
#

#   This is for the package xdmsc, after installing and
#   and configuration you should remove the comment character
#   from the following line:
#7:3:respawn:+/etc/init.d/rx tty7


# modem getty.
# mo:235:respawn:/usr/sbin/mgetty -s 38400 modem

# fax getty (hylafax)
```

```
# mo:35:respawn:/usr/lib/fax/faxgetty /dev/modem

# vbox (voice box) getty
# I6:35:respawn:/usr/sbin/vboxgetty -d /dev/ttyI6
# I7:35:respawn:/usr/sbin/vboxgetty -d /dev/ttyI7

# end of /etc/inittab
```

The line, `id:5:initdefault:` is of great importance, as it identifies the default runlevel the system will initially attempt to go to after each boot. The lines beneath identify that at each runlevel, the shell script `rc` (beneath `/etc/rc.d`) is to run—using a different variable for each level. This script looks for other scripts within subdirectories of `/etc/rc.d` based on the runlevel: For example, there are `/etc/rc.d/rc0.d`, `/etc/rc.d/rc1.d`, and so on. Within those subdirectories are script files that start with either an "S" or a "K." Scripts that start with "K" identify processes/daemons that must be killed when changing to this runlevel, and scripts starting with "S" identify processes/daemons that must be started when changing to this runlevel.

Note

Startup and kill scripts are executed in numeric order.

Note

The 'si' entry runs the system's initialization script before the runlevel scripts.

The line, `ca::ctrlaltdel:/sbin/shutdown -r -t 4 now` defines what happens when Ctrl+Alt+Del is pressed. If the terminals get killed off, they are started up again thanks to the action of **respawn**. Other actions that can be specified are

- **boot**—To run at boot time
- **bootwait**—To run at boot time and prevent other processes until finished
- **kbrequest**—Send a request for keyboard action/inaction
- **off**—Don't run the command
- **once**—Only run the command once
- **ondemand**—Same as **respawn**
- **powerfail**—Run in the event of a **powerfailure** signal

- powerokwait—Wait until the power is okay before continuing
- sysinit—Run before any users can log on
- wait—Allow completion before continuing on

The init daemon is responsible for carrying out changes that need to be taken in relation to runlevels. This daemon is summoned by the init utility. (Remember, the init utility is also called by telinit and shutdown.)

The init daemon is the first service to come alive upon a boot, and it reads and executes entries in the /etc/inittab file. After completion, the init daemon stays active and respawns any processes that are supposed to run but die off, as well as interacting with the log files (utmp and wtmp from beneath /var or /etc).

If you modify the /etc/inittab file, the changes you make will not be active until the system reboots, or you run this command:

init q

LILO and GRUB

Two bootloaders are currently in use in Linux and supported in NLD: LILO and GRUB. The Linux Loader (LILO) enables Linux to coexist on your machine with other operating systems: Up to 16 images can be swapped back and forth to designate what operating system will be loaded on the next boot.

Note

NLD uses GRUB, by default, but can be configured to use LILO.

By default, LILO boots the default operating system each time, but you can enter the name of another operating system at the BOOT: prompt, or force the prompt to appear by pressing Shift, Ctrl, or Alt during the boot sequence. Entering a question mark (or pressing Tab) will show the available operating systems as defined in the /etc/lilo.conf file: This is a text file that can range from simple to complex based on the number of OSes you have. Changes can be made to the file and are active when you run /sbin/lilo.

Different options that can be used with the lilo command are

- -b to specify the boot device
- -C to use a different configuration file

- -D to use a kernel with a specified name
- -d to specify how long the wait should be in deciseconds
- -I to be prompted for the kernel path
- -i to specify the file boot sector
- -m to specify the name of the map file to use
- -q to list the names of the kernels (which are held in the /boot/map file)
- -R to set as a default for the next reboot
- -S to overwrite the existing file
- -s to tell LILO where to store the old boot sector
- -t to test
- -u to uninstall LILO
- -v to change to verbose mode

LILO is, in many ways, a last-generation utility. It is still in use, but is being surpassed in favor of GRUB.

GRUB is a multiboot loader that was originally created by Erich Stefan Boleyn and is now maintained by GNU. The name is an acronym for GRand Unified Bootloader, and the simplest way to get information on it is to use the info grub command.

Note

Whereas LILO requires that boot information be written to the drive or boot partition's boot sector beforehand, GRUB dynamically reads its configuration file each time you boot. GRUB provides substantially more flexibility than LILO in terms of booting other operating systems and is especially useful when dual booting because it can swap the system's idea of which disk is which.

GRUB, by default, installs in the /boot/grub directory, and the file menu.1st contains the boot information. Devices are referred to using the (hd0,1) syntax. The name of the device can always be broken into the four fields that each character stands for:

- The type of drive: h for IDE, or s for SCSI
- The type of device: d for disk
- The number of the disk expressed in numeric format
- The number of the partition

There must always be a minimum of two partitions: the filesystem itself (often referred to as root) and a swap partition. The swap partition is the memory and some hard drive space. The swap partition is always a minimum of the amount of RAM installed on the machine, but can be more. The ability to use a swap partition greater than the amount of installed RAM is known as using virtual memory.

The menu.1st file can be edited and changed with any editor, and the options are immediately available at boot time. More information on GRUB can be found at: http://www.gnu.org/software/grub/grub.html.

Related Boot Files and Utilities

There are a few other files and utilities to be aware of when discussing booting—the first of which is dmesg. This utility enables you to display bootup messages generated by the kernel and the system startup process. By default, when you type in **dmesg**, the messages are displayed from the kernel's message buffer to your screen. If there is a problem, however, and you want to save the messages for troubleshooting purposes, you can use this command:

```
dmesg > {filename}
```

The listing that is returned is rather lengthy, but it is important to check as it can be an invaluable aid in troubleshooting.

As you look at the file on your system, notice the order of operations as the system comes up. Notice, as well, how the first line identifies the kernel version and vendor.

Other files to be aware of are

- /var/log/messages
- utmp
- wtmp

The first file, messages, is written to by **cron** and other processes (any process that uses **syslogd** or **klogd**) and can be useful in troubleshooting problems. Some of the contents of this file are displayed by the **dmesg** command.

The utmp and wtmp files are log files that act as counterparts of each other and exist in /var/run and /var/log, respectively. By default, when the system comes up, entries are written to utmp, and when the system goes down, entries are written to wtmp.

The `last` command can be used to look at the most recent entries in `wtmp`—showing users and system state changes:

```
$ last
root      pts/0                      Mon Oct  9 14:58   still logged
in
root      :0                         Mon Oct  9 14:21   still logged
in
reboot    system boot  2.2.10        Mon Oct  9 14:15
(03:01)
root      pts/1                      Mon Oct  9 11:35 - down
(02:15)
root      pts/0                      Mon Oct  9 11:35 - down
(02:15)
root      :0                         Mon Oct  9 11:34 - down
(02:16)
reboot    system boot  2.2.10        Mon Oct  9 11:33
(02:16)
root      pts/0                      Tue Oct  3 11:18 - crash
(6+00:15)
root      :0                         Mon Oct  2 16:31 - 11:28
(6+18:56)
reboot    system boot  2.2.10        Mon Oct  2 16:23
(6+21:26)
root      :0                         Mon Sep 25 16:32 - 17:20
(00:48)
reboot    system boot  2.2.10        Mon Sep 25 16:29
(00:51)
root      :0                         Mon Sep 25 16:18 - 16:25
(00:06)
reboot    system boot  2.2.10        Mon Sep 25 16:06
(00:18)

wtmp begins Mon Sep 25 16:06:45 2000
```

Summary

This chapter focused on the topics you need to know to pass questions related to the booting and initialization of the Linux operating system. We also examined the different runlevels and how to change from one to another.

## CHAPTER 10

Linux Administration

This chapter focuses on the basics of Novell Linux Desktop 9 administration. It is important for you to know the topics in this chapter in order to function as an administrator.

Creating and Managing Users

During the installation of the operating system, at least one user (root/superuser) must be added to the system, and you are also prompted to add at least one more user. The root user is the most powerful user on the system and literally able to do almost anything. After the installation, it is almost always necessary to add additional users and modify variables associated with existing ones. Both tasks will be examined further in this section.

You can add users at the command line or through YaST (which is discussed in the "Working with Security and Users" section in Chapter 5, "Working with YaST"). To understand what is involved, however, it is important to know the files the operating system uses to deal with users, regardless of the way in which you administer them. The first file of importance is the /etc/passwd file. Fields are delimited by colons, and an example would resemble the following:

```
root:x:0:0:root:/root:/bin/bash
bin:x:1:1:bin:/bin:
daemon:x:2:2:daemon:/sbin:
adm:x:3:4:adm:/var/adm:
lp:x:4:7:lp:/var/spool/lpd:
sync:x:5:0:sync:/sbin:/bin/sync
shutdown:x:6:11:shutdown:/sbin:/sbin/shutdown
halt:x:7:0:halt:/sbin:/sbin/halt
mail:x:8:12:mail:/var/spool/mail:
news:x:9:13:news:/var/spool/news:
```

```
uucp:x:10:14:uucp:/var/spool/uucp:
operator:x:11:0:operator:/root:
games:x:12:100:games:/usr/games:
gopher:x:13:30:gopher:/usr/lib/gopher-data:
ftp:x:14:50:FTP User:/home/ftp:
man:x:15:15:Manuals Owner:/:
majordom:x:16:16:Majordomo:/:/bin/false
postgres:x:17:17:Postgres User:/home/postgres:/bin/bash
mysql:x:18:18:MySQL User:/var/lib/mysql:/bin/false
nobody:x:65534:65534:Nobody:/:/bin/false
edulaney:x:1000:100:emmett:/home/edulaney:/bin/bash
kdulaney:x:1001:100:karen:/home/kdulaney:/bin/tcsh
sdulaney:x:1002:100:spencer:/home/sdulaney:/bin/zsh
```

The seven fields can be broken down as follows:

- The login name of the user—This must be unique per system, but is free text and can be edited and modified with any editor at any time. Among the entries shown in the example, **bin** is the owner of executables, **daemon** is used for system services, and **adm** owns the log files. Other entries are users (such as **edulaney**) or individual services (such as **ftp**).

Note

If you modify this field with a text editor, you must be extremely careful to make the same modification in /etc/shadow, or you will lock out the user. This can be a fatal error if the account in question is for root.

- The password—This can be an encrypted entry held within this field, or an "x." In the case of the latter, the single character merely indicates that the values are stored elsewhere—in the /etc/shadow file.

Note

Placing the passwords in the shadow file adds additional security. Everyone can read the passwd file, but only the root user can read the shadow file.

- The numerical user ID (UID)—This is an incremental number unique for every user and is how the operating system truly references the user. (Remember that the login name is changeable text.) The root user is always number 0, and maintenance/service accounts use small numbers (typically up to 99). Regular user accounts start at 1,000 and increment from there. For security reasons, you can rename root to any other text value, but the number 0 is always the identifier.

- The numerical group ID (GID)—This identifies the default group associated with the user. The **root** group is always 0, and lower numbers are
  used for system groups. Regular users are assigned groups at a beginning
  number listed in the **/etc/login.defs** file.

- This field traditionally contains the user's full name but can be any free
  text used for descriptive purposes—One of the main utilities that look at
  this field is **finger**, which simply returns information about a user to
  anyone querying.

- The home directory of the user—This is where the users start when they
  log in and where files are held to define their environmental variables.

- The shell to use for the user—If no data is in this field, the default shell
  is used.

The **/etc/shadow** file is used to hold the password and information about the
aging parameters. Here's an example:

```
root:awYeiEwzMpfo6:11144:0::7:7::
bin:*:10547:0::7:7::
daemon:*:10547:0::7:7::
adm:*:10547:0::7:7::
lp:*:10547:0::7:7::
sync:*:10547:0::7:7::
shutdown:*:10547:0::7:7::
halt:*:10547:0::7:7::
mail:*:10547:0::7:7::
news:*:10547:0::7:7::
uucp:*:10547:0::7:7::
operator:*:10547:0::7:7::
games:*:10547:0::7:7::
gopher:*:10547:0::7:7::
ftp:*:10547:0::7:7::
man:*:10547:0::7:7::
majordom:*:10547:0::7:7::
postgres:*:10547:0::7:7::
mysql:*:10547:0::7:7::
nobody:*:10547:0::7:7::
edulaney:awOVvUAsWpigo:11144:0::7:7::
kdulaney:awzIG94wrzGqY:11144:0::7:7::
sdulaney:awf7Zbxwu.NmQ:11144:0::7:7::
```

The eight fields are

- The login name of the user, which is the only field that must match with
  the **/etc/passwd** file.

- An encrypted hash of the password. If no password has been defined on system accounts, an asterisk (*) is often used. If no password is defined on newly created accounts, an exclamation mark (!) often appears. Under no conditions can this field be left blank for a functioning user.

- The day the password was last changed, expressed in the number of days that have passed since 1/1/1970. An entry of **12711**, for example, would mean 12,711 days had passed and it is now October 19, 2004.

- Minimum password age expressed in how many days a user must wait between being allowed to make password changes. A value of **0** means that he can make changes as often as he likes.

- Maximum password age expressed in how many days a user is allowed to keep this password. A value of **90** would mean that the password must be changed every 90 days, whereas **99999** (the default) essentially means that no change is required.

- The number of days before the password expires when a warning starts appearing to change the password. This is usually **7**.

- The number of days after the password expires to wait before disabling the account. This field is often blank.

- The expiration date for the password, again in days since 1/1/1970. This field is often blank.

Creating User Accounts at the Command Line

Note

Adding users through YaST, the graphical interface, is discussed in the "Working with Security and Users" section in Chapter 5.

New users can be created manually or by using command-line utilities. To do so manually, simply append an entry to the **/etc/passwd** file. (It is strongly recommended that you make a backup copy of the file before changing.) You can leave the password field blank, and then assign a password using the **passwd** utility. If you simply leave it blank, it is a valid account without a password:

```
$ cat >> /etc/passwd
evan::504:100:EvanD:/home/evan:/bin/bash
{press Ctrl+D}
$
$ passwd evan
New user password: {enter password}
```

```
Retype new user password: {enter password again}
passwd: all authentication tokens updated successfully
$
$ tail -1 /etc/passwd
evan:petKv.fLWG/Ig:504:100:EvanD:/home/evan:/bin/bash
$
```

NOTE

Any user can use the passwd utility to change his password. Only the root user, however, can use it to change the password of another user.

Notice that this method places the encrypted password in the /etc/passwd file itself and does not use the /etc/shadow file. Provided that the home directory exists, and the user is the owner of it, the user can now be an authenticated user.

A utility provided with Linux (most vendors also have their own utilities as well) to simplify this process is **useradd**. You must use options with the utility, and a key one is **-D** to display default settings. Here's an example:

Note

The useradd utility is intended for use when su'd to root. A typical user will get an error message when he attempts to use it.

```
$ useradd -D
GROUP=100
HOME=/home
INACTIVE=-1
EXPIRE=
SHELL=/bin/bash
SKEL=/etc/skel
GROUPS=dialout,uucp.video,audio
$
```

These are the defaults that will be used when a new user is created with this utility. The defaults come from the text file /etc/login.defs. Therefore, the following sequence is possible:

```
$ useradd kerby
$ tail -1 /etc/passwd
kerby:x:1002:100::/home/kerby:/bin/bash
$ tail -1 /etc/shadow
kerby:!:12711:0:99999:7:::
```

```
$
$ passwd kerby
New user password: {enter password}
Retype new user password: {enter password again}
passwd: all authentication tokens updated successfully
$ tail -1 /etc/shadow
kerby:M3cMnQDwHjRD6:12711:0:99999:7:::
$
```

Note

Many default values for the local user account, such as password aging policies, are stored in /etc/login.defs. This file is used by many of the password-related utilities for finding default values. The file is well commented and worth looking through.

The /etc/default/useradd file holds a handful of other default values that are also used by that utility when creating local users. If the same setting exists in /etc/login.defs and /etc/default/useradd, those settings in /etc/login.defs are used.

Neither of these files are used when LDAP accounts or nonlocal users are created.

Note that the /etc/shadow file is used, and the values used to create the entries in the two files come directly from the defaults, which are shown in Table 10.1.

TABLE 10.1
Defaults for /etc/shadow

DEFAULT	FILE RESULT
GROUP	Becomes the fourth field of passwd
HOME	Becomes the sixth field of passwd, with the %s variable becoming the name given on the command line (which becomes the first field of both passwd and shadow)
SHELL	Becomes the seventh field of passwd
PASS variables	Entered into appropriate fields of shadow

The SKEL variable was not used in this example. By default, useradd will make the entries in the passwd and shadow files, but will not create the home directory for the user. If you use the -m option, useradd will also create the home directory for the user and copy files from the SKEL location (a skeleton, or template of files that you want copied for every new user) into the new directory. In typical NLD implementations, /etc/skel holds the following files:

- `.bash_history`
- `.bashrc`
- `.dvipsrc`
- `.emacs`
- `.exrc`
- `.fonts`
- `.kermrc`
- `.muttrc`
- `.profile`
- `.urlview`
- `.xcoralrc`
- `.xemacs`
- `.xim.template`
- `.xinitrc.template`
- `.xtalkrc`
- Documents
- bin
- public_html

The hidden files here are used for processing (setting up variables, environment, and so on) with the various shells or setting up variables for editors (`.emacs` is for emacs, `.kermrc` is for kermit, `.muttrc` is for the mutt mail reader, and so on).

A number of options can be used with **useradd** to override default settings, and they include the following:

- `-c` to specify the free text (fifth field of **passwd**) associated with the user. Most Linux implementations default to an empty entry here or a variation of their name.
- `-d` to specify a home directory different from **/home/{username}**.
- `-e` to change expiration date (format: mm/dd/yyyy).
- `-f` for the variable defining how many days after expiration the account becomes disabled. The default of `-1` prevents it from being disabled even after expiration.
- `-g` to specify a different GID.
- `-r` for a system directory.

- -s to choose a different shell.
- -u to specify a UID: By default, the next available number is used. If you try to use a number that is already in use, the utility fails and identifies which user already has that number.

SWITCHING BETWEEN passwd AND shadow

In the manual example for creating a new user, the encrypted password appears in the /etc/passwd file and not the /etc/shadow file. If you want to do manual additions, and still use /etc/shadow, the pwconv utility can be irreplaceable. This utility reads the entire passwd file and converts new entries into shadow file entries.

The opposite of pwconv is pwunconv u, which takes entries from the shadow file and places them in the appropriate format in the passwd file. As a final step, pwunconv removes the shadow file completely.

THE su UTILITY

The entries in the passwd file represent valid accounts that can log in. Any user can sit at the system and give the correct username and password combination to log in as that user. Any user already logged in can also use the su utility (*su* stands for *substitute userID*) to change identity to another user if he knows the other user's password. This creates a subshell, if you will, in which one user becomes another, and can revert to his own identity by typing **exit**.

Although there are dozens of harmful reasons why a user might want to become another, there are also very legitimate reasons as well. If su is given without a user name following it, it tries to make the user the superuser (root), needing the password for that account. Therefore, as an administrator, it is possible for you to log in as a typical user without root permissions and begin your day. The lack of root permissions can be a blessing as it can keep you from deleting entries you unintentionally typed, and so on. When a user comes up with a problem, you can use su to become root—with all rights and privileges as if you had logged in as such—fix the user's problem, and then exit back to your regular account again.

USING sudo

Another utility, sudo, works the same as su but can be limited by entries in the /etc/sudoers configuration file. The entries in this file can limit which users can use sudo and can even limit which actions sudo can perform in the new shell.

Read the comments in the /etc/sudoers file to understand how to configure this file.

Managing User Accounts

Note

Managing users through YaST, the graphical interface, is discussed in the "Working with Security and Users" section in Chapter 5.

After an account has been created, you can manage and modify it manually or through the use of utilities. For example, if a user named Karen Dulaney gets married, and her name changes to Karen Brooks, you can edit the **passwd** and **shadow** files and change the first field of each from **kdulaney** to **kbrooks**. Because the same UID is in place, all files and such associated with her continue to remain so. The home directory can be renamed, and the change made in **passwd** as well. (It is always recommended that home directory and username match for administrative purposes.)

As another example, if Karen gets promoted to administration, it might be necessary to remove her from the **users** group and place her in the **root** group. This can also be accomplished by manually editing the **/etc/passwd** file and changing the GID field. Similar examples can be given, endlessly, for each field within the files.

Note

The usermod utility should be used by su or the root user. Typical users will get an error message when they attempt to use it.

Just as **useradd** is intended to simplify the addition of users to the system—and avoid manual entries—**usermod** is meant to simplify changing existing values. Options/flags must be used with the utility, and these are the possibilities:

- **-c** to replace the descriptive text with a new value.
- **-d** to alter the home directory.
- **-e** to change the password expiration date.
- **-f** to set the inactive parameter.
- **-G** to change secondary group membership. More than one group can be given as long as commas separate entries.
- **-g** to change the GID.
- **-l** to change the login name.
- **-m** (must be used with **-d**) to make the new home directory.
- **-p** to change the password.

- -s for a different shell.
- -u to change the UID.

Aside from the text description, most of the values require the user to not be logged in while the change is made. Here's an example of a change:

```
$ grep krist /etc/passwd
kristin:petKv.fLWG/Ig:506:100:kristin:/home/kristin:/bin/bash
$ usermod -l kristen kristin
$ grep krist /etc/passwd
kristen:petKv.fLWG/Ig:506:100:kristin:/home/kristin:/bin/bash
$ ls -l /home
drwxr-xr-x 4 evan    users 1024 Jul 6 11:16 evan
drwxr-xr-x 4 kristin users 1024 Aug 8 10:29 kristin
drwxr-xr-x 4 spencer users 1024 Jul 6 11:16 spencer
$ usermod -d /home/kristen -m kristen
$ ls -l /home
drwxr-xr-x 4 evan    users 1024 Jul 6 11:16 evan
drwxr-xr-x 4 kristin users 1024 Aug 8 10:29 kristin
drwxr-xr-x 4 spencer users 1024 Jul 6 11:16 spencer
$ grep krist /etc/passwd
kristen:petKv.fLWG/Ig:506:100:kristin:/home/kristen:/bin/bash
$
```

The usermod utility has the -p option to allow for the changing of passwords, but that can be accomplished more commonly with the passwd utility discussed earlier. The standalone utility is safer in that it requires you to enter the value twice, and thus helps prevent entering a value that is off by one character from what you were thinking (preventing you from logging in).

If a large number of passwords need to be changed (think system break-in), you can do a batch change with the chpasswd utility. To use it, create a text file with one entry per line. Each line consists of the username and new password, separated by a colon. For example,

```
$ cat > changes
kristen:spea23ker
evan:pho78ne
kdulaney:fla98sh
{Ctrl+D}
$
$ chpasswd < changes
$
```

The passwords are in clear text, and for that reason, you will want to remove the batch file from your system as soon as possible. An alternative is to use encrypted passwords and use the -e option with chpasswd.

Note

It is a good idea to encourage users to use good passwords. Good passwords consist of at least six characters, which are a mix of letters, characters, and numbers and would not be easily guessed.

Removing Users

When a user account is no longer needed, there are a number of ways you can deal with the situation. The first question you have to address is why the account is no longer needed. When you know that, you can formulate a plan for dealing with it. Table 10.2 offers some scenarios and methods of proceeding.

TABLE 10.2
Solutions for Unneeded User Accounts

PERCEIVED REASON FOR NOT NEEDING ACCOUNT	PROPOSED SOLUTION
User has been temporarily transferred to another division	If it is a temporary situation, you do not want to delete the account—doing so will remove all references that might be needed later. To temporarily disable the account, edit the /etc/passwd file and place a pound sign (#) at the beginning of the line. This will make the entire line a comment and disable the account.
	A second method of quickly disabling an account is to put an asterisk (*) at the beginning of the user's password entry in /etc/shadow.
User's password has been compromised by a hacker	Change the password to another value to keep the other party out. For further security, rename the login name and home directory.
User has left the organization	Remove the account from /etc/passwd and /etc/shadow and delete the home directory.

The **userdel** utility can also be used to remove the user. This utility removes the user from system files (**passwd** and **shadow**), but you must still remove any files associated with them.

Tip

You can use userdel's −r option to remove the user's home directory and mail spool files.

Working with Groups

Just as it is important to know the parameters behind user variables to understand how to work with them, you must also understand group constructs. The primary file holding group information is **/etc/group**, an example of which would be

```
root::0:
wheel::10:
bin::1:bin,daemon
daemon::2:bin,daemon
sys::3:bin,adm
adm::4:adm,daemon
tty::5:
disk::6:
lp::7:daemon,lp
mem::8:
kmem::9:
operator::11:
mail::12:mail
news::13:news
uucp::14:uucp
man::15:
majordom::16:
database::17:
mysql::18:
games::20:
gopher::30:
dip::40:
utmp::45:
ftp::50:
nobody::65534:
users::100:
```

There are four fields to each entry in the file. The first field is the text name (maximum of eight characters) associated with the group (used for `ls -l` listings and the like). The third field is the GID that must be unique on the system. The second field—blank in all cases by default—holds a password that can be required for use. The fourth field can be used to list the members of the group.

Creating a New Group

Note

Adding groups through YaST, the graphical interface, is discussed in the "Working with Security and Users" section in Chapter 5.

To create a new group, you can manually edit the `/etc/group` file and append an entry to it. If you do so, you must be certain to use a unique text name and GID number. The **groupadd** utility can also be used to simplify the operation:

```
$ groupadd -g 101 sales
$ tail -1 /etc/group
sales:!:101:
$
```

The `-g` option is used to specify the GID number to use. If the number is not unique, the utility will fail. As a general rule, GIDs 0–99 are reserved for system groups:

```
$ groupadd -g 101 marketing
groupadd: GID 101 is not unique.
$
```

Similarly, if you attempt to reuse a group name, the utility fails:

```
$ groupadd -g 102 sales
groupadd: Group `sales' already exists.
$
```

Only a few other options are available with **groupadd** besides `-g`. Chief among them, the `-o` option can be used to create a non-unique group (allowing the same gid to be used). The `-p` option allows you to specify a password, and `-r` creates a system group.

To further define your group, you can resort to manual editing or use the **gpasswd** utility. When issued with only the name of a group, it prompts for a password to associate with the group:

```
$ gpasswd sales
Changing the password for group sales
New Password: {enter value}
Re-enter new password: {enter value again}
$ tail -1 /etc/group
sales:QJHexo2Pbk7TU:101:
$
```

If you tire of the password, or find it unwieldy, the -r option can be used to remove it.

```
$ gpasswd -r sales
$ tail -1 /etc/group
sales::101:
$
```

The exclamation point appears in the second field as a placeholder to identify that other users can join, and so on. You cannot add or delete more than one user at a time with gpasswd.

Picking a Group

When a user is a member of more than one group, his default group is the one defined by the fourth field of the /etc/passwd file. The id utility will show information about the user, including all the groups the user is a member of:

```
$ id
uid=501(edulaney) gid=100(users) groups=100(users),101(sales)
$
```

Note

There are a number of reasons why it might be necessary to be a member of multiple groups. Typically, this is done to share files and occasionally to execute group-specific applications.

To change groups, use the newgrp utility and the name of the other group you want to make your default. Non-group members trying to become a part of the group have to give a password, whereas group members do not:

```
$ id
uid=501(edulaney) gid=100(users) groups=100(users),101(sales)
$ newgrp sales
$ id
uid=501(edulaney) gid=101(sales) groups=100(users),101(sales)
$ newgrp marketing
```

```
Password: {enter value}
$ id
uid=501(edulaney) gid=102(marketing) groups=100(users),
101(sales),102(marketing)
$
```

Modifying Groups

Note

Modifying groups through YaST, the graphical interface, is discussed in the "Working with Security and Users" section in Chapter 5.

After groups have been created, you can modify their entries by manually editing the files, using **gpasswd** or the **groupmod** utility. This tool allows you to change values (name and GID) associated with the group. The parameters that can be used with **groupmod** include

- -g to specify a new GID
- -n to change the name of the group to a new text value
- -o to allow a duplicate group ID number to be used
- -p to specify a password
- -A to add a user to the group
- -R to remove a user from the group

For example,

```
$ tail -1 /etc/group
sales:x:101:edulaney,kristen,kerby,martha
$ groupmod -g 105 sales
$ tail -1 /etc/group
sales:x:105:edulaney,kristen,kerby,martha
$
$ groupmod -n business sales
$ tail -1 /etc/group
business:x:105:edulaney,kristen,kerby,martha
$
```

When groups are no longer needed, they can be deleted by manually removing the lines from the files or by using the **groupdel** command. The utility cannot be used if any user has the group as his default group, and it only removes the entry from /etc/group.

Working with PAM

To increase security, Pluggable Authentication Modules (PAM) can act as intermediaries between users and applications. Once a user is authorized in PAM,
he is free to access the applications that are available to him. The beauty of this
arrangement is that you can change any one element in the process, and not
affect anything else. For example, suppose that you are requiring users to enter
a password to authenticate themselves, and then giving them access to 10
applications. You can change the authentication method from a password to a
fingerprint scan, and then allow them access to the applications without having
to reconfigure anything but the authentication method. PAMs provide a flexible
framework that makes it easy for administrators to change and add system
authentication mechanisms without modifying the applications that require and
use authentication.

Global files are located beneath /etc/security. Individual configuration files
for PAM modules are located beneath /etc/pam.d, as shown in Figure 10.1.

FIGURE 10.1
Configuration files exist for each program that uses PAM modules.

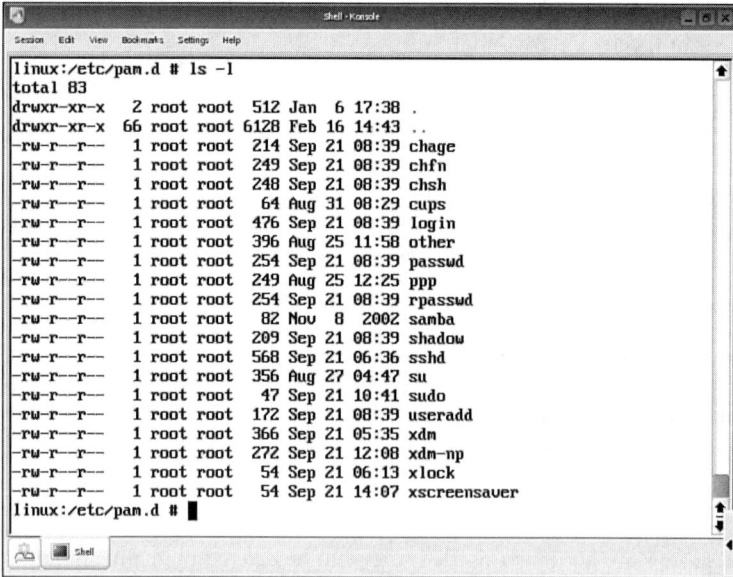

Notice that the names which appear here have the same name as the utility with which they are associated. When a user uses one of these applications, a check is made in this directory for an associated configuration file. If found, it is read and acted upon.

Some of the configuration files are only a single line, whereas some are more lengthy. Figure 10.2 shows the contents of the **su** configuration file.

FIGURE 10.2
The configuration file for su.

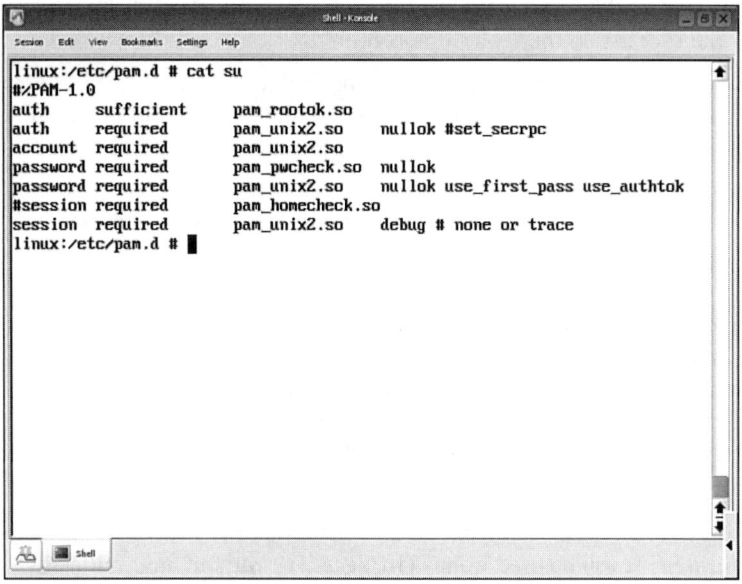

```
linux:/etc/pam.d # cat su
#%PAM-1.0
auth        sufficient      pam_rootok.so
auth        required        pam_unix2.so        nullok #set_secrpc
account     required        pam_unix2.so
password    required        pam_pwcheck.so      nullok
password    required        pam_unix2.so        nullok use_first_pass use_authtok
#session    required        pam_homecheck.so
session     required        pam_unix2.so        debug # none or trace
linux:/etc/pam.d # ▮
```

There are four fields to each line in the file. The first field identifies the module type, whereas the second is the control flag. The third field lists the modules to use, and the fourth field (which is optional) lists any arguments that are needed.

The four possible values for the module type are

- account—This identifies a need to see if the user has permission to use the service he wants to.
- auth—This identifies a need to check the user's authenticity. This is most often accomplished with a password.

- password—This allows a change in the access/authentication token. Usually, a change is done by issuing a password.

- session—This is the module type used to govern the session between the application and the user.

The four possible values for the control flags are

- optional—No adverse consequences are associated with the success/ failure of this flag.

- required—The flag must be marked successful before being allowed to continue. Any other associated flags are processed upon failure, and then the user is told there was a problem.

- requisite—Similar to required, except that no other associated flags are processed upon a failure and the user is immediately told that there was a problem.

- sufficient—If the flag is successful, no other modules need to be processed. (This is sufficient.) If there is a failure, there are no direct consequences.

The modules themselves are identified in the third field and reside in /lib/security on most systems and /lib64/security on 64-bit platforms. The arguments that can be passed are any that are needed, with the most common being **debug** and **nullok**. The **debug** argument is used to enable debugging, whereas **nullok** is used to enable empty passwords to be counted as legitimate entities.

Looking at the first line in Figure 10.2, it states that the **pam_rootok.so** module (third field) will be used from /lib/security without any arguments (fourth field) to authorize (first field) via an authentication request that must be sufficient (second field) to continue on. This is what you would expect with the **su** utility when changing from one user to another, and it makes logical sense.

The /usr/share/doc/packages/pam/ directory holds the documentation for PAM on NLD 9. There is a README file in the main directory and beneath the modules subdirectory. An Administrators' Guide can be found in a variety of formats beneath subdirectories for **txt**, **pdf**, and **html**.

Configuring System Logs

Log files can easily be an administrator's best friend or worst enemy. They can monitor the system and report on administrative and security issues 24 hours a day, seven days a week, creating fingerprints that allow you to see what is happening and by whom. On the other hand, if improperly implemented, they monitor so much information that you spend days looking through thousands of lines of unneeded entries trying to find a single item; they eat up precious disk space; and they serve little purpose.

The key to using log files effectively is to know what each of them does. When you know that, you can realistically set your expectations and look for necessary data without being overwhelmed.

The Log Daemon

Although individual applications can have their own logging features, there is a log service specifically running just for the operating system. The service responsible for adding entries to the log files is the **syslogd**—the system log **daemon**—which is spawned by the **init** daemon. When started, **syslogd** reads the **/etc/syslog.conf** file to see what to monitor. Very descriptive in nature, each line consists of the item you want to monitor followed by a period (**.**) and the priority, whitespace, and the location of the log file.

You can use a comma (**,**) to separate multiple entries. You can also use a semicolon (**;**) to denote exceptions to the rule. This is the required syntax:

```
item.priority;exceptions log_file
```

Note

The **syslog** daemon reads the **syslog.conf** file by default. You can, however, modify the startup files so that **syslogd** starts with the **-f** option, allowing you to use another configuration file in place of **/etc/syslog.conf**.

The comments throughout the file do a great job of explaining the other options and recording/routing. The 10 valid values for the priority field, in the order of priority from highest to lowest, are

- debug
- info
- notice
- warning
- err—for error
- crit—for critical
- alert

- `emerg`—for emergency
- `*`–everything
- `none`

Note

Remember that when you specify a priority, that priority represents a minimum. Messages are generated at that, or any higher, priority. If you want it to only log for that priority, you can use the equal sign (=). For example,

`*.=err /var/log/errors`

If you want to specifically not get a type of priority, but get all others, you can use the exclamation point (!). For example, to log all news messages except those that are critical, you could use

`news.*;news.!=crit`

The location field can be anything. Some valid entries would include

- `*`—everywhere
- `/dev/console`—to notify the current console user
- `/var/log/{name of log file}`

Because the `/etc/syslog.conf` file is read by `syslogd` at startup, if you make changes to the file, you must restart the daemon for the changes to be active.

Files to Know

A number of log files exist by default, which you should be familiar with. Table 10.3 summarizes the main ones beneath `/var/log`.

TABLE 10.3
Log Files

FILE	PURPOSE
`lastlog`	Shows the last time each user logged in (is read by the `lastlog` command)
`mail or maillog`	Mail messages
`messages`	The big one: where most events are logged by default
`news or news.all`	News messages

FILE	PURPOSE
uucp	uucp events
wtmp	Used by the `last` command; the counterpart to /var/run/utmp, keeping track of logins and logouts

There are a few executables to be aware of in terms of logging. The first is `logger`. This utility must be followed by the name of the file to write to as well as a message. It will then insert that message in the log file. For example

```
$ pwd
/var/log

$ logger hey
$ tail -1 messages
Oct 20 20:34:58 linux logger: hey
$
```

Each entry starts with the date and time, and is followed by the name of the system, the caller, a colon (:), and the message. You can add notes to yourself in this file and quickly locate them when you need to know when something happened

```
$ logger taking system down to replace graphics card
$
```

And later,

```
$ grep "graphics card" messages
Oct 20 20:38:36 linux logger: taking system down to replace graphics card
$
```

The next executable to be aware of is `logrotate`. This utility reads configuration files and compresses or deletes log files as specified. The `gzip` utility is used for the compression, and actions can take place daily, weekly, monthly (all courtesy of `cron`), or when set sizes are obtained.

At any time, an administrator can archive, delete, or compress log files manually. The sole purpose of `logrotate` is simply to automate the process. Commands that can be used with this utility include

- `compress`
- `copytruncate`
- `create`
- `daily`

- `delaycompress`
- `errors`
- `extension`
- `ifempty`
- `include`
- `mail`
- `mailfirst`
- `maillast`
- `missingok`
- `monthly`
- `nocompress`
- `nocopytruncate`
- `nocreate`
- `nodelaycompress`
- `nomail`
- `nomissingok`
- `noolddir`
- `notifempty`
- `olddir`
- `postrotate`
- `prerotate`
- `rotate`
- `size`
- `weekly`

The text file `/var/lib/logrotate.status` will show the status of the utility in terms of the files it interacts with. On a normal NLD system, `logrotate` is run on a daily basis as a cron job with files rotated on a weekly basis. Configuration of the utility is done by modifying entries. The `/etc/logrotate.conf` file and the man pages for `logrotate` should be consulted before any changes are made.

Monitoring the System

It is important to be able to quickly identify the status of your server and know that it is working as it should. There are a number of ways you can identify this. Most often, you want to first know that the system booted properly. Boot messages are written to the /var/log/boot.msg file.

The dmesg command can be used to display the contents of the kernel's ring buffer.

Hardware-related information is stored in temporary files beneath /proc and can be viewed from there. The names of most of the files telegraph the information they hold—dma, for example, holds information on the Direct Memory Access modules. In the 2.6 Linux kernel, which is used by NLD, block, bus, class, devices, firmware, and power are in /sys and not /proc.

The hwinfo utility can be used to see a list of information about the installed devices. If you use the -log option, you can specify a file for the information to be written to. The hdparm utility can be used to see and change hard disk parameters. A plethora of options are available, and just entering **hdparm** without any other parameters will show those to you. For example, Figure 10.3 shows a test of the hard drive's performance.

FIGURE 10.3
Checking the hard drive performance with hdparm.

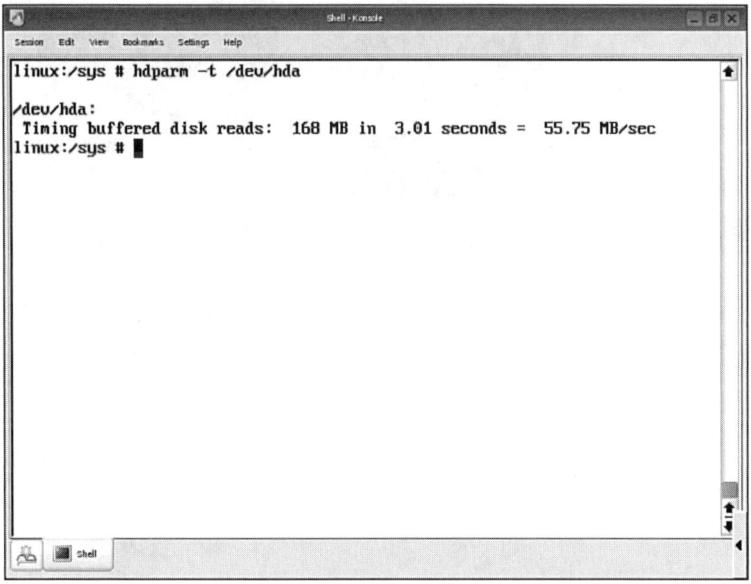

Note

Many of the hdparm parameters can be dangerous if misused. You should very carefully read the man page for this utility before using it.

The lspci utility can show information about the PCI buses, listing all PCI devices.

The KDE System Guard can offer a quick snapshot of the system load and process table, as shown in Figure 10.4. This tool is started by choosing System from the main menu, and then Monitor, and KDE System Guard.

FIGURE 10.4
The KDE System Guard offers a quick overview of the system.

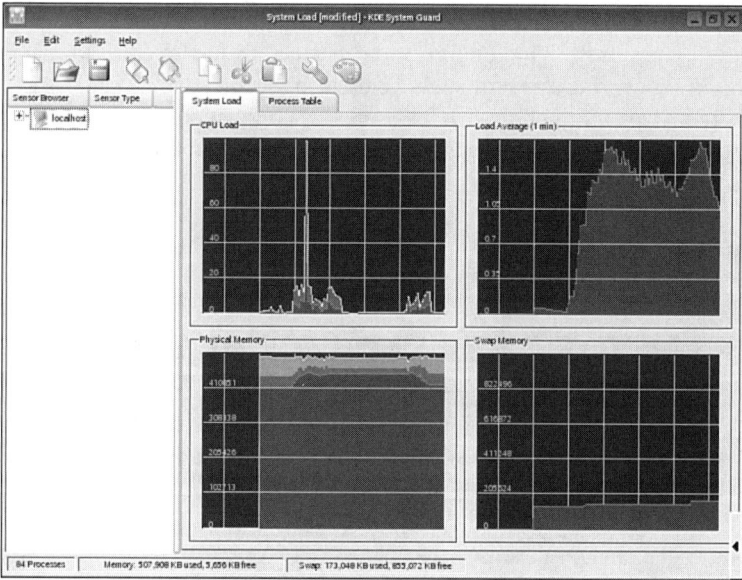

The KDE Info Center (System, Monitor, Info Center) offers another view of all the hardware devices and configuration parameters, as shown in Figure 10.5.

The suseplugger, shown in Figure 10.6, offers yet another way to access this information. This tool is started from the command line with the command **suseplugger**, and it is often already running as indicated by a small icon in your panel.

FIGURE 10.5
The KDE Info Center allows quick access to device parameters.

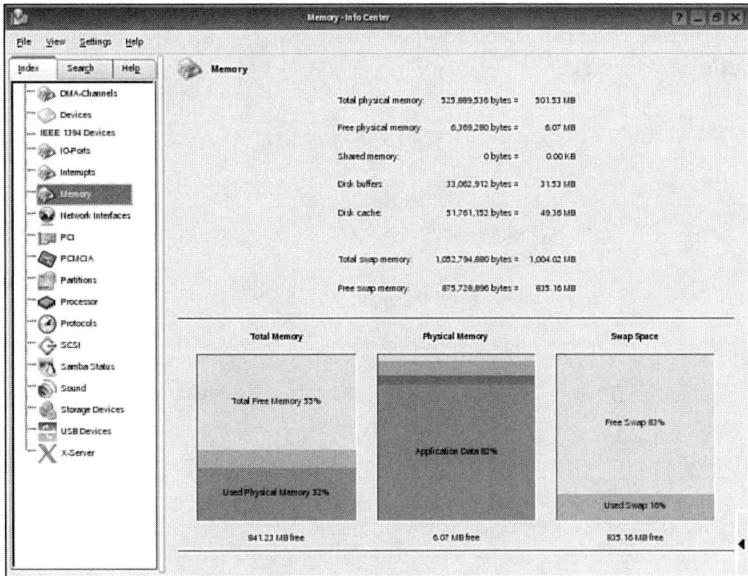

FIGURE 10.6
The suseplugger offers another venue to hardware information.

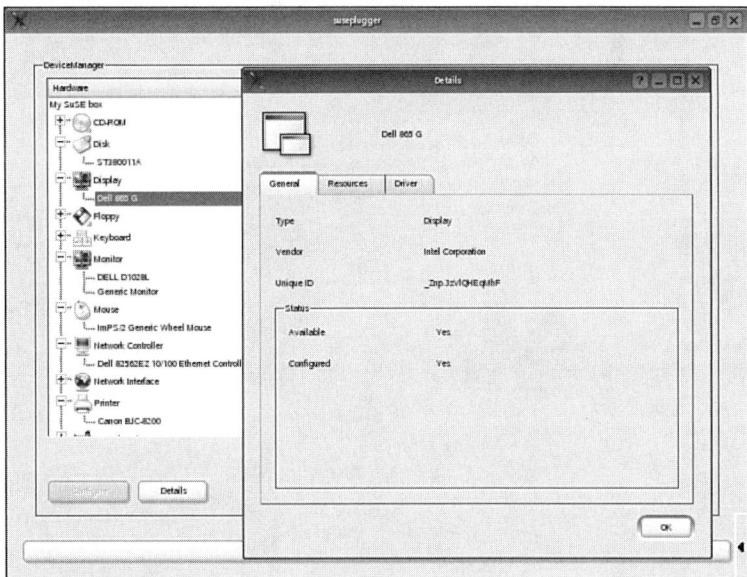

Summary

This chapter focused on the topics you need to know to perform basic Linux administration. The next chapter looks at networking—an integral part of any computing environment.

## CHAPTER 11

Networking

This chapter focuses on the fundamentals of networking. In this chapter, you'll learn about the TCP/IP networking protocol and how to configure it. This chapter builds on those concepts, and you'll learn about some of the services that run on TCP/IP.

TCP/IP Background

The Transmission Control Protocol/Internet Protocol (TCP/IP) is an industry-standard suite of protocols designed to be routable and efficient. TCP/IP was originally designed as a set of wide area network (WAN) protocols for the purpose of maintaining communication links and data transfer between sites in the event of an atomic/nuclear war. Since those early days, development of the protocols has passed from the hands of the government and has been the responsibility of the Internet community for some time.

The evolution of these protocols from a small four-site project into the foundation of the worldwide Internet has been extraordinary. But despite more than 25 years of work and numerous modifications to the protocol suite, the inherent spirit of the original specifications is still intact. TCP/IP has the following advantages over other protocols:

- An industry-standard protocol. Because TCP/IP is not maintained or written by one company, it is not proprietary or subject to as many compatibility issues. The Internet community as a whole decides whether a particular change or implementation is worthwhile.

- A set of utilities for connecting dissimilar operating systems. Many connectivity utilities have been written for the TCP/IP suite, including the File Transfer Protocol (FTP) and Terminal Emulation Protocol (Telnet).

- A scaleable, cross-platform client-server architecture. Consider what happened during the initial development of applications for the TCP/IP protocol suite. Vendors wanted to be able to write their own client/server applications—for instance, SQL Server and Simple Network Management Protocol (SNMP). The specification for how to write applications was also up for public perusal. Which operating systems would be included? Users everywhere wanted to be able to take advantage of the connectivity options promised through using TCP/IP, regardless of the operating system they were currently running.

- Access to the Internet. TCP/IP is the de facto protocol of the Internet and allows access to a wealth of information that can be found at thousands of locations around the world. To connect to the Internet, though, a valid IP address is required.

The Four Layers of TCP/IP

TCP/IP maps to a four-layer architectural model. This model is called the Internet Protocol Suite and is broken into the Network Interface, Internet, Transport, and Application layers. Each of these layers corresponds to one or more layers of the OSI model, which it predates. The Network Interface layer corresponds to the Physical and Data Link layers. The Internet layer corresponds to the Network layer. The Transport layer corresponds to the Transport layer, and the Application layer corresponds to the Session, Presentation, and Application layers of the OSI model.

Each of the four layers of the model is responsible for all the activities of the layers to which it maps.

The Network Interface layer is responsible for communicating directly with the network. It must understand the network architecture being used, such as token-ring or Ethernet, and provide an interface enabling the Internet layer to communicate with it. The Internet layer is responsible for communicating directly with the Network Interface layer.

The Internet layer is primarily concerned with the routing and delivery of packets through the Internet Protocol (IP). All the protocols in the Transport layer must use IP to send data. The Internet Protocol includes rules for how to address and direct packets, fragment and reassemble packets, provide security information, and identify the type of service being used. However, because IP is not a connection-based protocol, it does not guarantee that packets transmitted onto the wire will not be lost, damaged, duplicated, or out of order. This is the responsibility of higher layers of the networking model, such as the Transport layer or the Application layer. Other protocols that exist in the Internet layer are the Internet Control Messaging Protocol (ICMP), Internet Group Management Protocol (IGMP), and the Address Resolution Protocol (ARP).

The Transport layer maps to the Transport layer of the OSI model and is responsible for providing communication between machines for applications. This communication can be connection based or non-connection based. The primary difference between these two types of communications is whether there is a mechanism for tracking data and guaranteeing the delivery of the data to its destination. Transmission Control Protocol (TCP) is the protocol used for connection-based communication between two machines providing reliable data transfer. User Datagram Protocol (UDP) is used for non-connection–based communication with no guarantee of delivery.

The Application layer of the Internet Protocol Suite is responsible for all the activities that occur in the Session, Presentation, and Application layers of the OSI model. Numerous protocols have been written for use in this layer, including Simple Network Management Protocol (SNMP), File Transfer Protocol (FTP), Simple Mail Transfer Protocol (SMTP), as well as many others.

The interface between each of these layers is written to have the capability to pass information from one layer to the other.

The interface between the Network Interface layer and the Internet layer does not pass a great deal of information, although it must follow certain rules. Namely, it must listen to all broadcasts and send the rest of the data in the frame up to the Internet layer for processing, and if it receives any frames that do not have an IP frame type, they must be silently discarded.

The interface between the Internet layer and the Transport layer must be capable of providing each layer full access to such information as the source and destination addresses, whether TCP or UDP should be used in the transport of data, and all other available mechanisms for IP. Rules and specifications for the Transport layer include giving the Transport layer the capability to change these parameters or to pass parameters it receives from the Application layer down to the Internet layer. The most important thing to remember about all of these boundary layers is that they must use the agreed-upon rules for passing information from one layer to the other.

Primary Protocols

Six primary protocols are associated with TCP/IP:

- Transmission Control Protocol (TCP)
- User Datagram Protocol (UDP)
- Internet Protocol (IP)
- Internet Control Message Protocol (ICMP)
- Address Resolution Protocol (ARP)
- Internet Group Management Protocol (IGMP)

TRANSMISSION CONTROL PROTOCOL

The first protocol that lives in the Transport layer is the Transmission Control Protocol (TCP). This protocol is a connection-based protocol and requires the establishment of a session before data is transmitted between two machines. TCP packets are delivered to sockets or ports. Because TCP uses a connection between two machines, it is designed to verify that all packets sent by a machine are received on the other end. If, for some reason, packets are lost, the sending machine resends the data. Because a session must be established and delivery of packets is guaranteed, there is additional overhead involved with using TCP to transmit packets.

TCP requires a connection, or session, between two machines before any data is transferred. TCP exists within the Transport layer, between the Application layer and the IP layer, providing a reliable and guaranteed delivery mechanism to a destination machine. Connection-based protocols guarantee the delivery of packets by tracking the transmission and receipt of individual packets during communication. A session is capable of tracking the progress of individual packets by monitoring when a packet is sent, by indicating in what order it was sent, and by notifying the sender when it is received so that more can be sent.

After the TCP session has been created, the machines begin to communicate just as people do during a phone call. During the initialization of a TCP session, often called the "three-way handshake," both machines agree on the best method to track how much data is to be sent at any one time, acknowledgment numbers to be sent upon receipt of data, and when the connection is no longer necessary because all data has been transmitted and received. Only after this session is created does data transmission begin.

To provide reliable delivery, TCP places packets in sequenced order and requires acknowledgments that these packets reached their destination before it sends new data. TCP is typically used for transferring large amounts of data, or when the application requires acknowledgment that data has been received. Given all the additional overhead information that TCP needs to keep track of, the format of a TCP packet can be somewhat complex.

TCP uses the concept of sliding windows for transferring data between machines. Sliding windows are often referred to in the Linux\UNIX environment as *streams*. Each machine has both a send window and a receive window that it uses to buffer data and make the communication process more efficient. A window represents the subset of data currently being sent to a destination machine, and is also the amount of data being received by the destination machine. At first, this seems redundant, but it really isn't. Not all data sent is guaranteed to be received, so the packets must be kept track of on both machines. A sliding window enables a sending machine to send the window data in a stream without having to wait for an acknowledgment for every single packet.

USER DATAGRAM PROTOCOL

The second protocol that lives in the Transport layer is the User Datagram Protocol, or UDP. This protocol is a non-connection–based protocol and does not require a session to be established between two machines before data is transmitted. UDP packets are still delivered to sockets or ports, just as they are in TCP. But because UDP does not create a session between machines, it cannot guarantee that packets are delivered or that they are delivered in order or retransmitted if the packets are lost. Given the apparent unreliability of this protocol, some might wonder why a protocol such as UDP was developed.

Sending a UDP datagram has very little overhead involved. A UDP datagram has no synchronization parameters or priority options. All that exists is the source port, destination port, the length of the data, a checksum for verifying the header, and then the data.

There are actually a number of good reasons to have a transport protocol that does not require a session to be established. For one, very little overhead is associated with UDP, such as having to keep track of sequence numbers, Retransmit Timers, Delayed Acknowledgment Timers, and retransmission of packets. UDP is quick and extremely streamlined functionally; it's just not guaranteed. This makes UDP perfect for communications that involve broadcasts, general announcements to the network, or real-time data.

Another really good use for UDP is in streaming video and audio. Not only does the unguaranteed delivery of packets enable more data to be transmitted (because a broadcast has little to no overhead), but also the retransmission of a packet is pointless.

INTERNET PROTOCOL

A number of protocols are found in the Internet layer, including the most important protocol in the entire suite, the Internet Protocol (IP). This is probably the most important protocol because the Transport layer cannot communicate at all without communicating through IP in the Internet layer.

The most fundamental element of the Internet Protocol is the address space that IP uses. Each machine on a network is given a unique 32-bit address called an Internet address, or IP address. Addresses are divided into five categories, called classes, that are discussed later in this chapter.

IP receives information in the form of packets from the Transport layer, from either TCP or UDP, and sends out data in what are commonly referred to as datagrams. The size of a datagram depends on the type of network being used, such as token-ring or Ethernet. If a packet has too much data to be transmitted in one datagram, it is broken into pieces and transmitted through several datagrams. Each of these datagrams has to then be reassembled by TCP or UDP.

INTERNET CONTROL MESSAGE PROTOCOL

Internet Control Message Protocol (ICMP) is part of the Internet layer and is responsible for reporting errors and messages regarding the delivery of IP datagrams. It can also send "source quench" and other self-tuning signals during the transfer of data between two machines without the intervention of the user. These signals are designed to fine-tune and optimize the transfer of data automatically. ICMP is the protocol that warns you when a destination host is unreachable or how long it took to get to a destination host.

ICMP messages can be broken down into two basic categories: the reporting of errors and the sending of queries. Error messages include the following:

- Destination unreachable
- Redirect
- Source quench
- Time exceeded

ICMP also includes general message queries. The two most commonly used are the following:

- Echo request
- Echo reply

The most familiar tool for verifying that an IP address on a network actually exists is the Packet Internet Groper (PING) utility. This utility uses the ICMP echo request and reply mechanisms. The echo request is a simple directed datagram that asks for acknowledgment that a particular IP address exists on the network. If a machine with this IP address exists and receives the request, it is designed to send an ICMP echo reply. This reply is sent back to the destination address to notify the source machine of its existence. The PING utility reports the existence of the IP address and how long it took to get there.

INTERNET GROUP MANAGEMENT PROTOCOL

Internet Group Management Protocol (IGMP) is a protocol and set of specifications that allows machines to be added and removed from IP address groups, using the class D range of addresses. IP allows the assignment of class D addresses to groups of machines so that they can receive broadcast data as one functional unit. Machines can be added and removed from these units or groups, or they can be members of multiple groups.

Note

Unicast messages are those sent to one host. Multicast messages are those sent to a number of hosts. Broadcast messages are those sent to all hosts. Understanding this distinction is helpful when discussing networking.

ADDRESS RESOLUTION PROTOCOL

Unless IP is planning to initiate a full broadcast on the network, it must have the physical address of the machine to which it is going to send datagrams. For this information, it relies on Address Resolution Protocol (ARP). ARP is responsible for mapping IP addresses on the network to physical addresses in memory. This way, whenever IP needs a physical address for a particular IP address, ARP can deliver. But ARP's memory does not last indefinitely, and occasionally IP will ask for an IP address that is not in ARP's memory. When this happens, ARP has to go out and find one.

ARP is responsible for finding a map to a local physical address for any local IP address that IP might request. If ARP does not have a map in memory, it has to go find one on the network. ARP uses local broadcasts to find physical addresses of machines and maintains a cache in memory of recently mapped IP addresses to physical addresses. Although this cache does not last indefinitely, it enables ARP to not have to broadcast every time IP needs a physical address.

As long as the destination IP address is local, ARP simply sends a local broadcast for that machine and returns the physical address to IP. IP, realizing that the destination IP address is local, simply formulates the datagram with the IP address above the physical address of the destination machine.

Protocols and Ports

The Transport layer uses port numbers to transfer data to the Application layer. These ports enable a host to support and track simultaneous sessions with other hosts on the network. There are over 65,000 definable ports, and Table 11.1 lists the most common assignments.

TABLE 11.1
Port Numbers Used by the Common Services

PORT	SERVICE	PURPOSE
20, 21	FTP	Transfers files from one host to another
23	Telnet	Connects to a host as if on a dumb terminal for administrative purposes
25	SMTP	Simple Mail Transfer Protocol
53	DNS	Domain Name System
80	WWW	The World Wide Web service
110	POP3	The Post Office Protocol (version 3) for retrieving email
119	NNTP	The Network News Transfer Protocol
139	NetBIOS	Used to translate Windows-based names to IP addresses
143	IMAP	The Internet Mail Access Protocol, which can be used in place of POP3
161	SNMP	Simple Network Management Protocol

The /etc/services file holds definitions for common ports. An ASCII file maps text names to services. The Internet Assigned Numbers Authority (IANA) assigns lower number ports, but administrators might assign higher numbers freely.

TCP/IP Host Configuration

To configure TCP/IP on a host, you must know/configure three values. The three needed values are

- IP address
- Subnet mask
- Default gateway

Note

Technically, you need to configure IP and subnet. Gateway is optional and only needed if you want to move off your subnet.

Each of these three values is examined in the following sections.

IP Address

Every host on a TCP/IP network must have a unique IP address. An IP address is made up of values from a 32-bit binary number. Because it is next to impossible to memorize 32-bit binary numbers, IP addresses are usually written in the form of four decimal number octets. The first octet identifies the "class" of address that it is, which determines the number of hosts available on the network as shown in Table 11.2.

TABLE 11.2
Available Host IP Addresses

CLASS	ADDRESS	NUMBER OF HOSTS AVAILABLE	DEFAULT SUBNET MASK
A	01–126	16,777,214	255.0.0.0
B	128–191	65,534	255.255.0.0
C	192–223	254	255.255.255.0
D	224–239	Used only for multicasting and cannot be assigned to individual hosts	
E	240–255	Reserved addresses that cannot be issued	

The first octet cannot be 127 because the address 127.0.0.1 is reserved for a loopback address to always signify the current host. Depending on the class, the second through fourth octets are used to identify the network and the host.

It is important to understand that the IP address must be unique within the realm of the network the host communicates with. If the host is connected only to three other machines, each of the three machines must have a unique value. If the host connects to the Internet, the address must be unique within the scope of the Internet.

Subnet Mask

The subnet mask, to oversimplify, tells whether the network has been sub-divided into smaller networks, or all the hosts can be found on one wire. The default value is based on the class of the network as shown in Table 11.2. If you deviate from this value, you are divvying your possible hosts from one network to multiple networks. This allows you to better isolate and find your hosts, but the trade-off is that you have fewer possible hosts available to use (a result of using up some of your binary numbers to signify the network and leaving fewer for the host). Table 11.3 illustrates this trade-off.

It is important to understand that when a subnet value is used, it limits the possible values that can be used for the IP address by taking away some of the bits (thus values) that could otherwise have been used. For example, if you have a class C address of 201.1.1, and are not subnetting, the values that can be used in the fourth field are 1–254 (made up of possible values from eight binary digits). On the other hand, if you are using a subnet of 192 (made by using two binary bits), six bits are left and you therefore have a maximum of 62 host addresses on two subnet ranges. The ranges that can be used are: 65–126 and 129–190.

Default Gateway

The default gateway is an optional field if you want to communicate beyond your subnet. It used to hold the IP address of the router. If a client connects to an ISP through a dial-up connection (such as a standalone Linux machine dialing from home), the ISP fills in the address here.

To summarize: the IP address must be unique for every host; all hosts on that subnet share the subnet value; and the default gateway is shared by every host that uses that router to get beyond the local network.

Supplying Values

The needed values for TCP/IP configuration can be entered manually each time you add a host to the network, or you can use the DHCP (Dynamic Host Configuration Protocol) service. With DHCP, you do not need to enter any values when adding new hosts to the network. A server hosting the DHCP Daemon (dhcpd) holds a range of addresses—known as a scope—and can "lease" IP addresses out to clients. The lease duration is configurable—from a short time period up to forever. As long as forever is not used, the client will regularly attempt to renew the lease it is using if possible. If the server does not hear it, the client will try again at regular intervals all the way up until the lease expires. When the lease expires, it goes back into the scope and the client must obtain another lease anew. After every expiration, when a client requests an address, it will always attempt to get the one it had last time if it is available.

TABLE 11.3
Subnet Mask Values

ADDITIONAL BITS REQUIRED	SUBNET ADDRESS	MAXIMUM NUMBER OF NETWORK	MAXIMUM NUMBER OF HOSTS—C NETWORK	MAXIMUM NUMBER OF HOSTS—B NETWORK	MAXIMUM NUMBER OF HOSTS—A NETWORK
0	0	0	254	65,534	16,777,214
2	192	2	62	16,382	4,194,302
3	224	6	30	8,190	2,097,150
4	240	14	14	4,094	1,048,574
5	248	30	6	2,046	524,286
6	252	62	2	1,022	262,142
7	254	126	invalid	510	131,070
8	255	254	invalid	254	65,534

Other TCP/IP Configuration

There are a number of configuration files and utilities to be aware of. The files to know are as follows:

- **/etc/HOSTNAME**—This file holds the name of the host and domain on a single line. If networking is not configured, the entry will read

  `noname nodomain nowhere`

  On some implementations, this is **/etc/hostname**.

- **/etc/hosts**—This ASCII file is used to list IP addresses and text names. It can convert the test (host) names to the IP addresses on the network. This file is suitable for use only on small networks as it must exist on every host in the network and must constantly be updated when each host is added to the network. On large networks, you want to avoid using the **hosts** file and use the DNS (Domain Name System) service instead.

- **/etc/sysconfig/network**—This directory holds the configuration files for the known networks the host can communicate with.

- **/etc/sysconfig/network/routes**—This file is the configuration file used to hold routing information.

The following are the utilities to know for network system administration in a pinch:

- **arp**—ARP, as a utility, can be used to see the entries in the Address Resolution table, which maps network card addresses (MAC addresses) to IP addresses (see Figure 11.1). You can check to see if the IP addresses you believe should be in the table are there and if they are mapped to the computers they should be. Usually, you do not know the MAC addresses of the hosts on your network. However, if you cannot contact a host, or if a connection is made to an unexpected host, you can check this table with the ARP command to begin isolating which host is actually assigned an IP address.

- **dig**—This utility works with DNS (discussed later in this chapter) and looks up entries on DNS name servers. The output of this utility is shown in Figure 11.2.

- **domainname**—In Novell Linux Desktop, this utility is actually just a link to **hostname**, passing it the parameters to show the domain name used by the host instead of the hostname. It can be used to set the domain name as well.

FIGURE 11.1
The arp utility IP to physical name resolution.

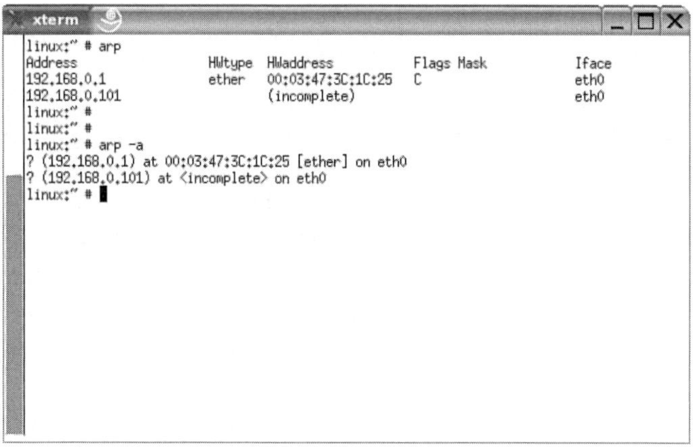

```
xterm
linux:~ # arp
Address                 HWtype  HWaddress           Flags Mask      Iface
192.168.0.1             ether   00:03:47:3C:1C:25   C               eth0
192.168.0.101                   (incomplete)                        eth0
linux:~ #
linux:~ #
linux:~ # arp -a
? (192.168.0.1) at 00:03:47:3C:1C:25 [ether] on eth0
? (192.168.0.101) at <incomplete> on eth0
linux:~ #
```

FIGURE 11.2
The dig utility displays name resolution statistics.

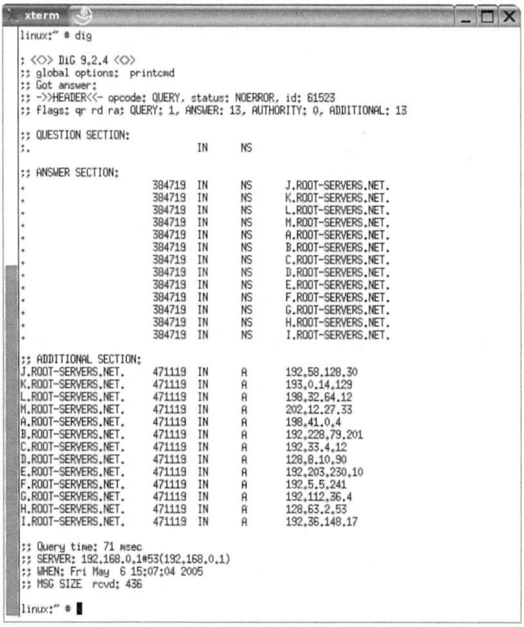

```
xterm
linux:~ # dig

; <<>> DiG 9.2.4 <<>>
;; global options:  printcmd
;; Got answer:
;; ->>HEADER<<- opcode: QUERY, status: NOERROR, id: 61523
;; flags: qr rd ra; QUERY: 1, ANSWER: 13, AUTHORITY: 0, ADDITIONAL: 13

;; QUESTION SECTION:
;.                              IN      NS

;; ANSWER SECTION:
.                       384719  IN      NS      J.ROOT-SERVERS.NET.
.                       384719  IN      NS      K.ROOT-SERVERS.NET.
.                       384719  IN      NS      L.ROOT-SERVERS.NET.
.                       384719  IN      NS      M.ROOT-SERVERS.NET.
.                       384719  IN      NS      A.ROOT-SERVERS.NET.
.                       384719  IN      NS      B.ROOT-SERVERS.NET.
.                       384719  IN      NS      C.ROOT-SERVERS.NET.
.                       384719  IN      NS      D.ROOT-SERVERS.NET.
.                       384719  IN      NS      E.ROOT-SERVERS.NET.
.                       384719  IN      NS      F.ROOT-SERVERS.NET.
.                       384719  IN      NS      G.ROOT-SERVERS.NET.
.                       384719  IN      NS      H.ROOT-SERVERS.NET.
.                       384719  IN      NS      I.ROOT-SERVERS.NET.

;; ADDITIONAL SECTION:
J.ROOT-SERVERS.NET.     471119  IN      A       192.58.128.30
K.ROOT-SERVERS.NET.     471119  IN      A       193.0.14.129
L.ROOT-SERVERS.NET.     471119  IN      A       198.32.64.12
M.ROOT-SERVERS.NET.     471119  IN      A       202.12.27.33
A.ROOT-SERVERS.NET.     471119  IN      A       198.41.0.4
B.ROOT-SERVERS.NET.     471119  IN      A       192.228.79.201
C.ROOT-SERVERS.NET.     471119  IN      A       192.33.4.12
D.ROOT-SERVERS.NET.     471119  IN      A       128.8.10.90
E.ROOT-SERVERS.NET.     471119  IN      A       192.203.230.10
F.ROOT-SERVERS.NET.     471119  IN      A       192.5.5.241
G.ROOT-SERVERS.NET.     471119  IN      A       192.112.36.4
H.ROOT-SERVERS.NET.     471119  IN      A       128.63.2.53
I.ROOT-SERVERS.NET.     471119  IN      A       192.36.148.17

;; Query time: 71 msec
;; SERVER: 192.168.0.1#53(192.168.0.1)
;; WHEN: Fri May  6 15:07:04 2005
;; MSG SIZE  rcvd: 436

linux:~ #
```

- ethereal—This utility is not installed by default, but can be added to the system. Once added, it offers a graphical interface with which you can monitor network traffic. This same functionality is inherently available at the command line using the **tcpdump** utility.

Tip

As an analogy, what Apache is to web servers, Ethereal is becoming to network monitoring. An excellent packet sniffer and decoder, it is the subject of a number of texts. You should visit the Ethereal home page (http://www.ethereal.com) to download the latest version and peruse the most current documentation.

- ftp—The File Transfer utility, operating on the File Transfer Protocol, is used to send files back and forth between a local and remote host.

- hostname—This simple utility shows the name of the host. It can also be used with a number of parameters, as shown in Figure 11.3.

FIGURE 11.3
The hostname utility can be used to see or set the hostname.

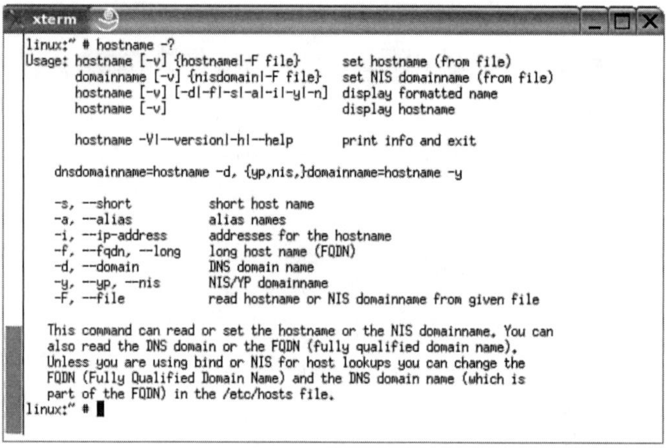

```
linux:" # hostname -?
Usage: hostname [-v] {hostname|-F file}        set hostname (from file)
       domainname [-v] {nisdomain|-F file}      set NIS domainname (from file)
       hostname [-v] [-d|-f|-s|-a|-i|-y|-n]    display formatted name
       hostname [-v]                            display hostname

       hostname -V|--version|-h|--help          print info and exit

       dnsdomainname=hostname -d, {yp,nis,}domainname=hostname -y

       -s, --short        short host name
       -a, --alias        alias names
       -i, --ip-address   addresses for the hostname
       -f, --fqdn, --long long host name (FQDN)
       -d, --domain       DNS domain name
       -y, --yp, --nis    NIS/YP domainname
       -F, --file         read hostname or NIS domainname from given file

       This command can read or set the hostname or the NIS domainname. You can
       also read the DNS domain or the FQDN (fully qualified domain name).
       Unless you are using bind or NIS for host lookups you can change the
       FQDN (Fully Qualified Domain Name) and the DNS domain name (which is
       part of the FQDN) in the /etc/hosts file.
linux:" #
```

- ifconfig—This utility is used to configure the TCP/IP parameters on the command line. The syntax is: **ifconfig interface options**. Thus, to configure the IP address of **201.13.12.65** for the first Ethernet card, the command would be **ifconfig eth0 201.13.12.65**, and this would use the default subnet mask. To do the same configuration with a subnet mask of 192, the command becomes `ifconfig eth0 201.13.12.65 netmask 255.255.255.192`. To simply see the current configuration, enter the name of the utility without any parameters, as shown in Figure 11.4.

FIGURE 11.4
The `ifconfig` utility displays IP configuration information.

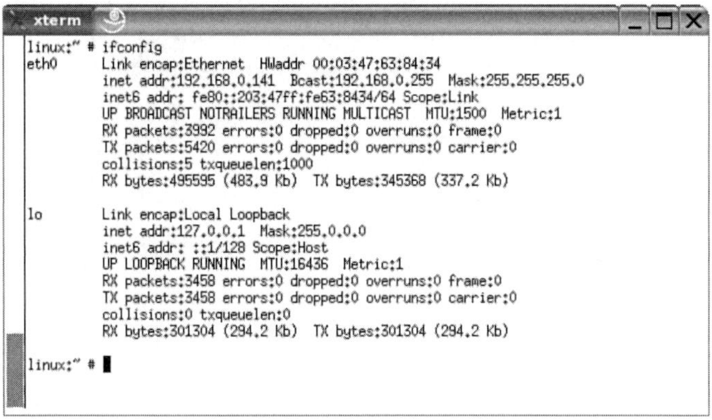

```
xterm
linux:~ # ifconfig
eth0      Link encap:Ethernet  HWaddr 00:03:47:63:84:34
          inet addr:192.168.0.141  Bcast:192.168.0.255  Mask:255.255.255.0
          inet6 addr: fe80::203:47ff:fe63:8434/64 Scope:Link
          UP BROADCAST NOTRAILERS RUNNING MULTICAST  MTU:1500  Metric:1
          RX packets:3992 errors:0 dropped:0 overruns:0 frame:0
          TX packets:5420 errors:0 dropped:0 overruns:0 carrier:0
          collisions:5 txqueuelen:1000
          RX bytes:495595 (483.9 Kb)  TX bytes:345368 (337.2 Kb)

lo        Link encap:Local Loopback
          inet addr:127.0.0.1  Mask:255.0.0.0
          inet6 addr: ::1/128 Scope:Host
          UP LOOPBACK RUNNING  MTU:16436  Metric:1
          RX packets:3458 errors:0 dropped:0 overruns:0 frame:0
          TX packets:3458 errors:0 dropped:0 overruns:0 carrier:0
          collisions:0 txqueuelen:0
          RX bytes:301304 (294.2 Kb)  TX bytes:301304 (294.2 Kb)

linux:~ # 
```

- **ifup** and **ifdown**—These two utilities are used to start or stop a precon-figured network interface. To see the status (either started or stopped), you can use the **ifstatus** command. Figure 11.5 shows the commands available with this utility.

FIGURE 11.5
A number of options are available for use with the `ifstatus` utility.

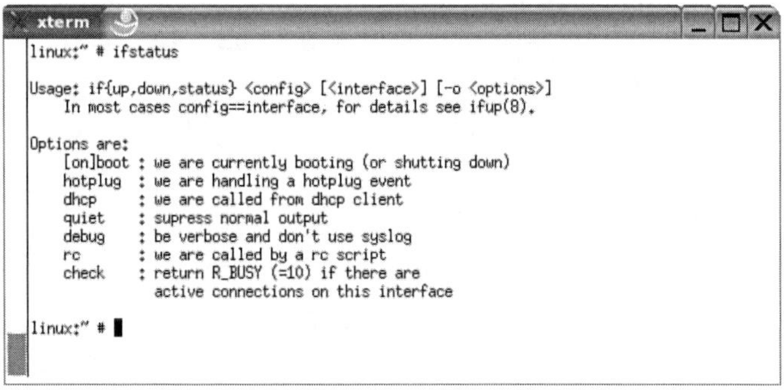

```
xterm
linux:~ # ifstatus

Usage: if{up,down,status} <config> [<interface>] [-o <options>]
    In most cases config==interface, for details see ifup(8).

Options are:
    [on]boot : we are currently booting (or shutting down)
    hotplug  : we are handling a hotplug event
    dhcp     : we are called from dhcp client
    quiet    : supress normal output
    debug    : be verbose and don't use syslog
    rc       : we are called by a rc script
    check    : return R_BUSY (=10) if there are
               active connections on this interface

linux:~ # 
```

- netcat—This utility can be used to establish a connection between two hosts. You can use the -h option to see a list of all available parameters. The most basic operation, however, is to open a port on one host with a command such as netcat -1 -p 16000, which puts port 16000 in listen mode. Following this, you establish a connection with that host on another by using the command netcat {hostname to connect to} 16000. The connection will stay established until you press Ctrl+C.

- netstat—This command shows the statistics of the TCP and UDP protocols. Executing netstat without switches displays protocol statistics and current TCP/IP connections. When you have determined that your base level communications are working, you will need to verify the services on your system. This involves looking at the services that are listening for incoming traffic and/or verifying that you are creating a session with a remote station. The netstat command will allow you to do this. Figure 11.6 shows part of the display from this utility.

FIGURE 11.6
The netstat utility displays information on network connectivity.

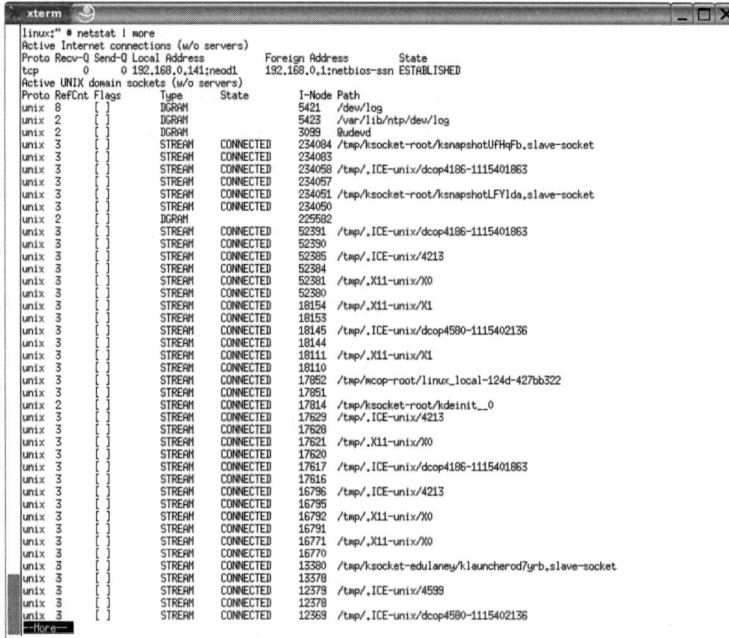

NOTE

To see the options available for netstat, as you do with most other utilities, use the -? option.

- **ping**—This utility will send echo messages to a host to see if it is reachable. If it is, the ICMP protocol on the remote host will echo the response. If it is not reachable, the resulting error message will indicate that.

- **route**—This utility is used to see and configure routing. If you give the route command with no parameters, it displays the current routing table. Figure 11.7 shows a sample output from this command on Novell Linux Desktop as well as a list of the options that it works with.

FIGURE 11.7
The display from the route utility shows the routing table.

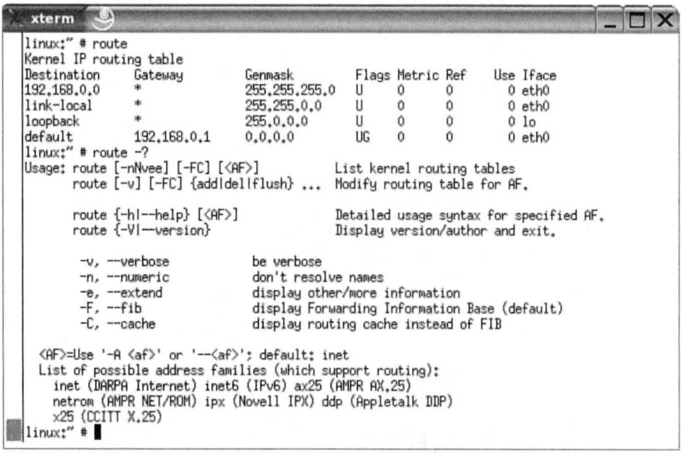

```
linux:~ # route
Kernel IP routing table
Destination     Gateway         Genmask         Flags Metric Ref    Use Iface
192.168.0.0     *               255.255.255.0   U     0      0        0 eth0
link-local      *               255.255.0.0     U     0      0        0 eth0
loopback        *               255.0.0.0       U     0      0        0 lo
default         192.168.0.1     0.0.0.0         UG    0      0        0 eth0
linux:~ # route -?
Usage: route [-nNvee] [-FC] [<AF>]           List kernel routing tables
       route [-v] [-FC] {add|del|flush} ...  Modify routing table for AF.

       route {-h|--help} [<AF>]              Detailed usage syntax for specified AF.
       route {-V|--version}                  Display version/author and exit.

       -v, --verbose       be verbose
       -n, --numeric       don't resolve names
       -e, --extend        display other/more information
       -F, --fib           display Forwarding Information Base (default)
       -C, --cache         display routing cache instead of FIB

  <AF>=Use '-A <af>' or '--<af>'; default: inet
  List of possible address families (which support routing):
    inet (DARPA Internet) inet6 (IPv6) ax25 (AMPR AX.25)
    netrom (AMPR NET/ROM) ipx (Novell IPX) ddp (Appletalk DDP)
    x25 (CCITT X.25)
linux:~ #
```

- **tcpdump**—This command-line utility allows you to monitor network traffic and analyze packets flowing through an interface in promiscuous mode. The -i option is used to specify an interface. The command tcpdump -i eth0, for example, turns on promiscuous mode for the first Ethernet interface and immediately begins displaying data to the terminal until you break out of it. The -c option can be used to specify that you only want to listen to a certain number of packets. tcpdump -i eth0 -c

32, for example, will display the output for the next 32 packets and then exit. At the end of the display, it will report how many packets were captured, how many were received by filter, and how many were dropped by the kernel, as illustrated in Figure 11.8.

FIGURE 11.8
The `tcpdump` utility shows how many packets were captured, received, and dropped.

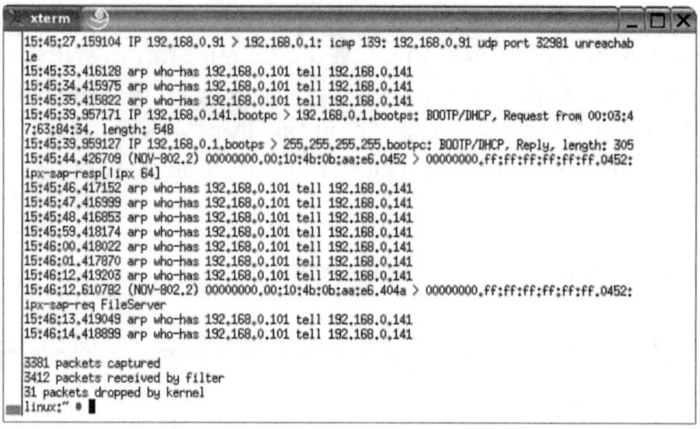

- `telnet`—Allows you to establish a connection with a remote host. This is often used for administrative purposes.

- `traceroute`—This is a much-enhanced version of the `ping` utility and is used in place of it. Not only will it show that the remote host is reachable, but also it shows the path that was taken to reach the host. Figure 11.9 shows the route a client takes to reach the pearson.com server.

Configuring Routes

Three types of routes exist to help IP packets make their way to their final destination:

- Host routes
- Network/gateway routes
- Default routes

The purpose behind any route is to point the way for the data to find its target, and the tool to use with routes is simply the **route** utility. To add a route, use the **route add** command. To delete a route, use the **route del** command.

FIGURE 11.9
The traceroute utility shows how hops must be made to reach a server.

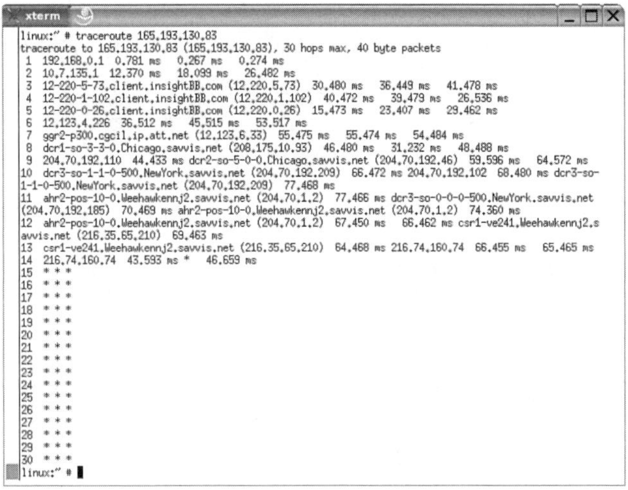

```
xterm
linux:" # traceroute 165,193,130,83
traceroute to 165,193,130,83 (165,193,130,83), 30 hops max, 40 byte packets
 1  192,168,0,1  0,781 ms   0,267 ms   0,274 ms
 2  10,7,135,1  12,370 ms   18,099 ms   26,482 ms
 3  12-220-5-73,client,insightBB,com (12,220,5,73)  30,480 ms   36,449 ms   41,478 ms
 4  12-220-1-102,client,insightBB,com (12,220,1,102)  40,472 ms   39,479 ms   26,536 ms
 5  12-220-0-26,client,insightBB,com (12,220,0,26)  15,473 ms   23,407 ms   29,462 ms
 6  12,123,4,226  36,512 ms   45,515 ms   53,517 ms
 7  ggr2-p300,cgcil,ip,att,net (12,123,6,33)  55,475 ms   55,474 ms   54,484 ms
 8  dcr1-so-3-3-0,Chicago,savvis,net (208,175,10,93)  46,480 ms   31,232 ms   48,488 ms
 9  204,70,192,110  44,433 ms dcr2-so-5-0-0,Chicago,savvis,net (204,70,192,46)  59,596 ms   64,572 ms
10  dcr3-so-1-1-0-500,NewYork,savvis,net (204,70,192,209)  66,472 ms 204,70,192,102  68,480 ms dcr3-so-
1-1-0-500,NewYork,savvis,net (204,70,192,209)  77,468 ms
11  ahr2-pos-10-0,Weehawkennj2,savvis,net (204,70,1,2)  77,466 ms dcr3-so-0-0-0-500,NewYork,savvis,net
(204,70,192,185)  70,469 ms ahr2-pos-10-0,Weehawkennj2,savvis,net (204,70,1,2)  74,360 ms
12  ahr2-pos-10-0,Weehawkennj2,savvis,net (204,70,1,2)  67,450 ms   66,462 ms csr1-ve241,Weehawkennj2,s
avvis,net (216,35,65,210)  69,463 ms
13  csr1-ve241,Weehawkennj2,savvis,net (216,35,65,210)  64,468 ms 216,74,160,74  66,455 ms   65,465 ms
14  216,74,160,74  43,593 ms *   46,659 ms
15  * * *
16  * * *
17  * * *
18  * * *
19  * * *
20  * * *
21  * * *
22  * * *
23  * * *
24  * * *
25  * * *
26  * * *
27  * * *
28  * * *
29  * * *
30  * * *
linux:" #
```

Configuring Networking Services

Within Linux, there is a superdaemon known as **init**, which is responsible for bringing up the services required at specific runlevels and maintaining the integrity of the system. The **init** daemon will start and stop other daemons such as the system logger (**syslogd**), the swapper (**kswapd**), and so on. One of the daemons it starts is a superdaemon over networking services: **xinetd** (also known as the extended Internet Services Daemon).

The **xinetd** daemon is a replacement for **inetd** that offers a vast improvement in security. The configuration options are now modularized. As an administrator, you should know that this daemon is a replacement for **inetd** and can be downloaded from a number of sites and used in place of the original.

Note

As a general rule, any process with a last character of "d" is a daemon.

When started, the **xinetd** looks at its configuration file, **/etc/xinetd.conf**, and determines from it what additional services it is responsible for; **xinetd.conf** provides the settings as well as the includes for the files in the **/etc/xinetd.d** directory—where the service files actually live. By default, this file exists on every host whether it is used or not: If it is not used, most of the lines are commented out.

This file has the capability to call settings from other files and need not be self-contained. If you change any of the settings in this file, you must restart the xinetd before the changes will be recognized. There are a number of ways to do this—including rebooting the system, starting and stopping networking, and so on. The simplest way of doing so, however, is to kill the xinetd daemon with

/etc/rc.d/xinetd restart

or

/etc/rc.d/xinetd reload

Then the daemon will restart—rereading the configuration file when it does.

Note

More information on the daemon can be found at http://www.xinetd.org/. The HowTo can be found at http://www.debianhowto.de/howtos/en/xinetd/c_xinetd.html.

The /etc/services File

This file was mentioned earlier in this chapter, but its real usefulness is that it is checked to determine what port a particular service is to use. This ASCII file exists on every host by default, and divides the entries into three fields:

- Service—Whatever name also appears in the /etc/xinetd.conf file.

Tip

Information about services that require starting/stopping is actually in separate files beneath the /etc/xinetd.d directory.

- Port—What port to use.
- Alias(es)—These are optional and constitute other names the service is known as.

It is important to know that the ports appearing by default in the file are *common port* assignments for those services. An administrator can change the port a service is using for security, or other purposes. This still allows the service to run, but now requires the user using it to know of—and specify—the new port.

One of the best examples of this is the www service, which runs on port **80** by default. If you make a website available to the world, using the Fully Qualified Domain Name (FQDN) of www.ds-technical.com, anyone in the world can enter that address and reach your site by making a call to port **80**. On the other hand, if you want the site to be up, and accessible from anywhere, yet only used by your employees in the outback, you can move the www service to one not being used by anything else—**15000**, for example. Now, anyone entering www.ds-technincal.com will still be hitting port **80** and unable to find the www service there. Your employees will use www.ds-technincal.com:15000 and be able to operate as they would at a regular website.

Network Access

You can limit access to your network host to explicitly named machines via the use of either a `hosts.allow` file or a `hosts.deny` file,: both of which reside in the `/etc` directory. The syntax within these files is the same:

```
daemon: group
```

and they either limit who is allowed in (to those specifically named in the `.allow` file) or limit who cannot come in (to those specifically named in the `.deny` file). The use of such variables as **ALL** to indicate all services or **ALL EXCEPT** to indicate all but a particular service are allowed in both files.

By default, both files exist on a host, though their lines are commented out. To recap,

- `hosts.allow` is used to specifically list the names of other hosts that can access this machine through any of the `/usr/sbin/tcpd` services. Figure 11.10 shows the default copy of this file.

- `hosts.deny` is used to specifically list the names of other hosts that cannot access this machine through the `/usr/sbin/tcpd` services.

Working with NFS, smb, and nmb

These topics address sharing. The three subcomponents of this section have only a passing familiarity with each other, but all fall within the broad category of file/directory sharing.

FIGURE 11.10
The `hosts.allow` file can be used to limit access from other hosts.

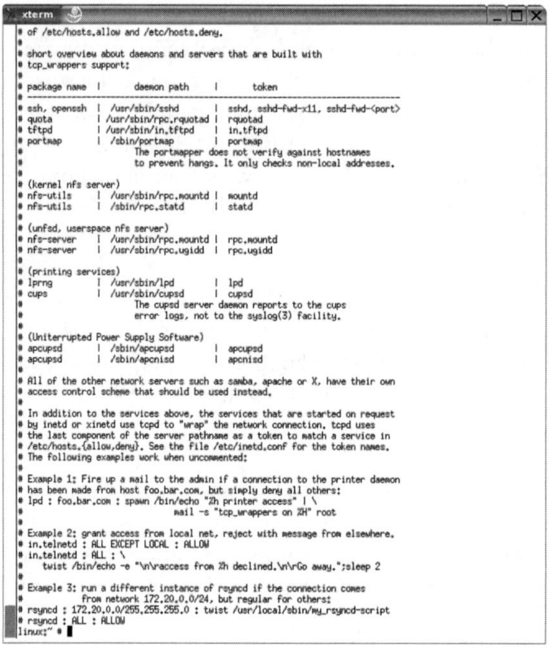

```
# of /etc/hosts.allow and /etc/hosts.deny.
#
# short overview about daemons and servers that are built with
# tcp_wrappers support:
#
# package name |       daemon path      |       token
# ----------------------------------------------------------------------
# ssh, openssh |  /usr/sbin/sshd        |  sshd, sshd-fwd-x11, sshd-fwd-<port>
# quota        | /usr/sbin/rpc.rquotad |  rquotad
# tftpd        | /usr/sbin/in.tftpd    |  in.tftpd
# portmap      |  /sbin/portmap         |  portmap
#                       The portmapper does not verify against hostnames
#                       to prevent hangs. It only checks non-local addresses.
#
# (kernel nfs server)
# nfs-utils    |  /usr/sbin/rpc.mountd |  mountd
# nfs-utils    |  /sbin/rpc.statd      |  statd
#
# (unfsd, userspace nfs server)
# nfs-server   |  /usr/sbin/rpc.mountd |  rpc.mountd
# nfs-server   |  /usr/sbin/rpc.ugidd  |  rpc.ugidd
#
# (printing services)
# lprng        |  /usr/sbin/lpd        |  lpd
# cups         |  /usr/sbin/cupsd      |  cupsd
#                       The cupsd server daemon reports to the cups
#                       error logs, not to the syslog(3) facility.
#
# (Uniterrupted Power Supply Software)
# apcupsd      |  /sbin/apcupsd        |  apcupsd
# apcupsd      |  /sbin/apcnisd        |  apcnisd
#
# All of the other network servers such as samba, apache or X, have their own
# access control scheme that should be used instead.
#
# In addition to the services above, the services that are started on request
# by inetd or xinetd use tcpd to "wrap" the network connection. tcpd uses
# the last component of the server pathname as a token to match a service in
# /etc/hosts.{allow,deny}. See the file /etc/inetd.conf for the token names.
# The following examples work when uncommented:
#
# Example 1: Fire up a mail to the admin if a connection to the printer daemon
# has been made from host foo.bar.com, but simply deny all others:
# lpd : foo.bar.com : spawn /bin/echo "%h printer access" | \
#                                mail -s "tcp_wrappers on %H" root
#
# Example 2: grant access from local net, reject with message from elsewhere.
# in.telnetd : ALL EXCEPT LOCAL : ALLOW
# in.telnetd : ALL : \
#    twist /bin/echo -e "\n\raccess from %h declined.\n\rGo away.";sleep 2
#
# Example 3: run a different instance of rsyncd if the connection comes
#              from network 172.20.0.0/24, but regular for others:
# rsyncd : 172.20.0.0/255.255.255.0 : twist /usr/local/sbin/my_rsyncd-script
# rsyncd : ALL : ALLOW
linux:~ #
```

NFS

NFS is the Network File System and the way in which partitions are mounted and shared across a Linux network. NFS falls into the category of being a Remote Procedure Call (RPC) service. NFS uses three daemons— `nfsd`, `portmap`, and `rpc.mountd`—and loads partitions configured in the `/etc/exports` file. This file exists on every host, by default, but is empty. Within this file, you must specify the directories to be exported and the rights to it.

Tip

The default copy of this file supplied with the system contains nothing but comments that point you to the correct man page to find the syntax used within this file.

The NFS server can be started with the `/etc/init.d/nfsserver start` command, and the daemons `rpc.nfsd` and `rpc.mountd` are spawned. `rpc.nfsd` is the service daemon, whereas `rpc.mountd` acts as the `mount` daemon.

Problems with NFS generally fall into two categories: errors in the `/etc/exports` listings (fixed by editing and correcting them) or problems with the daemons. The most common problem with the daemons involves their not starting in the correct order. The `portmap` daemon must begin first, and is the only daemon needed on a host that accesses shares but does not offer any.

Note

Shares can only be mounted through /etc/fstab or manually using the `mount` command.

NIS

The Network Information Service (NIS) acts as a giant phone book, or Yellow Pages, to resources distributed across the network. NIS acts so much like a directory, in fact, that most of the files and utilities begin with the letter `yp` as a carryover from when it was known as that. The three components of NIS are

- Master server—There must be at least one running the `ypserv` program and holding the configuration files.

- Slave servers—These are optional and not used in small networks. When used, they act as intermediaries on behalf of the master server in processing requests.

- Clients—These run the `ypbind` program and retrieve data from the server.

An NIS network is organized into domains with the `/etc/defaultdomain` file defining the domain and `/etc/yp.conf` holding the server address. Common resources mapped with NIS include user information (`/etc/passwd`), group information (`/etc/group`), and services (`/etc/services`), though you can add many more.

The number of utilities to know to work with NIS are

- `ypdomainname`—Shows the name of the NIS domain
- `ypmatch`—Queries the key field of a map and shows the results
- `yppasswd`—Changes the user password on the NIS server
- `yppoll`—Shows the ID number of the NIS map
- `ypwhich`—Shows the NIS server the client uses

SMB

SMB stands for Server Message Block and is the protocol used for sharing resources on a Microsoft Windows-based network (Windows 95, Windows 98, Windows NT, Windows 2000, and so on). The resources shared can be directories, printers, or other devices. In order for Linux to access shared resources on a Windows-based network (we will use NT as an example), it is necessary to have Linux communicating via the same SMB protocol.

Unfortunately, the SMB protocol was not always native with many implementations of Linux, though it could almost always be added. Samba is a free program that can be found at www.samba.org (from which you must first choose your country). Almost every major Linux distribution today—including Novell Linux Desktop—includes Samba and supports SMB. Figure 11.11 shows the protocol stack when SMB is used.

FIGURE 11.11
SMB runs in the Application/Service layer.

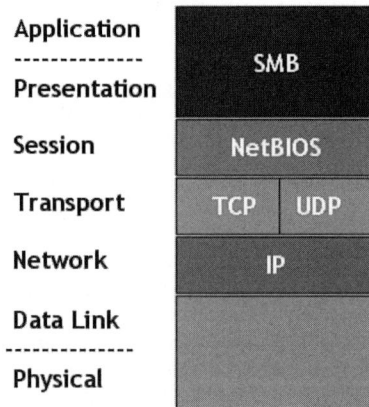

Samba makes the Linux host an SMB-client using values found in the /etc/samba/smb.conf file. When the Linux host is installed and configured, the Linux host (providing permissions are adequate) can access any shared SMB resources on the NT network: directory, printer, and so on.

Note

Though the concept is the same, when you configure the shares, you must configure them separately. Printer shares are configured by setting up a path to the resource, whereas directory shares are configured using *settings*.

When the objects can be reached, they are mounted to make them accessible, and you use them as if they resided locally.

SMB support is native to NLD, and you can access shared resources through NLD without needing to do anything further. Figure 11.12 shows the Windows Network appearing within the network browsing feature. Clicking on this brings up SMB and any Windows-based networks become visible, as shown in Figure 11.13.

FIGURE 11.12
The services installed by default allow you to see Windows-based networks.

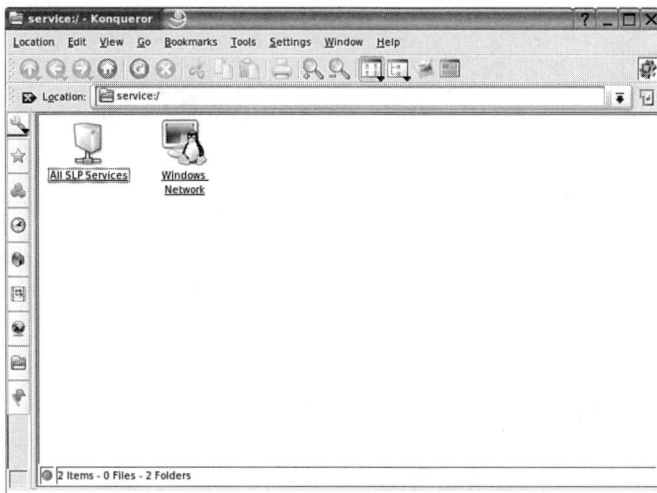

Consult www.samba.org for any information on configuration or troubleshooting of this service.

NMB

In the Windows-based world, NetBIOS names are often used to identify computers. Although using SMB enables Linux computers to share files, communicating with those resources if NetBIOS names are used is not possible without something to resolve the names. That is where NMB comes into play. The NetBIOS Message Block enables Linux to identify the resources on Windows-based networks by the names that they are known as on those resources.

Samba includes both the **smbd** daemon and **nmbd** daemon to enable resources to be referenced and accessed. Users on the Windows systems will be able to click on their Network Neighborhood icon and see the resources there that exist on Linux machines as if they were on fellow Windows-based systems.

FIGURE 11.13
Choosing a Windows-based network automatically brings up the SMB service.

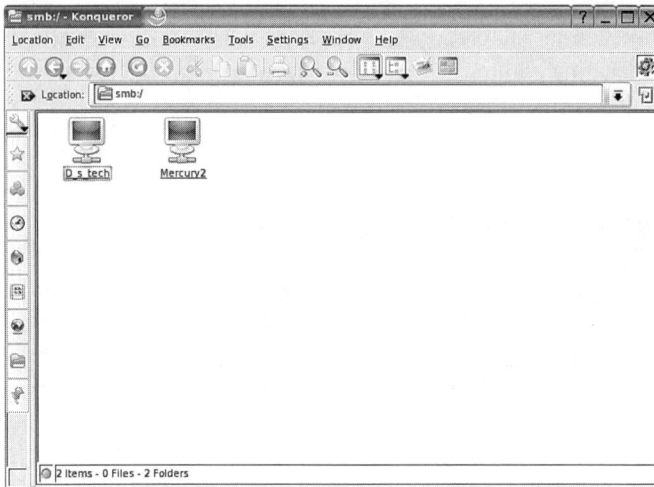

The `smb.conf` file is used for configuration of all Samba parameters including those for the NMB daemon. Figure 11.14 shows a default copy of this file.

Working with the IP Tool

NLD includes the `ip` utility to let you see and change the current network configuration. Though the options offered are many, the choices are very simplistic.

To see the current configuration, the command `ip address show` is used. The output of the `ifconfig` command is identical to the output `ip address show` will display.

Substituting "add" for "show," you can add to the settings, and using "del" allows you to delete existing settings.

The command `ip link show` will show the hardware address of every Ethernet device, and to work with the routing table, use the following commands:

- `ip route show` to see the current routing table
- `ip route add` to add a route
- `ip route add default` to add a default route
- `ip route delete` to delete a route

FIGURE 11.14

The smb.conf file is used to configure Samba parameters.

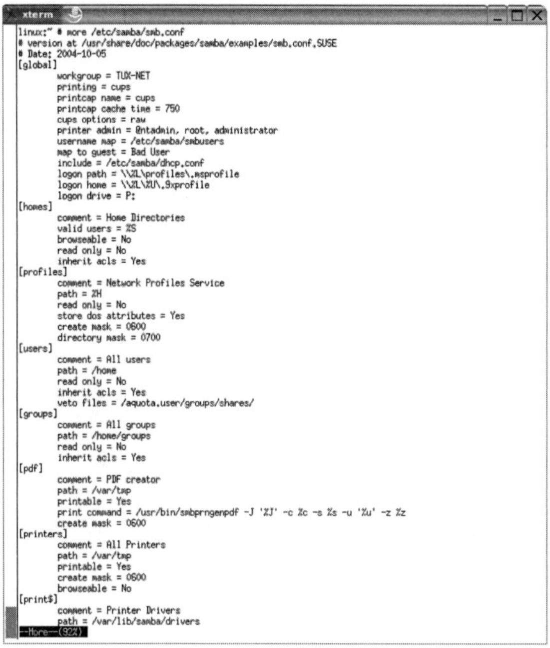

```
xterm
linux:~ # more /etc/samba/smb.conf
# version at /usr/share/doc/packages/samba/examples/smb.conf.SUSE
# Date: 2004-10-05
[global]
        workgroup = TUX-NET
        printing = cups
        printcap name = cups
        printcap cache time = 750
        cups options = raw
        printer admin = @ntadmin, root, administrator
        username map = /etc/samba/smbusers
        map to guest = Bad User
        include = /etc/samba/dhcp.conf
        logon path = \\%L\profiles\.msprofile
        logon home = \\%L\%U\.9xprofile
        logon drive = P:
[homes]
        comment = Home Directories
        valid users = %S
        browseable = No
        read only = No
        inherit acls = Yes
[profiles]
        comment = Network Profiles Service
        path = %H
        read only = No
        store dos attributes = Yes
        create mask = 0600
        directory mask = 0700
[users]
        comment = All users
        path = /home
        read only = No
        inherit acls = Yes
        veto files = /aquota.user/groups/shares/
[groups]
        comment = All groups
        path = /home/groups
        read only = No
        inherit acls = Yes
[pdf]
        comment = PDF creator
        path = /var/tmp
        printable = Yes
        print command = /usr/bin/smbprngenpdf -J '%J' -c %c -s %s -u '%u' -z %z
        create mask = 0600
[printers]
        comment = All Printers
        path = /var/tmp
        printable = Yes
        create mask = 0600
        browseable = No
[print$]
        comment = Printer Drivers
        path = /var/lib/samba/drivers
--More--(92%)
```

Note

Tunnel interfaces take the form sit*x*, where *x* is a number (sit is short for Simple Internet Transition). sit0 is used as a generic route between IPv4 and IPv6.

Summary

This chapter focused on the fundamentals of networking, and in particular TCP/IP. After providing background information on the protocol suite, the chapter examined the process of configuring the suite. This chapter also looked at a number of network services that are available for Linux.

## CHAPTER 12

Security

This chapter discusses security and issues related to it. The Novell Linux Desktop is an extremely secure operating system, when administered appropriately, and can easily meet the needs of even the most stringent computing environment.

Applying Common Sense

Common sense is always the guiding factor when applying security to a system, to a network, or to the Internet. If you apply no security whatsoever, you run the risk of someone accessing your data who otherwise should not. What they do with the data after accessing it is anyone's guess: They can use it to underbid you or steal trade secrets, they can mischievously delete it, or they can alter it in a myriad of ways.

On the other hand, if you apply too much security to a system, you make it too difficult to use. For example, to prevent anyone from seeing the files on a system, simply unplug the system and then smash the hard drive with a hammer. Although no one would disagree that it is overkill, it accomplishes the purpose.

Somewhere between no security and total security resides a level of comfort that you must find and apply. That level depends on such factors as the value of the data you are securing, the type of access (local, remote, dial-in) that users use, and so on. That level of comfort can always be changing, as well being as acted on by extraneous factors. For example, if you've just heard that another division in your company is having trouble with break-ins, you will want to increase your security, and so on.

Under all conditions, some commonsense rules should be applied:

- Remember that the entire environment is only as secure as its weakest component. For example, if you make NLD as secure as possible, yet store the user data files on a server that is not secure, you are not running a secure environment at all.

- Secure the physical environment. If host machines are providing services and are not used by users sitting in front of them, there is no reason why those machines need to be sitting in the middle of the office. Move those machines to secured wiring closets and reduce the risk of someone simply sitting down in front of them and accessing data.

- Pay attention to ambient factors. Data does not just get corrupted by users—it can get corrupted by system failures as well. To reduce system failures—and hence potential data corruption—pay attention to such items as proper electrical feeds (use an uninterruptible power supply— UPS), and don't run wiring over objects that can cause electromagnetic interference (EMI), such as fluorescent lighting or electrical motors. Pay attention to moisture conditions, and so on.

- Before you install any software, verify that the software is clean. This can prevent you from adding rogue processes to a good machine. There are a number of ways in which you can attempt to do this: Verify the check-sum to make certain that no corruption occurred during downloading (and download only from trusted sites), list the contents of a package and verify it against what should be there, and so on. The best method, however, is to install the software on a standalone machine and verify that it works as it should before installing it on a production machine.

TIP

Building applications from source code is also a good way of verifying their integrity.

- Require all users to use passwords and create a suitable password policy. Make sure that those passwords are not just single characters (6–8 characters is a good minimum), and implement regular expirations. Remember that passwords are changed with the `passwd` command, and you can disable accounts by adding characters to the user's entry in the `/etc/passwd` file.

- Use shadow entries for passwords. This applies to both users and groups. Shadowing merely moves the passwords from files that can be accessed by all users into files that can only be accessed by the root user and adds additional security. Novell Linux Desktop, by default, uses shadowing, but it can always be reversed.

- Routinely check the log files and make certain that only logins and logouts (which can be seen with `last`) are not suddenly showing odd times. If users start accessing the system at 3:00 in the morning when they have never done so before, be certain to follow up and verify that it is indeed that user who is accessing the system and not someone else. While on the subject, routinely check all log files—they are there for a purpose, and they can alert you early on to situations you need to catch before they become uncontrollable.

- Disable *any* accounts that need not be in current use. This is true for both user and group accounts and provides one less door by which entry can be gained.

- Assign authentication to dial-in access. PPP is the most commonly used dial-in protocol on TCP/IP. It allows for authentication using PAP—the Password Authentication Protocol—which does not encrypt passwords and allows plain text to be sent—leaving the door open for anyone snooping to intercept. Thankfully, it also has the capability to authenticate with CHAP—Challenge Handshake Authentication Protocol—which encrypts the passwords and makes them much less valuable if intercepted.

- Use TCP wrappers to reduce the traffic that you are allowing to come in across the network: Novell Linux Desktop uses TCP wrappers by default via `xinetd`. A wrapper (which works with the `/etc/hosts.deny` and `/etc/hosts.allow` files) is a rule determining who can come in. Using a wrapper, you can reduce the allowed hosts to only those that are local or only rule out unknown hosts, or any other combination needed to meet your needs.

- Regularly run a check to see which files have permissions involving SGID or SUID. There should be an indisputable reason for their existence, or they should not exist at all. If a user cannot run a process as himself, what level of comfort do you have giving him higher-level permissions to run jobs? What if the process should crash and he is left as that user?

- Verify correct usage of sudo through the configuration of the `/etc/sudoers` file. This provides a secure way of granting higher-level privileges to users.

- Related to the preceding one—always use the minimal user and group ownership for any file or daemon that runs with SUID or SGID permissions, respectively. If a daemon can function properly without being owned by root, that ownership change should be made.

- Use the secure shell (`ssh`) in place of `telnet` for remote logins. `telnet` (port 23) uses plain text passwords, whereas `ssh` (port 22) uses encryption and provides more security. `ssh`, although not included with some releases, is included with Novell Linux Desktop.

- Use an appropriate `umask` value to make default permissions for newly created files and directories as minimal as possible.

The majority of these rules are discussed in the previous chapters or constitute common sense. Always think through both the possibilities and the ramifications when considering adding security to a host or a network.

Working with `iptables`

Although it's somewhat of a generalization, it can be said that `ipfwadm` goes with the Linux kernel 2.0.x and previous, and `ipchains` replaced it in 2.2.x. Although `ipchains` is still available—and still in use in many locations—`iptables` basically superseded it as of 2.4.x.

`iptables` is a generic implementation of packet filtering that can function in both stateful and stateless modes. More information on `iptables` can be found in the tutorial at http://iptables-tutorial.frozentux.net/.

Host Security

The best way to secure a host is to know everything you can about it. When you set up a host to provide web services, its purpose is to deliver web content and pages to users. That host has no business providing DHCP addresses to clients—or even the ability to do so—in this situation.

The `/etc/xinetd.conf` file holds a list of the default services that are started on a host when networking is started. (Real service settings are in the files in the `/etc/xinet.d` directory.) Carefully audit the services that will start and verify that they will not jeopardize the system or the network by opening a door by which unwelcome guests can enter your site. Audit, as well, the log files created by the `syslogd` to see what services are starting, and if they are encountering any problems forcing them to die off, restart, and so on.

You should, as an administrator, regularly keep track of security-related developments and problems as they occur in the world and respond to them accordingly. For example, if your entire network is made up of the XYZ implementation of Linux and it is suddenly reported that versions of XYZ have a bug that provides an open door for anyone typing "wizard" at a login prompt, you had best know about the situation and formulate a plan of response quickly.

You can keep on top of security issues by monitoring your vendor's site as well as those of CERT (originally an acronym for Computer Emergency Response Team) at www.cert.org. Now a division of Carnegie Mellon Software Engineering Institute, CERT had 3,734 reported incidents in 1998. In 1999, that number almost tripled to 9,859. For 2003 (the last reporting period for which cert will issue incident numbers), that number escalated to more than 137,000.

As the number of incidents reported has grown, so too has the number of vulnerabilities and related statistics. If you suspect a problem on your own network and need to contact CERT, you can do so via email at cert@cert.org or through regular mail at

CERT Coordination Center
Software Engineering Institute
Carnegie Mellon University
Pittsburgh, PA 15213-3890

It is also highly recommended that you subscribe to the BUGTRAQ mailing list, which can be done by sending an email to listserv@securityfocus.com with a blank subject and in the body indicate "SUBSCRIBE BUGTRAQ."

When security problems are found, the most common solution is an update of the affected binaries. These are almost always available at the vendor's site, and you will want to obtain and install them immediately. The only way to deal with a threat is to eliminate it as expeditiously as possible.

Note

Whenever you make any changes to the system, you should always fully document what you have done in a method that you can readily refer back to should unforeseen problems occur later. You should also do complete backups before making any major changes.

User-Level Security

If you give a user root-level permissions to the whole network, the scope of the damage he can cause is equal to that of the whole network. If you give the user very limited permissions to only one machine, the amount of potential damage he can cause is severely limited. Although this objective repeats everything else that has been discussed, it focuses on how to limit the user.

One of the main methods to limit the user is to use the rule of always granting him minimal permissions needed to do his job. It is always better to give someone not enough and then have to go back and give him a little more, than to give him too much and find out the hard way.

As an example, using the rm command while intending to delete only a few files and inadvertently using recursive commands to delete far too much can be an irreversible error. When that happens, the system administrator assuredly wishes she had given fewer permissions and had those actions denied.

It is also important to place other limits on the users as well. You can limit such things as

- The amount of storage space the users are allowed on the system. This is accomplished by implementing quotas.
- The processes they can run. The `ulimit -u` command is used to place restrictions on this and will limit the maximum number of processes a single user can have at any one time.

Tip

The user default is 7,168.

- Their memory usage. The `ulimit -v` command will allow you to specify a maximum amount of virtual memory that is available to a shell.

Tip

The default is unlimited.

Note

The `ulimit` specifications should be placed in /etc/profile to apply to all users.

With `ulimit`, mentioned in several points in the preceding list, you can specify that values are either H (hard) or S (soft). If they are hard values, they can never be increased. If they are soft values—the default—they can be increased. Options that can be used with `ulimit` other than those already listed include

- `-a` to show all current limits
- `-f` to specify the maximum size of files created by a shell
- `-t` to specify the maximum CPU time that can be used (in seconds)
- `-n` for the maximum number of open files. This setting can be viewed, but not set.

An example of the command in action follows:

```
# ulimit -a
core file size (blocks)    0
data seg size (kbytes)     unlimited
file size (blocks)         unlimited
```

```
max memory size (kbytes) unlimited
stack size (kbytes)      8192
cpu time (seconds)       unlimited
max user processes       256
pipe size (512 bytes)    8
open files               1024
virtual memory (kbytes)  2105343
#
```

YaST Settings

One of the simplest ways to configure security within Novell Linux Desktop is through YaST. Figure 12.1 shows the Security and Users options that are available.

FIGURE 12.1
The options available for Security and Users in YaST.

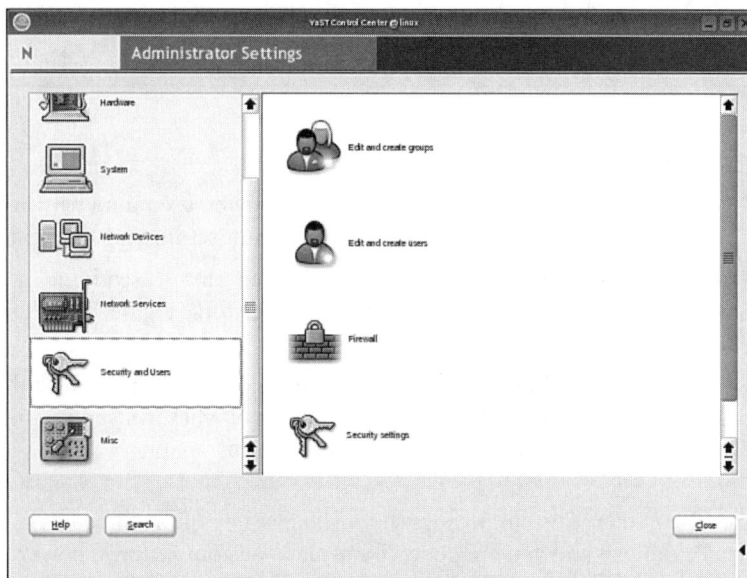

Choosing Security, you arrive at the screen shown in Figure 12.2. You can also get here quickly from the command line with the command: yast2 security.

FIGURE 12.2
You can choose the security level that you want to use.

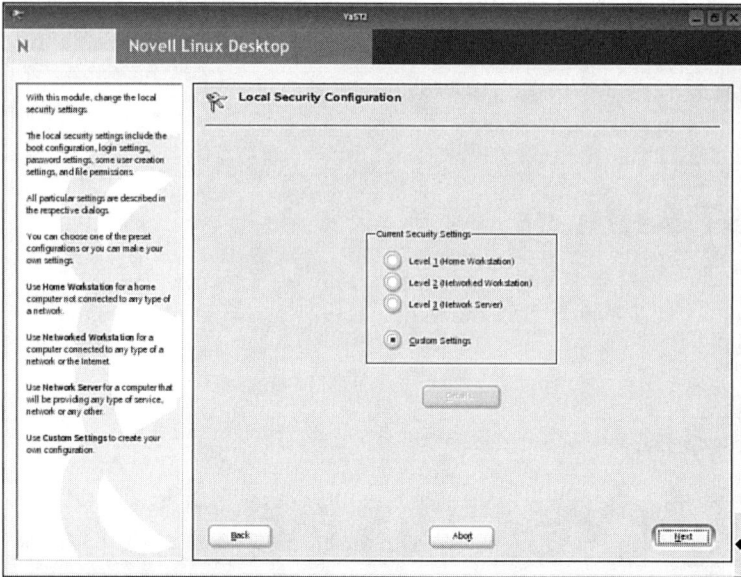

Three predefined security levels are available:

- Level 1 (Home Workstation)—This should only be used if no networking at all is employed. Figure 12.3 shows the default settings for this option.

- Level 2 (Networked Workstation)—This setting can be used for a workstation connecting to the Internet or a network. Figure 12.4 shows the default settings for this option.

- Level 3 (Network Server)—This level is recommended for any host that is offering a service to the network, regardless of what that service might be. Figure 12.5 shows the default settings for this option.

You can also choose Custom Settings. If you choose any of the three levels, merely click Finish and you are done. If you click Custom Settings, however, the Finish button changes to Next, and you can configure the options shown in Figure 12.6.

FIGURE 12.3
The default settings for Level 1.

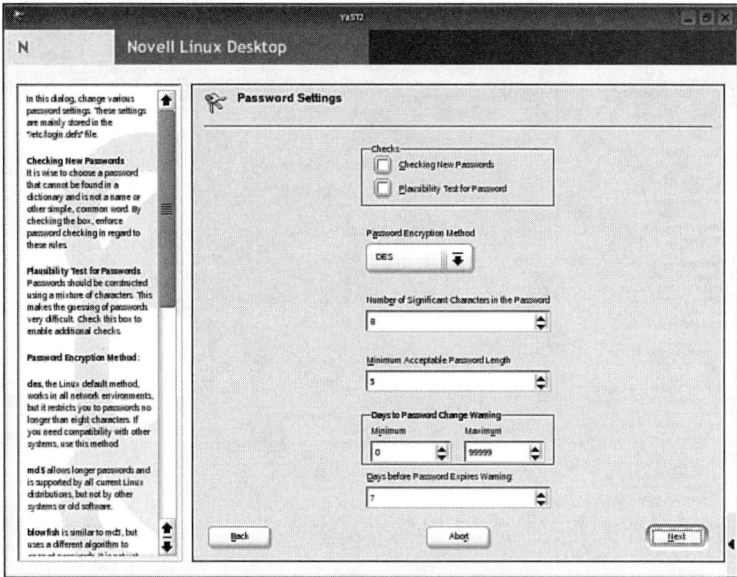

FIGURE 12.4
The default settings for Level 2.

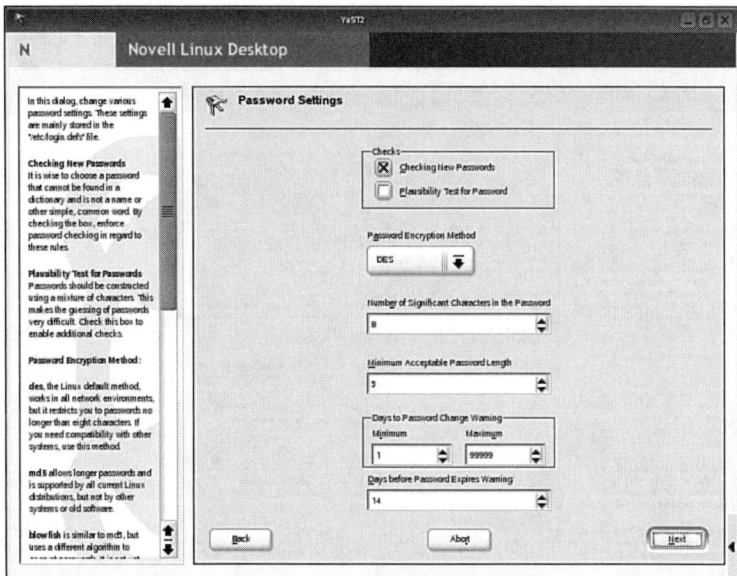

FIGURE 12.5
The default settings for Level 3.

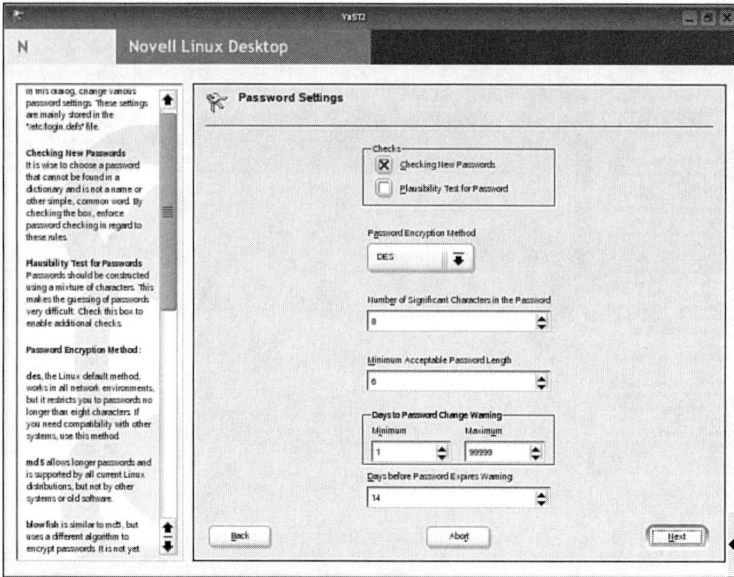

FIGURE 12.6
The first of the Custom Settings possibilities.

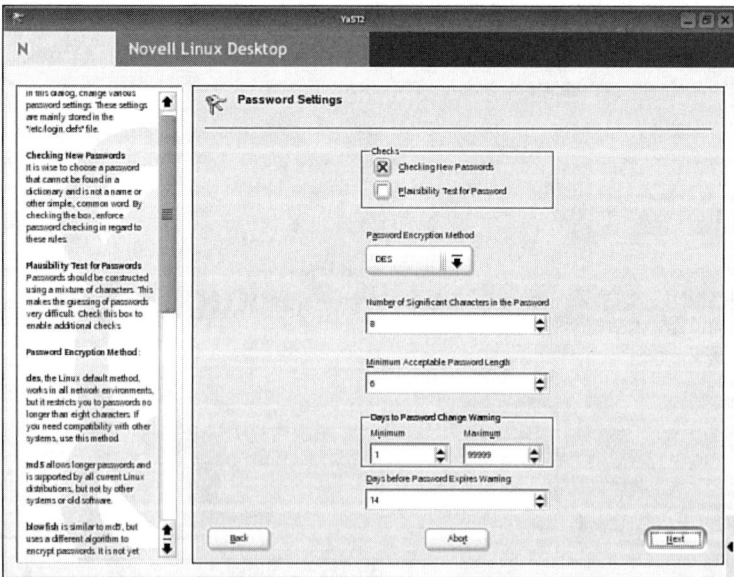

Click Next, and you can then configure the boot permissions, as shown in Figure 12.7.

FIGURE 12.7
You can customize the boot options.

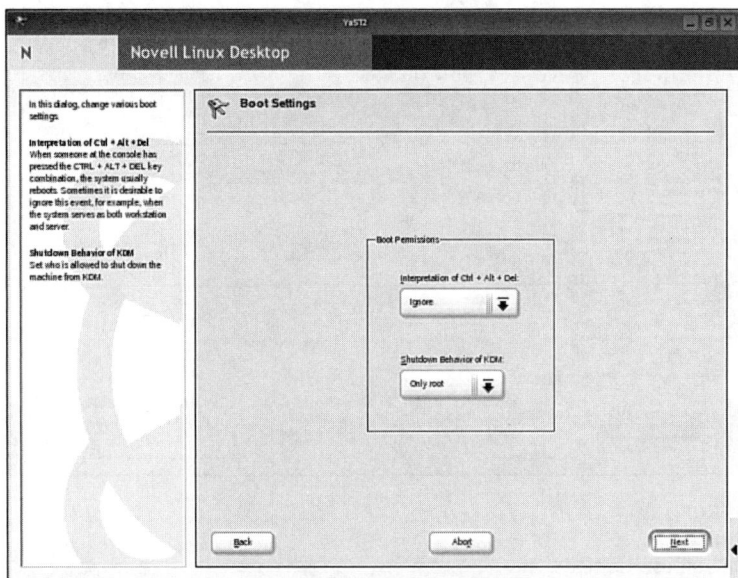

Following this, you can configure the login settings (see Figure 12.8) and the user settings (see Figure 12.9).

Miscellaneous settings (see Figure 12.10) round out the possibilities. On this screen, the Next button changes to Finish and your configuration settings are applied.

Maintaining Effective Backups

Every system has the capability (sad to say) to crash. When it does, the operating system can be reinstalled from the media it came upon and you can start over. What cannot be reinstalled from that media is all the data you've created since the system was started up. Enter the lifesaving backups.

FIGURE 12.8
The initial login settings.

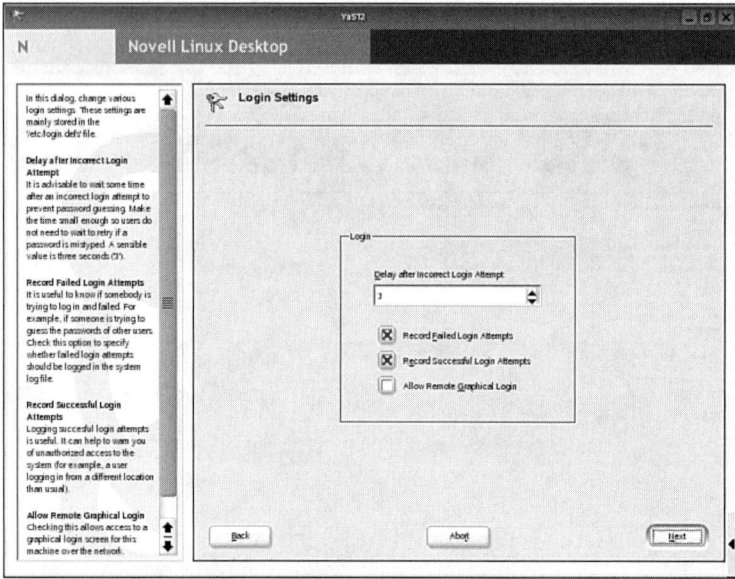

FIGURE 12.9
The default user settings.

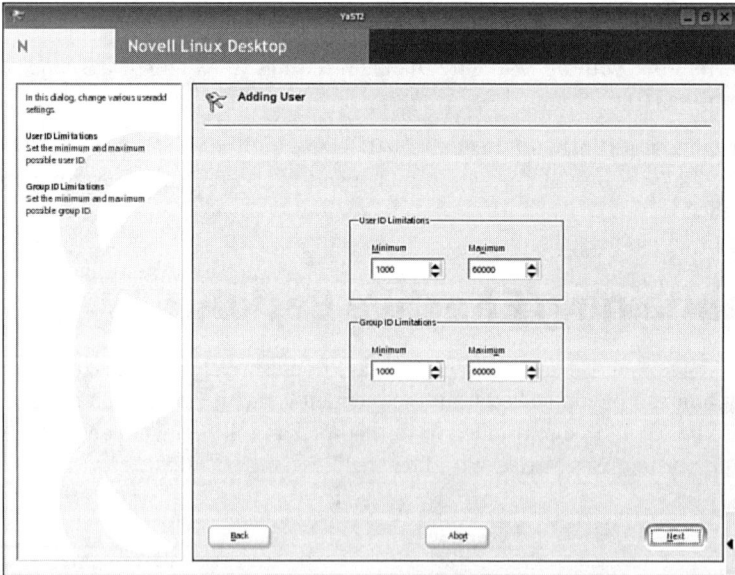

FIGURE 12.10
The default miscellaneous security settings.

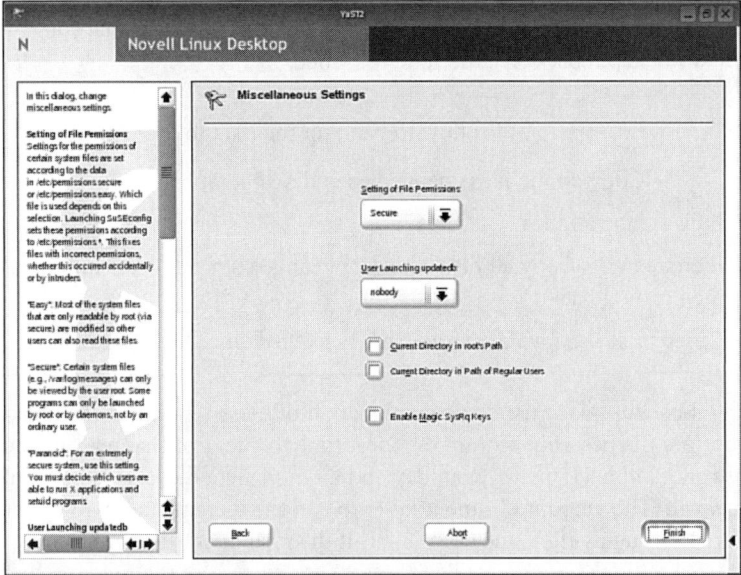

The true definition of backups is copies of your data stored on removable media. (You can copy files from one drive to another, but they are no good if the system gets hit by fire.) In recent times, the definition has become a bit broadened to include technologies such as clusters and such.

Although the removable media can be anything from floppy disks to DVD-RWs, most of the time, magnetic tapes are the preferred medium. Most tapes allow you to store several gigabytes of data and provide a cheaper, more reusable media than other possibilities.

One of the first things to realize is that one tape, used over and over, does not provide a good backup strategy. You need to use multiple tapes, to be able to recover in the event of the failure of one, and rotate them. You need to store copies in safe locations, including offsite (in case the entire building is blown away in a tornado). Logs should be kept of what is on each tape to allow you to quickly identify what is there.

Note

It is important to understand the difference between backups and archives. Archives are files you copy from your system to store elsewhere and would not put back on the system if it crashes. Backups are files on the system that you need and would put back on if the system crashed.

There are several strategies for how to back up the data to the tapes:

- Daily—Copy all the files changed each day to a tape
- Full—Copy all files
- Incremental—Copy all files added or changed since the last full or incremental backup
- Differential—Copy all files added or changed since the last full backup

Most real backup plans use some combination of these types. For example, full backups are the best, but require the most time to run. For that reason, you might run a full backup every Sunday and an incremental every other evening of the week. The amount of time it takes to run the incrementals will be much shorter and roughly the same each night. If the system crashes on Friday, however, it will take quite a while to restore as you restore the full tape from Sunday, and then the incremental from Monday, the incremental from Tuesday, the one from Wednesday, and the one from Thursday (a total of five tapes).

Another possibility would be to do a full backup on Sunday and a differential each night. The amount of time to do the differentials will get longer each night, but if the system crashes on Friday, you only need two tapes: Sunday's full and Thursday's differential.

There are also two other types of backups recognized: copy and partial. A copy backup is simply a copy of a file to the media (think of copying one file to a floppy). A partial backup is just a copy of all the files within a single directory.

Just as important as a good backup strategy and adherence to it is the knowledge that you can restore the data if you have to. This can only come from verifying that on a regular basis. Every so often, when a backup is completed, run a restore operation and verify that you can read back the data in its original form.

Utilities to Know

Linux includes a number of utilities that can be used to do your backups: `tar` and `cpio`. The `tar` utility (tape archiver) will combine multiple files into a single file that can be copied to the media. The syntax for it is

`tar {options} {target_file} {source_files}`

Both the target file and source files can be paths (such as `/dev/tape`). The options include

- `c` to create a new file
- `d` to compare contents and display the differences between the target and source
- `f` to specify a file
- `p` to keep the permissions
- `r-` to append to an existing file
- `t` to show the names of the files in the tar file
- `u` to only add files that are new
- `v` to run in verbose mode
- `x` to extract files

Examples of common commands follow.

To create a new `tar` file on the tape and do so in verbose mode

`tar cvf /dev/tape {files}`

To extract/restore the files from the `october.tar` backup file

`tar xf october.tar`

The `cpio` utility is used to copy in or out. There are three basic actions it can do, and one must be specified:

- `-i` to extract from an archive
- `-o` to make a new archive
- `-p` to print/pass through the files

Options that can be used with it are

- `d` to create directories if they are needed
- `f` to specify a file

- **t** to show the contents
- **u** to overwrite existing files
- **v** to run in verbose mode

Some examples follow.

To read in files from a tape and display them as it is operating (verbose mode)

```
cpio -iv < /dev/tape
```

The following example will find all files on the system starting with "ead" and copy them beneath the **/home/ead** directory, creating all the needed sub-directories in the process:

```
find / -name ead* | cpio -pdv /home/ead
```

dd

The device-to-device (**dd**) utility is used to copy a file from one device to another. It goes beyond that in functionality, however, for it can convert a file during the copy process from one format to another. It can convert from EBCDIC to ASCII (and reverse), change uppercase to lowercase (and reverse as well), and work with bytes, blocks, or keywords.

The most common use for **dd** is copying files to and from removable media, and you must use arguments that can include

- **bs**—block file size
- **if**—input file
- **of**—output file

Related Utilities

Backup utilities allow you to copy files from the system to the backup media, or vice versa. There are also utilities designed to reduce/compress data so that it takes up less space. The most common of these are **gzip** (to compress) and **gunzip** (to uncompress). The contents of the **gzip** file can be seen (without uncompressing) by using the **zcat** utility in place of **cat**.

Two others that exist on some systems are

- bzip2 (and its counterpart, bunzip2). You can see the contents of the file with bzcat and recover a damaged file with bzip2recover.
- compress (and its counterpart, uncompress)

Summary

This chapter focused on the topic of security. It looked at how common sense applies to all areas of this topic, and then examined settings that can be configured in YaST, as well as the importance of backups.

## CHAPTER 13

Living with Novell Linux Desktop

Novell Linux Desktop was designed to be the best open-source desktop operating system on the market. Although it sounds like a lofty aspiration, it is an objective the product not only meets, but also exceeds.

NLD can function well as a desktop operating system on a stand-alone system or in a network of almost any type. It seamlessly interacts with Novell-based networks such as those running OES (Open Enterprise Server) and SLES (SUSE Linux Enterprise Server), as well as networks running Microsoft-based servers and those running Unix and other variations of Linux as well.

In this chapter, we will look at several different scenarios in which NLD can be deployed.

NLD as a Standalone Operating System

The vast majority of this book discusses features of Novell Linux Desktop that make it an excellent choice for the operating system on a standalone PC, such as a laptop computer. It includes OpenOffice.org for all your office applications, and support is included for the standard Microsoft Office file formats.

Figure 13.1 shows the Office menu choices available with Novell Linux Desktop. Figure 13.2 shows the main screen of the word processor.

FIGURE 13.1
The Office options available in NLD.

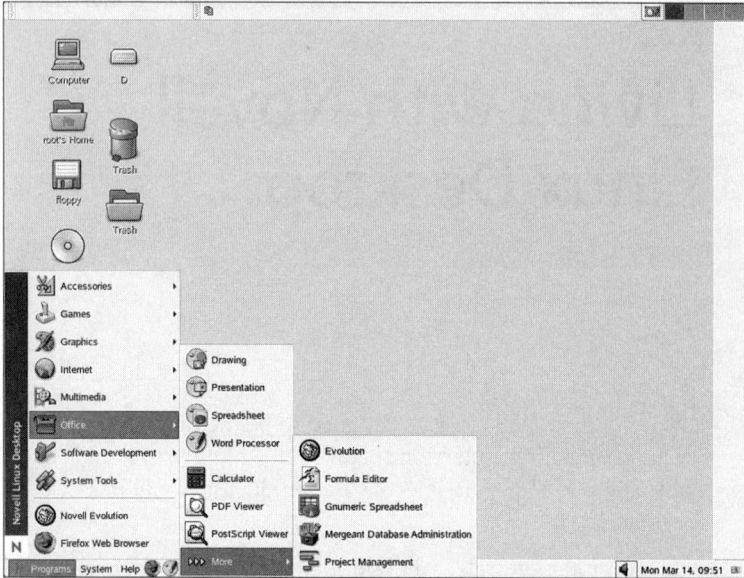

FIGURE 13.2
Working on a new document in OpenOffice.org.

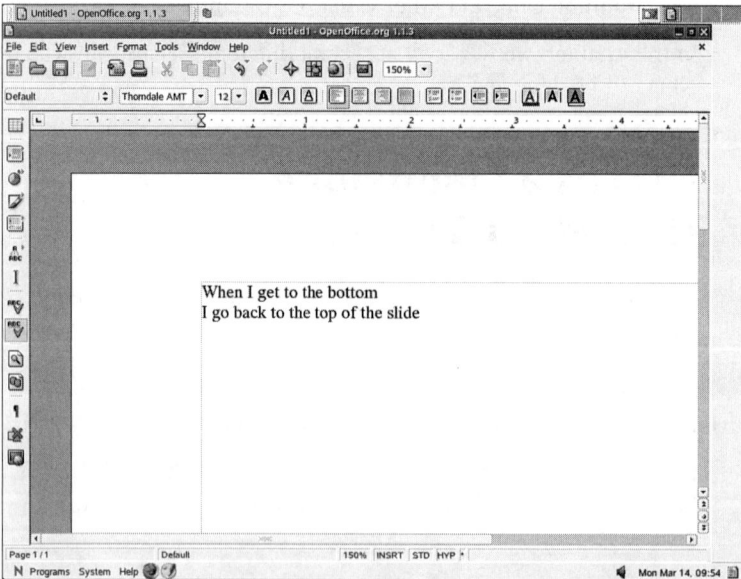

To start the word processor, you can click on the word processor icon, which appears by default on the panel or use the menu choices Programs, Office, Word Processor.

NLD in a Windows Environment

With native SMB support, NLD can readily join an existing Windows-based network, whether that network is a workstation-only environment or one running Windows Server 2000/2003. The only issue that occasionally occurs in adding NLD to such a network is the configuration of the printer.

The simplest method of so doing is to add the LPD service to the existing print server (a simple selection in all current Microsoft operating systems). After this is done, the printer will be visible when scanning for it in Administrator Settings, Hardware, Printer, and it can be selected.

TIP

From the Linux side, the alternative is to run Samba on your system and use that to print directly to Windows printers regardless of whether they support LPD.

NLD in a Novell Environment

Since Novell is the company behind the Linux Desktop, it stands to reason that NLD can not only function in an environment of Novell servers (NetWare, OES, or SUSE), but also it can excel. NLD can fully utilize such utilities and services as

- ConsoleOne—This network-compatible Java-based tool allows you to quickly and easily administer the network resources from a browser.

- iManager—This Web-based application can be used for managing, maintaining, and troubleshooting eDirectory from within your browser interface.

- iMonitor—This tool offers you monitoring and diagnostic capability from within a Web browser to all servers in your eDirectory tree.

- Remote Manager—The easiest way to think of this tool is to imagine that you are sitting at the server console. Remote Manager gives you all the functionality that would be available at the server console within a web browser.

Without much argument, it is the services that made NetWare a market leader. The following sections look at some of those services.

Directory Services

Since the days that Novell moved away from the bindery, one of the great strengths of NetWare has been its directory service—first known as NDS and now as eDirectory. The directory delineates the boundaries of your network and is truly one of the most important services any network can offer.

Often, icons of the globe are used in discussions of eDirectory, and this is for good reason. Given the scalability and robustness of eDirectory today, your network can easily span the world, and many do.

In its simplest form, you can think of eDirectory as an object-oriented, hierarchical, distributed—and replicated—database. In reality, it is that and so much more. It holds data—called objects—within a logical tree structure.

Each object is uniquely identified by the object name, or Common Name (CN) and an address that describes the location of the object within the tree, or Context. This combining the Common Name and Context creates what is known as the Distinguished Name. Mandatory and optional attributes are used to round out the description of the objects.

There are four important benefits that eDirectory offers the network:

- Discovery—The ability to search for objects or properties of objects.
- Relationship—This allows information to become global and removes the need to connect separately to each server by requiring authentication at the network level instead of the server level.
- Security—Rights can be granted to users or groups, and all security can be managed across the network within eDirectory—canceling the need to create a separate infrastructure. Every object within the tree can have an Access Control List (ACL) attribute that holds information about which trustees have access to the object and the attributes for the object.
- Storage—eDirectory can store network data in its distributed database and protect it from corruption through fault tolerance and other features.

The version numbers of eDirectory have incremented rapidly over the years, with each successive version offering more features than its predecessors. To see the version you are currently running, you can query the DS module using the console commands VERSION or MODULE DS.

It has been said that eDirectory is "the heart and soul of NetWare." In so many ways, that is true for it is not truly possible to have NetWare without eDirectory, but this service is only the tip of the iceberg as to what NetWare offers, as the following sections illustrate.

Storage Services

The need for local area networks sprang from a need for ways to share files and resources. To this day, NetWare still includes an outstanding network filing system offering the latest in file storage technology. Two key elements fall within this category: Novell Storage Services (NSS), and iFolder.

Each of these is explored in the following sections.

NOVELL STORAGE SERVICES

Novell Storage Services (NSS) is a 64-bit file storage and management system that uses free space from multiple storage devices to create an unlimited number of volumes. NSS can integrate with Novell Clustering Services to configure servers in a multimode cluster that enable network resources to be dynamically transferred from one server to another on-the-fly.

NSS uses five hierarchical components:

- partitions—Segments of storage deposits configured for a specific operating system.
- storage deposits—Free space that can be gathered from unpartitioned areas of storage devices and organized into partitions.
- storage devices—Hard drives, CD-ROM drives, and offline storage media.
- storage pools—A quantity of file system space that is obtained from one or more storage devices.
- volumes—These can be logical volumes, traditional volumes, or read-only volumes.

NSS uses overbooking (which allows the sum of the size of each volume in a partition to exceed the partition size) and journaling. The journaling keeps track of file system transactions and notes whether they are completed or undone to enable the file system to recover after a crash.

IFOLDER

iFolder is the user interface tool that allows users to access applications and data through a Java-enabled web browser. iFolder lets you access your files from anywhere and at anytime across the Web. iFolder uses LDAP (Lightweight Directory Access Protocol) for user authentication and stores files in encrypted form.

The iFolder Client can synchronize data (sending only the blocks of data that have changed between the local directory with the centralized iFolder server). The Client encrypts all files sent to and from the iFolder server and runs on Windows 95, 98, Me, NT, and 2000 workstations. After the user logs in, he sees iFolder icons on his desktop (a shortcut to his files) and in the Windows system tray (which offers access to iFolder user account information and configuration parameters).

The iFolder Server runs on NetWare or Windows NT/200x and provides the infrastructure needed by the clients. It stores the encrypted files and uses LDAP for authentication purposes. Before users can start using iFolder, you have to enable their User objects. This is done from the User Management button in the iFolder Server Management, and you can choose to grant permission to individual users or groups.

Print Services

In the early days of networking, it used to be the case that you could run the wiring and set the network up in a short period of time, and then spend days trying to get the printing service to properly function. Those days are long gone.

Novell iPrint is the latest tool for printing. Being web enabled, it allows mobile users to print from almost any remote locations to almost any printing devices through the Internet. The users just use their web browser to point, click, and print.

iPrint builds on the Novell Distributed Print Services (NDPS) and combines it with the Internet Printing Protocol (IPP) to form a powerful service. It uses Secure Socket Layers (SSL) for secure encryption of all data and even allows non-Novell clients to print to NetWare printers.

iPrint consists of the following software components:

- Broker—Provides centralized management of printing services for all the printers on the network.
- Gateways—Handles communication between the Print Manager and the printer.
- Printer Agent—Software that manages an individual printer.
- Print Manager—Controls all printer agents installed on a server.

Configuration is accomplished in only a few steps:

1. Install iPrint on the Server
2. Start iManager
3. Create an NDPS Broker
4. Create and Load an NDPS Manager
5. Create NDPS Printers
6. Configure NDPS for Automatic Installation on Workstations

Printers are represented as icons on a map, and all redirection occurs in the background.

End User Services

Virtual Office is a new service from Novell that lets administrators create personalized user portals. Those user portals are then used by users to access their data and applications from a single website.

Virtual Office allows you to create virtual teams on-the-fly for when you need a group working on a project to suddenly all have access to resources through a shared portals.

The services are Java-based servlets or applications that are used to perform common network tasks

- eGuide—Offers a simplified screen for accessing phone numbers and related user information from eDirectory.

- E-mail and calendaring—Provides support for email applications and protocols such as GroupWise, Microsoft Exchange, and the POP3 and IMAP protocols.

- iPrint—As mentioned in the printing section earlier in this chapter, it provides access to Internet printing.

- NetStorage—Provides Internet-based access to file storage, including access to iFolder.

- Password—Provides links to where users can change their eDirectory password.

- ZENWorks—Provides integration with Novell ZENWorks for Desktops through the Virtual Office interface.

Administrative Services

Two key administrative services are worth paying attention to: iManager and Patch Management. Each of these services is discussed in the following sections.

IMANAGER

The iManager utility is the administrative tool of the future. It replaces many of the standalone utilities that existed in previous versions of NetWare and allows the administrator the ability to work with a tool that is platform independent and web browser based.

NOTE

One of the primary tools that iManager replaces for performing management tasks is ConsoleOne.

iManager runs at port 2200, by default, and can be accessed from the NetWare 6 Web Manager portal using the address HTTPS://{server IP address}:2200.

NOTE

Although you can use either a secure (HTTPS) or unsecure (HTTP) connection to access iManager, a secure connection is always recommended.

When it opens, the main page has three functional frames:

- Header Frame—Located at the top center, it contains these buttons: Home, Exit, Roles and Tasks, Configure, and Help.
- Navigation Frame—Along the left side, it has the links that pertain to whichever button is chosen in the Header frame.
- Main Content Frame—At the right side, it is the advanced administration area used for server management.

iManager uses Role-Based Services (RBS) to customize its interface based on assigned administrative roles. Although you can customize and add more, there are five default iManager role categories that are applicable to most networks:

- DHCP Management
- DNS Management
- eDirectory Administration—This can be customized further to container management, group management, and user management.

- iPrint Management—Nine tasks are available: Create Printer, Create Manager, Create Broker, Delete NDPS Object, Enable iPrint Access, Manage Printer, Manage Print Service Manager, Manage Broker, and Remote Print Manager Configuration.

- License Management

iManager uses Novell's exteNd Web services platform and runs on the Apache Web Server for NetWare. It is also possible to use iManager in "Simple" mode for compliance with federal accessibility guidelines. This mode offers the same functionality as "Regular" mode, but the interface is accessibility by those with disabilities. To use Simple mode, replace iManager.html with Simple.html in the URL.

PATCH MANAGEMENT

No matter how great software is, there are always going to be situations that can occur and do not show up until a particular set of circumstances exist. That set of circumstances can be anything from an abnormally high load of traffic, to hackers devoting all their time and energy to inflicting harm.

As an administrator, it is critically important that you keep abreast of current patches and updated modules for your network. It is imperative that you understand that your network consists not only of the servers you administer, but also every workstation, laptop, and device that connects to that network.

You can keep the servers up-to-date by checking the postings at http://support.novell.com. Select Product, Novell Linux Desktop, and you can find any available updates. Over time, patches are rolled into support packs, but not every patch or update is needed for every network. Patches and updates are also included on the Support Connection Library—a subscription CD service regularly produced by Novell Technical Services and mailed.

TIP

The easiest way to keep the system up-to-date is with the automatic update feature discussed in Chapter 2, "Installing Novell Desktop 9."

You can find patches and updates for your workstation applications by checking the sites of those vendors. Any network is only as strong as its weakest component, so you must keep all parts of the network updated and secure.

Basic Shell Tools

Regardless of what type of network—if any—you install NLD into, there are a number of tools and commands that can help you interact with the network or server from the command line. The majority of these have been mentioned throughout the book and are summarized here:

- bg—Move a job to the background
- cat—Displays the contents of a file
- cd—Changes from the current directory to another
- chgrp—Changes an entity's group association
- chmod—Changes an entity's permissions
- cp—Copies a file or directory
- cut—Extracts a field from each line of a file
- edquota—Creates quotas for users or groups
- fg—Moves a job to the foreground
- getfacl—Shows the Access Control List for a file
- grep—Displays lines that contain the given string
- head—Displays the beginning lines of a file
- jobs—Displays a list of jobs running in the background
- join—Combines columns from two files into a single display
- kill—Ends a process
- killall—Ends several processes
- locate—Finds a file from the locatedb database
- ls—Lists files and directories on the system
- mkdir—Makes directories
- mv—Renames/moves a file or directory
- nice—Starts a process at a priority other than the default
- paste—Puts the contents of two files in a single display
- ps—Shows the running processes
- pstree—Graphically depicts the relationship between processes
- pwd—Displays the current directory in absolute format
- quotaoff—Turns off user/group quotas
- quotaon—Turns on user/group quotas

- `renice`—Changes the priority of a running process
- `repquota`, `quota`, `quotacheck`, and `quotastats`—Views quota usage
- `rm`—Removes files and directories
- `rmdir`—Removes empty directories
- `sed`—Allows text to be changed before being displayed
- `setfacl`—Sets/modifies the Access Control List for a file
- `sort`—Sorts the lines of the file
- `tail`—Displays the last lines of a file
- `top`—Shows and monitors system information and processes
- `touch`—Changes the times associated with a file or creates a zero-sized file
- `umask`—A numerical variable subtracted from the default permissions when creating new files and directories
- `wait`—Suspends further processing until another process completes
- `wc`—Counts the number of words, lines, and characters/bytes within a file
- `which`—Finds a file from the path statement

Administrative Tools

The following tools—predominantly console commands—are used for basic administrative tasks:

- `bzip2/bunzip2`—Compresses/uncompresses files.
- `chpasswd`—Changes passwords with a batch file.
- `compress/uncompress`—Compresses/uncompresses files.
- `cpio`—Copies files to and from one location to another. It is typically used to create and extract file archives.
- `crontab`—Creates or edits a `crontab` file.
- `dd`—Copies files and is commonly used for cloning media or partitions or for translating files from one format or blocksize to another.
- `depmod`—Determines module dependencies.
- `df`—Sees the amount of disk free space.
- `dmesg`—Displays boot messages.

- **dmesg**—Prints out the bootup messages.
- **dpkg**—Debian package manager.
- **du**—Sees disk usage statistics.
- **fdisk**—Used to partition the disk and work with the partition table.
- **fsck**—Used to check the file system consistency status.
- **gpasswd**—Adds/modifies variables for an existing group.
- **groupadd**—Adds a new group to the system.
- **groupdel**—Removes a group from the system.
- **groupmod**—Changes variables on an existing group.
- **grub**—Linux boot loader.
- **gzip/gunzip**—Compresses/uncompresses files.
- **gzip**—Compresses files.
- **halt**, **shutdown**, **reboot**—Interfaces to shutdown.
- **hdparm**—Can be used to see and change hard disk parameters.
- **hwinfo**—Displays a list of information about an installed devices.
- **id**—Shows user variables.
- **init**—Changes the runlevel.
- **insmod**—Installs a module.
- **last**—Views the most recent entries in the **wtmp** file.
- **lastlog**—Shows the last time each user logged on.
- **ldconfig**—Updates and maintains the cache of shared library data and symbols for the dynamic linker.
- **ldd**—Shows what shared libraries a program is dependent upon.
- **lilo**—Configures the Linux Loader.
- **logger**—Writes an event in the log file.
- **logrotate**—Automates administration to log files.
- **lsmod**—Lists the loaded modules.
- **lspci**—Shows information about the PCI buses.
- **mail**—Checks to see if mail is queued.
- **mkfs**—Creates a filesystem.
- **mkreiserfs**—Creates a Reiser filesystem.
- **modinfo**—Prints information about a module.

- modprobe—Probes and installs a module and its dependents.
- mount—Mounts a filesystem.
- newgrp—Switches between default groups.
- passwd—Changes/sets the password for a user account.
- pwconv—Converts passwords into the shadow file.
- pwunconv—Removes passwords from the shadow file and places in passwd.
- rmmod—Removes a module.
- rpm—Red Hat Package manager.
- rsync—Copies directories from one host to another.
- runlevel—Shows the current runlevel of the system.
- shutdown—An interface to init with more options.
- su—Changes from one user account to another.
- tar—Copies files to or from a tape.
- tar—Creates and extracts files known as tarballs.
- telinit—Same as init.
- ulimit—Shows user limits currently imposed.
- umount—Unmounts a filesystem.
- useradd—Adds a new user to the system.
- userdel—Removes user accounts.
- usermod—Modifies user variables.

Networking Tools

The following tools—predominantly console commands—can help you troubleshoot issues with networking and the IP protocol:

- arp—Shows the entries in the Address Resolution table
- dig—Shows DNS entries
- domainname—Displays the domain name used by the host
- ftp —A utility for transferring files between hosts
- ifconfig—Displays the TCP/IP configuration parameters
- ifdown—Stops a preconfigured network interface

- `ifup`—Starts a preconfigured network interface
- `ifstatus`—Displays the status of a preconfigured network interface
- `netstat`—Displays network status information
- `ping`—Displays echo messages to show whether or not a host can be reached
- `route`—Displays the routing table
- `telnet`—A utility for establishing a connection with a remote host
- `traceroute`—Displays the route taken to reach a remote host

Miscellaneous Tools

The following tools are useful when looking to solve a very specific problem or find more information:

- `apropos`—Returns a short summary of information from `whatis`
- `at`—Allows you to schedule a job to run *at* a specified time
- `find`—Locates a file based on given criteria
- `fuser`—Used to monitor user access to files
- `info`—Shows the help information available on a command
- `KFind`—A graphical version of `find`
- `lsof`—Lists open files
- `man`—Displays the manual pages for a command/utility/file
- `whatis`—Returns information about the utility or command
- `whereis`—Lists all information it can find about locations associated with a file

Summary

This chapter looked at the integration of Novell Linux Desktop with other environments. It discussed using NLD in a standalone environment as well as in a Windows-based network and a Novell-based network.

Index

Symbols

B

C

D

E

SGID (Set Group ID), 211

sticky bit, 212

SUID (Set User ID), 211

w (write), 204

x (execute), 204

printing, 158-159

  CUPS (Common Unix Printing System), 159-160, 163-167

  lpadmin command, 162

  lpc command, 162

  lppasswd command, 163

  lpq command, 162

  lprm command, 162

profile, 177

relative addressing, 84-86

removing

  rm command, 217

  rmdir command, 217-218

renaming, 215

saving, 114-115

searching, 118

sending output to, 228

services, 294-295

shadow, 251-254

skel, 254

sorting, 80-82

standard output and input, 88-90

SuSE-release, 176

uncompressing, 318

utmp, 246

viewing contents of

  cat command, 76-77

  head command, 77-79

more command, 83

tail command, 77-79

wtmp, 246

X11, 176

Filesystem Hierarchy Standard (FHS), 173-174

filesystems. *See also* **files**

checking for errors, 194-196

creating, 190-191

directories, 173

  / (root), 174

  absolute addressing, 84-86

  adding to path, 66

  /bin, 175

  /boot, 175

  changing, 83-84

  copying, 212-215

  creating, 218-219

  /dev, 175-176

  eDirectory, 324-325

  /etc, 176-177

  home, 177

  /install, 182

  /lib, 177

  listing, 86-88

  /lost+found, 183, 196

  /media, 177

  /mnt, 178, 197-198

  moving, 215-216

  /opt, 178

  present working directory, displaying, 83-84

  /proc, 178-179

G

O

P

Z